King George County, Virginia

Deed Book Abstracts

1773–1783

Ruth and Sam Sparacio

HERITAGE BOOKS
2019

HERITAGE BOOKS

AN IMPRINT OF HERITAGE BOOKS, INC.

Books, CDs, and more—Worldwide

For our listing of thousands of titles see our website
at
www.HeritageBooks.com

Published 2019 by
HERITAGE BOOKS, INC.
Publishing Division
5810 Ruatan Street
Berwyn Heights, Md. 20740

International Standard Book Number
Paperbound: 978-1-68034-823-1

pp.
1028-
1029

THIS INDENTURE made this thirtyeth day of Decr: in the year of our Lord Christ one thousand seven hundred and seventy two Between the Reverend JOHN DIXON of the COLLEGE of WILLIAM and MARY of one part and ARTHUR MORSON of Town of FALMOUTH, Merchant, of other part. Witnesseth that said JOHN DIXON for sum of Thirty pounds current money to him in hand paid by ARTHUR MORSON by these presents doth bargain & sell unto ARTHUR MORSON his heirs one certain tract or half acre of land situated in County of King George and near the Town of FALMOUTH, Begining at a Stake at a litle distance from the Northwest corner of the FALLS RUN BRIDGE and on a line with the Southwest front of DAVID BRIGGS and GAWIN LAWSONs Lotts, thence N. 63 1/2 W. six poles to another Stake, thence N. 27 1/2 E. thirteen and one third poles to another Stake, thence So. 63 1/2 E. 6 poles to another Stake, and from thence S. 27 1/2 W. thirteen and one third poles to the begining; together with all houses ways and water courses belonging and the rents issues and profits thereof; To have & to hold the half acre of land together with all appurtenances to ARTHUR MORSON his heirs and JOHN DIXON for himself his heirs the half acres of land with its appurtenances against all persons shall warrant and forever defend by these presents: In Witness whereof the sd. JOHN DIXON hath hereunto set his hand and affixed his seal the day month and year above mentioned
Signed sealed & acknowledged in the presence of

    A. BUCHANAN; GERARD BANKS,   JOHN DIXON
    DAVID BRIGGS. JAMES CLELAND,
    JOHN URQUHART, THOMAS VOWLES

FALMOUTH. 30th December 1772. Received of ARTHUR MORSON thirty pounds current money being the within mentioned consideration money p me.
Witness A. BUCHANAN   JOHN DIXON
  At a Court held for King George County the 6th day of May 1773
JOHN DIXONs Indented Deed of Bargain and Sale to ARTHUR MORSON was proved by the Oaths of A. BUCHANAN, GERARD BANKS, DAVID BRIGGS & JAMES CLELAND & admitted to
Record   Test JOSEPH ROBINSON, Cl KG

p.
1030

THIS INDENTURE made the 21st day of December in the year one thousand seven hundred and seventy two; WHEREAS JOHN CANNADAY heretofore of Parish of Hanover in King George County having been in his lifetime and at the time of his death, seized and possessed in certain real and of certain personal Estate, on the 9th day of September 1772 duly made and published his Last Will and Testament in Writing, & therein did give and devise certain Lands and other Estate to certain of his Children but in the said Will the said Testator has made no provision for he has not even mentioned the name directly or indirectly of SUSANNAH, his then Wife, as believing that the Laws of this Colony wou'd sufficiently make a provision for her and the said Testator having so made his Will, soon after died without altering or revoking the same; NOW THIS INDENTURE Witnesseth that SUSANNAH CANNADY, Widow of the said Testator, agreeable to the Act of Assembly in such case made, hereby doth renounce the said Will or any other Will made by her late Husband & she hath & hereby doth declare that she will not accept receive or take any Legacy or Legacies to her given and bequeathed or any part thereof by any Will of her late Husband and she renounces the benefit and

advantage which she may claim by any last Will or Wills and she hereby claims and demands her Dower and Third part of all the Estate whereof her Husband died seized and possessed according to Law. In Witness whereof the said SUSANNAH CANNADY hath hereunto set her hand and seal the day & year first above written
Signed Sealed & Acknowledged in the presence of
      JOHN TRIPLETT, JOHN JARVIS,   SUSANNAH her mark X CANADAY
      WILL: BUSSELL JUNR. JOHN PLAYL
   At a Court held for King George County the 6th day of May 1773
SUSANNAH CANNADAYs Indented Deed renouncing her Husbands Will proved by the witnesses thereto and admitted to Record   Test

pp.   THIS INDENTURE made between WILLIAM NEWTON of the Parish of Brunswick
1031- and County of King George of one part and WILLIAM BRIDGES of County &
1032   Parish aforesaid of other part; Witnesseth this twenty ninth day of March in
       the year of our Lord one thousand seven hundred and seventy three that
WILLIAM NEWTON hath granted leas'd and set unto farm one hundred acres of Land lying in County and Parish aforesaid & bounded; Begining at a small red Oak standing near the FALL RUN and opposite to the lower side of a large Vallie, which Vallie is settled for the bounds of JOHN THOMAS SEAY, thence up the Vallie to the head thereof, thence over a Ridge to another large Vallie, thence up the Vallie to the Spring or Black Gum, thence Norwest to the old mark'd line, thence down the line to the FALL RUN, thence over the Run across low grounds and to the top of Hill, thence setting across along the sd. Ridge till coming opposite to the Red Oak, the first begining, to include the quantity of the Land be it more or less for the rents and dutyes hereafter mentioned and during the natural lives from the date hereof together with all houses orchards profits and appurtenances belonging; To have and to hold the tract of land to WILLIAM BRIDGES and his Wife, AMEY BRIDGES during their natural lives &c., any of them paying to WILLIAM NEWTON his heirs &c. the annual rent of five hundred & thirty pounds of tobo: according to Law and ten shillings sixpence cash; And also WILLIAM BRIDGES or any one of them to build one English fram'd dwelling House sixteen feet square with one outside Chimney, one Barn 32 by 20, one Corn House 10 by 8 feet square and to be kept in good repair during the time, also to plant one hundred Apple trees, one hundred Peach trees, twenty five Cherry trees, all to be sett at the usual distance and to be kpet under a lawfull fence; In Witness whereof we the said parties do bind our selves to each other in the penal sum of one hundred pounds Sterling money to be paid to the party observing; Sealed the day and year above written
Signed Sealed and Delivered in presence of us
      BENJAMIN NEWTON, VINCEN COX,   WM: NEWTON
      ABRAHAM NEWTON, WILLIAM BARBER,   WM: BRIDGES
      JOHN POLLARD SENR., JOHN ROBERTSON
      RICHARD BAYN
   At a Court held for King George County the 6th day of May 1773
WILLIAM NEWTONs Indented Deed of Lease for Lives to WILLM: BRIDGES proved by JOHN POLLARD, JOHN ROBERTSON & RICHARD BAYN & admitted to Record

p,   KNOW ALL MEN by these presents that I WILLIAM RANDOLPH of the County of
1033 King George for sum of Thirteen pounds, six shillings & nine pence half penny
       current money to me in hand paid by DAVID BRIGGS of the same County, by
these presents doth bargain and sell unto DAVID BRIGGS one cart & cart gears, one brindled Cow & one Calf, one Chest, one feather Bed & bedstead, a Pine Table, one sorrel

Horse know brand that I know of, one Dutch oven & one iron pot & a small white horse, which goods & chattles I do warrant and defend to DAVID BRIGGS his heirs the claim of any person; In Witness whereof the said WILLIAM RANDOLPH hath hereunto set his hand & seal this twenty ninth day of May one thousand seven hundred and seventy two Signed Sealed & Delivered in presence of
(interlined "a white horse" before signed)

    CHARLES ASHLEY   WILLIAM his mark X RANDOLPH
    JOHN ROBERTSON

KNOW ALL MEN by these presents that I WILLIAM RANDOLPH within mentioned as a further payment for the within mentioned sum of thirteen pounds, six shillings & nine pence half penny to DAVID BRIGGS within mentioned have bargained and sold one black Horse which I purchased of H. HOOE about ten years old near fourteen hand high which Horse I do warrant and defend to DAVID BRIGGS or his assigns against the claims of all persons; In Witness whereof I have hereunto set my hand and seal this twenty ninth day of January one thousand seven hundred & seventy three
This signed sealed and delivered in presence of

    ALEX: HANSFORD,   WM: RANDLE
    CHARLES ASHLEY   WILLIAM RANDOLPH

At a Court held for King George County the 1st day of October 1772.
WILLIAM RANDOLPHs Bill of Sale to DAVID BRIGGS proved by the Oath of JOHN ROBERT-SOIN & admitted to Record. June Court 1773, further proved by ALEXR: HANSFORD

pp. 1034-1035   THIS INDENTURE made this Fourteenth day of December in the year of our Lord God one thousand seven hundred & seventy two Between PATRICK and JEANE KENDRICK his Wife, of King George County of one part & MARY HORTON, their Daughter, of said County of other part; Witnesseth that PATRICK KENDRICK & JEANE his Wife for the natural love & affection which the said PATRICK KENDRICK hath and doth bear to his Daughter, the said MARY, and also for the consideration of the sum of five shillings current money by said MARY to said PATRICK in hand paid, by these presents do bragin sell and confirm unto MARY HORTON her heirs lawfully begotten of her body, for the want of such heirs to returne to WILLIAM KENDRICK, Son to PATRICK & JANE KENDRICK his Wife & his heirs all that tract of land containing seventy acres lying in County of King George & STAFFORD granted to MARY HORTON by Patent dated the six day of November in year one thousand seven hundred and seventy one & bounded; Begining at a mark'd Box Oak in the line of Capt. LAURENCE WASHINGTON, thence S. 15d. E. 182 poles to a stooping Box Oak, a corner of CARTERs Land, thence S. 39d. W. 67 poles to a small Box Oak by the Road side, thence No. 20 Wt. 62 poles to a Box Oak pointers, thence No. 87 W. 90 poles to ye said WASHINGTONs line, including 70 acres & all houses orchards profits & appurtenances belonging; To have & to hold the seventy acres of Land and other the premises & the appurtenances unto MARY HORTON or her heirs lawfully begotten of her body and for the want of such heirs to WILLIAM KENDRICK; Witness our hands and seals the day and year above written
And in the presence of

    JAMES BROWN,   PATRICK KENDRICK
    WILLIAM LAWSON   JANE her mark X KENDRICK

At a Court held for King George County the 3d. day of June 1773
PATRICK KENDRICK and JANE his Wifes Deed Indented to MARY HORTON, the said JANE being first privately examined, was ackd: and admitted to Record
               Test JOS: ROBINSON, Cl Cur

pp.   THIS INDENTURE made this fifth day of August in the year one thousand seven
1035-   hundred and seventy three Between THOMAS JETT and MAXIMILIAN ROBINSON,
1036   Trustees for LEEDS TOWN in County of King George, of one part and DANIEL
         RICHARDSON of County of King George of other part; Witnesseth that THOMAS
JETT and MAXIMILIAN ROBINSIN, for sum of five pounds current money of Virginia in
hand paid by DANIEL RICHARDSON by these presents doth bargain and sell unto DANIEL
RICHARDSON his heirs one lot or half acre of Land within the said Town of LEEDS num-
bered in the Plan of said Town (96), and bounded by EAST STREET and CAMERON STREET;
To have and to hold the lott or half acre of land unto DANIEL RICHARDSON his heirs; In
Witness whereof THOMAS JETT and MAXIMILIAN ROBINSON hath hereutno set their
hands and seals the year above written
Signed Sealed and Delivered in the presence of
         BURKETT DAVENPORT,   WILLIAM BOOTH,   MAXN: ROBINSON
         SAMUEL TODD,   FRANCIS his mark ✗ WALKER   THOMAS JETT
   At a Court held for King George County the 5th day of August 1773
MAXN. ROBINSON & THOS: JETT, Gent., Trustees of the Town of LEEDS, acknowledge this
their Indented Deed of bargain and sale to DANIEL RICHARDSON which is admitted to
Record

pp.   THIS INDENTURE made this Eleventh day of June in year of our Lord one thou-
1036-   sand seven hundred and seventy three Between THOMAS JETT and WILLIAM
1037   BERNARD of one part and COLLIN REDDOCK of the other part; Whereas JOHN ORR
         by his Indenture of Bargain and Sale bearing date the fourteenth day of JUne
one thousand seven hundred & sixty nine had granted and sold unto THOMAS JETT and
WILLIAM BERNARD their hiers among other things a certain parcel of land lying
partly in County of RICHMOND and partly in County of King George where JOHN ORR
formerly resided containing four hundred & fifty acres or thereabouts in Trust to be
sold for the payment of several demands against JOHN ORR in the said Indenture particularly specified as by said Indenture of Record in the County Court of King George
will appear; And Whereas THOMAS JETT and WILLIAM BERNARD pursuant of the sd.
Trust haveing agreed with COLLIN REDDOCK for sale of the tract of land with its appurtenances; THIS INDENTURE therefore Witnesseth that THOMAS JETT & WILLIAM BER-
NARD in consideration of sum of hundred pounds Sterling, by these presents do bargain & sell lunto COLLIN REDDOCK his heirs the tract of land with all its rights members & appurtenances; To have and to hold the tract of land and premises to COLLIN
REDDOCK his heirs; In Witness whereof THOMAS JETT and WILLIAM BERNARD have
hereunto set their hands and seals the day and year above written
Signed Sealed and Acknowledged in presence of
         RICHARD BERNARD, BIRKETT DAVENPORT   THOMAS JETT
         WILLIAM ROBINSON, THOS: HODGE   WILLIAM BERNARD
   Received the consideration within mentioned; Witness our hands the day and year
within mentioned
Witness BIRKETT DAVENPORT,   THOS: JETT
         THOS: HODGE, WILL: ROBINSON,   WM: BERNARD
         RICHD: BERNARD
   At a Court held for King George County the 5th day of August 1773
THOS: JETT & WILL: BERNARD, Gent., acknowledged this their Indented Deed of Bargain
and Sale to COLLIN REDDOCK and on the motion of the said REDDOCK is admitted to
Record   Test JOS: ROBINSON, Cl

pp.   THIS INDENTURE made the twelfth day of May in the year of our Lord one thou-
1038- sand seven hundred and seventy three Between SAMUEL SIMPSON of County of
1042   ALBEMARLE, Eldest Son & heir at Law of WILLIAM SIMPSON, late of King George
        County, deced., of one part and WILLIAM HEWITT of County of King George of
other part, Whereas WILLIAM SIMPSON was in his lifetime seized and possessed of a
certain tract of land in County of King George containing by estimation one hundred
acres and did by his Last Will and Testament dated the Eighteenth day of May in year of
our Lord one thousand seven hundred & forty nine duly recorded in said County Court,
give & devise the Land to his Wife, DIANA SIMPSON, during herlife & after her death to
be sold at Publick Auction and the money to be equally divided between his Son,
SAMUEL SIMPSON, his Daughter MARGARET DAFTON, and his two Sons in Law, JAMES
PEYTON & EVAN PEYTON, & Whereas DIANA SIMPSON has departed this life in the month
of Febry: last and said Land has been sold at Publick Auction to WILLIAM HEWITT for
the sum of seventy seven pounds, five shillings; NOW THIS INDENTURE WITNESSETH
that SAMUEL SIMPSON for sum of five shillings current money doth by these presents
bargain and sell unto WM: HEWITT the tract. of land which is bounded; Begining at a
white Oak standing in the head of a Branch called the WHITE OAK BRANCH and runing
thence Easterly to a line of FITZHUGHs Land, thence along that line to another line of
sd. FITZHUGH, thence with that line to the line of POLLARD (formerly KENYON), at a
corner tree, thence to the begining; which tract of land was conveyed by WILLIAM
FLOWERS to WILLIAM SIMPSON by Deed of Feoffment dated the Fourth day of March in
the year of our Lord one thousand seven hundred and Thirty nine as by said Deed recorded in the County of King George may appear; Together with all houses profits and
appurtenances belonging; To have and to hold the tract of land & premises with the
appurtenance unto WILLIAM HEWITT his heirs during the term of one whole year
paying one ear of Indian Corn on the Feast of St. Michael if demanded, to the intent that
by virtue of these presents and of the Statute for transferring uses into possession,
WILLIAM HEWITT may be in actial possession of the premises and be thereby enabled to
accept a release of the inheritance thereof; In Witness whereof the said SAMUEL SIMP-
SON hath hereunto set his hand and affixed his seal the day and year first above written
Sealed and Delivered in the presence of
     JAMES PEYTON,   SAMUEL SIMPSON
     EVAN PEYTON, BENJA: LEATCH
  At a Court held for King George County the 7th day of October 1773
This Indented Deed of Lease from SAMUEL SIMPSON to WILLIAM HEWITT proved by the
Oaths of JAMES PEYTON, EVAN PEYTON & BENJAMIN LEACH, witnesses thereto and is
admitted to Record
      THIS INDENTURE made the Thirteenth day of May in the year of our Lord one
thousand seven hundred & seventy three Between SAMUEL SIMPSON of County of ALBE-
MARLE, Eldest Son & Heir at Law of WILLIAM SIMPSON, late of King George County,
deced., of one part and WILLIAM HEWITT of County of King George of other part;
Whereas (this Indenture continues repeating the passing of the land to SAMUEL SIMPSON as
described in the above Lease to WILLIAM HEWITT, the highest bidder for seventy seven pounds five
shillings; NOW THIS INDENTURE WIT-NESSETH that SAMUEL SIMPSON in consideration of
the sum of twenty five pounds, fifteen shillings (being the proportional part of the
price to be paid for the Land) to him in hand paid by WILLIAM HEWITT doth bargain
and sell unto WILLIAM HEWITT (in his actual possession now being by virtue of a
bargain and sale to him made for one year and by force of the Statute for transferring
uses into possession) and to his heirs the tract of which which is bounded; (the description of the bounds of the land repeated as in the Lease); To have and to hold the tract of land

and premises with appurtenances unto WILLIAM HEWITT his heirs discharged from all incumbrances; And SAMUEL SIMPSON and his heirs the land and premises to WILLIAM HEWITT his heirs from the claim of every person shall warrant and forever defend by these presents: In Witness whereof the said SAMUEL SIMPSON hath hereunto set his hand and affixed his seal the day & year above written
Sealed & Delivered in presence of
  JAMES PEYTON   SAMUEL SIMPSON
  EVAN PEYTON, BENJA: LEATCH
 Received of WILLIAM HEWITT the sum of twenty five pounds, fifteen shillings being the consideration within mentioned
  JAMES PEYTON,   SAMUEL SIMPSON
  EVAN PEYTON, BENJAMIN LEATCH
 At a Court held for King George County the 7th day of October 1773
An Indented Deed of Release & Receipt from SAMUEL SIMPSON to WILLIAM HEWITT proved by the Oaths of JAMES PEYTON, EVAN PEYTON and BENJAMIN LEATCH & is admitted to Record

pp THIS INDENTURE made the third day of April in the year of our Lord Christ one
1042- thousand seven-hundred seventy & three Between GEORGE SLAUGHTER and
1044 MARY his Wife of County of CULPEPER of one part and RICHARD LEWIS of County of King George of other part; Witnesseth that GEORGE SLAUGHTER hath this day bargained and sold unto RICHARD LEWIS hisheirs one half of certain lotts of land in the Town of FALMOUTH known by the numbers /23 & 34/ in the platt of said Town, lately purchased by said SLAUGHTER of WILLIAM KNOX and bounded; Begining at the West corner of Lott No. 29, now the property of JAMES BUCHANAN on the front of CAROLINE STREET, thence extending Westerly along said Street five poles to a line dividing this from an equal quantity of ground sold this day to ALEXR. WODROW by me, thence along the said line sixteen poles to ANN STREET, thence along ANN STREET Easterly five poles to the Corner of Lot No. 35, the property of JAMES BUCHANAN, thence along said BUCHANANs line sixteen poles to the begining; containing one half acre or Lott of Ground with appurtenances thereunto belonging; with all houses profits and advantages appertaining free and clear from the claim of GEORGE SLAUGHTER and MARY his Wife their heirs in consideration of the sum of Sixty pounds current money of Virginia To have and to hold the said lotts of ground and GEORGE SLAUGHTER and MARY his Wife release all their estate right and demand thereto warranting and forever defending the same to RICHARD LEWIS his heirs; In Witness whereof the said GEORGE SLAUGHTER and MARY his Wife have hereunto set their hands and seals the day and year first above written
Sealed Signed and Delivered in presence of
  JAMES BUCHANAN,   GEORGE SLAUGHTER
  HANCOCK LEE   MARY SLAUGHTER
  JOHN ROBERTSON) witness to George
  ALEXR. WODROW   ) Slaughters signing
  BENJAMIN ROBERTS younger; JAMES PEYTON,
  JOHN LEE, JOHN EUSTACE
 Received of RICHARD LEWIS the sum of sixty pounds current money of Virginia being the consideration within mentioned
Test JAMES BUCHANAN,   GEORGE SLAUGHTER
  HANCOCK LEE, JOHN ROBERTSON

At a Court held for King George County the 7th of October 1773
An Indented Deed of Feofment from GEORGE SLAUGHTER & Uxr. to RICHARD LEWIS
proved by the witnesses and admitted to Record
                    Test   JOS: ROBINSON, C. KGC

p.   THIS INDENTURE made the Twentieth day of May one thousand seven hundred
1045   and seventy three Between DAVID BRIGGS of King George County of one part
          and JAMES JONES of King George County of other part; Witnesseth that JAMES
JONES for sum of Eighty pounds & five pence three farthings doth bargain. sell and
confirm unto DAVID BRIGGS one Negro man named Harry about forty years of age, to
have and to hold the Negro man unto DAVID BRIGGS his heirs, Provided nevertheless
that if JAMES JONES do well and truly pay DAVID BRIGGS his Attorney the aforesaid sum
and Interest, Then this Instrument of Writing to be void, otherwise to remain in force
and virtue; In Witness whereof the said JAMES JONES hath hereunto set his hand and
seal the day and year above written
Signed Sealed and Delivered in presence of
        CHARLES ASHLEY,   JAMES JONES
        LAUCHN: MACKINTOSH,
        WILLIAM WINLOCK
    At a Court held for King George County the 7th day of October 1773
JAMES JONES acknowledges this his Mortgage to DAVID BRIGGS which is admitted to
Record

pp.   THIS INDENTURE made the nineteenth day of August in year of our Lord one
1046-   thousand seven hundred & seventy three Between THOMAS SHARPE of County of
1048   King George in Colony & Dominion of Virginia and HANNAH his Wife of the first
          part, JAMES ROBINSON of the Town of FALMOUTH and aforesaid County, Mer-
chant and Factor for Messrs. ANDREW COCKRANE, WILLIAM CUNNINGHAME & COMPANY
of the City of GLASGOW in the Kingdom of Great Britain of the second part and the said
Messrs. ANDREW COCKRANE, WILLIAM CUNNINGHAM & COMPANY of the third part;
Witness that THOMAS SHARPE for sum of Four hundred and forty four pounds, five
shillings & eight pence currt. money of Virignia to him in hand paid by JAMES ROBIN-
SON on behalf of said ANDREW COCKRANE, WILLIAM CUNNINGHAM & COMPANY, by these
presents said THOMAS SHARPE and HANNAH his Wife do bargain and sell unto ANDREW
COCKRANE, WILLIAM CUNNINGHAM & COMPANY that tract of land on which the said
SHARPE now lives, will'd to him by his Father, LINCEFIELD SHARPE, deceased, joining
what my Father sold BRYON O'BANNON and gave to my Brother, LINCEFIELD SHARPE, also
to the land of RICHARD SEVAN EDWARDS containing by estimation one hundred and
seventy acres be the same more or less with all houses gardens profits and appurte-
nances belonging; To have and to hold the premises with appurtenance unto JAMES
ROBINSON his heirs to the use of ANDREW COCKRANE, WILLIAM CUNNINGHAM and COM-
PANY their heirs; Provided nevertheless and it is agreed by and between the parties to
these presents tht if THOMAS SHARPE his heirs shall pay unto ANDREW COCKRANE,
WILLIAM CUNNINGHAM and COMPANY or their certain Factor and Attorney, the sum of
Four hundred and forty five pounds, five shillings and eight pence with lawfull
Interest for the same on the nineteenth day of August one thousand seven hundred and
seventy three, Then this present Indenture shall cease and become void; In Witness
whereof the sd. parties to these presents have hereunto interchangeably set their
hands and affixed their seals this nineteenth day of August one thousand seven hundred and seventy three

Sealed & Delivered in presence of
     ADAM NEWALL   THOMAS SHARPE
     WILLIAM LOVE   HANNAH her mark ⅄ SHARPE
     GEORGE HOLT, DAVID BRIGGS,   JAMES ROBINSON
     A. BUCHANAN, HANCOCK LEE
    At a Court held for King George County the 7th day of Octr. 1773 (1774 in text)
An Indented Deed of Mortgage from THOMAS SHARPE and HANNAH his Wife to JAMES
ROBINSON for the use of ANDREW COCKRANE, WILLIAM CUNNINGHAM & COMPY. was
proved as to the said THOMAS by the Oaths of HANCOCK LEE, DAVID BRIGGS & ANDREW
BUCHANAN, and on the motion of the said ROBINSON is admitted to Record

pp.   THIS INDENTURE made the 18th day of June one thousand seven hundred &
1049   seventy three Between JOHN COCKSHUTT and others, Trustees of Mr. JOHN BLAND,
1050   of LONDON, Mercht., of the one part and REUBIN PAYNE of County of King George
      of other part; Witnesseth that REUBIN PAYNE for sum of twenty two pounds, one
shilling and eight pence current money to him in hand paid, hath bargained and sold
unto JOHN COCKSHUTT and others, Trustees of Mr. JOHN BLAND, one Bay Mare about ten
years old branded on the near buttock W.E., three red Cows, one Bull and red Heifer
mark'd differently, three feather beds and furniture; To have and to hold the goods &
chattles unto JOHN COCKSHUTT and others, Trustees of Mr. JOHN BLAND of LONDON,
Mercht., Provided however that if REUBIN PAYNE shall pay to JOHN COCKSHUTT and
others, Trustees of Mr. JOHN BLAND, the aforesaid Debt and Interest from the date
hereof then this Instrument of Writing to be void otherwise to remain in force. In
Witness whereof the said REUBIN PAYNE hath hereunto set his hand and seal the day
and year above written
Sign'd Sealed & Delivered in presence of
     DAVID BRIGGS, CHARLES ASHLEY,   REUBIN PAYNE
     ALEXR: HANSFORD, WILLIAM SWETNAM
    At a Court held for King George County 7th day of October 1773
REUBIN PAYNE acknowledged this Mortgage to JOHN COCKSHUTT and others and is
admitted to Record

p.   KNOW ALL MEN by these presents that I JOHN PECK of County of King George
1050   for sum of twenty three poudns, one shilling and eight pence current money to
      me in hand paid by WILLIAM BOON, Deputy Sheriff, do by these presents bar-
gain and sell unto ye sd. WILLIAM BOON the following Negroes, stocks of Horses, cattle,
sheep, hoggs & household furniture, vizt., Negro Ben, Alice, Heathy, Clary, James,
Tom & Sarger, one horse, one black mare three years & three lambs, three cows, one
yearling and one Calf and twenty hoggs, two feather beds and furniture, one desk, two
tables, six chairs, six pewter dishes, one dozen pewter plates, five pewter basons, six
knives and forks, one Chest, three iron pots & pott hooks, one Dutch oven, one iron pot
rack, two pales, two piggins, and one Gun and one bell; To have & to hold the goods and
chattles unto WILLIAM BOON his heirs and JOHN PECK the said goods and chattles, together with the future increase of the Negroes and stocks unto WILLIAM BOON against the
claim of all persons will warrant and forever defend and I do hereby put WILLIAM
BOON in full possession by delivering the Bell before mentioned in name of the whole;
In Witness whereof I have hereunto set my hand and seal the Sixth day of March one
thousand seven hundred and seventy three

Sealed & Delivered in presence of
     SAML: PECK,
     GEORGE his mark Ⅹ JOHNSON
     SAML: TODD

                            JOHN PECK

At a Court held for King George County the 7th day of October 1773
JOHN PECKs Indented Mortgage to WILLIAM BOON proved by the witnesses thereto and admitted to Record

pp.   THIS INDENTURE made the third day of April in the year of our Lord one thou-
1051- sand seven hundred and seventy three Between GEORGE SLAUGHTER and MARY
1053 his Wife of County of CULPEPER of one part and ALEXR: WODROW of Town of
       FALMOUTH in County of King George of other part; Witnesseth that GEORGE
SLAUGHTER hath this day bargained and sold unto ALEXR: WODROW his heirs one half of
certain two lots of ground in Town of FALMOUTH known by numbers /28 & 32/ in the
Platt of said Town and lately purchased by GEORGE SLAUGHTER of WILLIAM KNOX and
bounded; Begining at the corner of Lot No. 28 where CAROLINE STREET intersects with
CAMBRIDGE STREET, thence along CAMBRIDGE STREET to the corner of Lot No. 34, where
ANN STREET intersects with CAMBRIDGE STREET, sixteen poles, thence along ANN STREET
five poles, thence through the middle of the two lots sixteen poles to CAROLINE STREET,
thence along CAROLINE STREET five poles to the begining; containing one half acre or
lot of ground with the appurtenances belonging and the rents issues and profits thereof; which lots of ground GEORGE SLAUGHTER for sum of four hundred and ninety
pounds current money bargained and sold unto ALEXR: WODROW, his heirs; To have and
to hold free and clear from all claim demand or title of any person warranting and for
ever defending the same unto ALEXR: WODROW his heirs; In Witness whereof, GEORGE
SLAUGHTER and MARY his Wife have hereunto set their hands and seals the day and
year first above written
Sealed Signed and Delivered in presence of
     JAMES BUCHANAN,   GEORGE SLAUGHTER
     HANCOCK LEE   MARY SLAUGHTER
     JOHN ROBERTSON   ) witness to George
     RICHARD LEWIS   ) Slaughter signing
     RICHARD LEWIS   )
     BENJAMIN ROBERTS, JOHN LEE)
     JAMES PEYTON, JOHN EUSTACE)
  Received of ALEXANDER WODROW the sum of one hundred and ninety pounds currt.
money of Virginia, being the consideration within mentioned
Test   JAMES BUCHANAN,   GEORGE SLAUGHTER
     HANCOCK LEE,   JOHN ROBERTSON
  At a Court held for King George County the 7th day of Octr: 1773
GEORGE SLAUGHTER & Wifes Indented Deed of Feoffment to ALEXR: WODROW proved by
three witnesses & admitted to Record
               Test JOS: ROBINSON, Cl. KGC

pp.   THIS INDENTURE made this 18th day of June one thousand seven hundred and
1053- seventy three Between THOMAS PEED of Parish of (blank) in County of RICH-
1055 MOND of one part and THOMAS JETT of County of King George and Parish of
       Hanover of other part; Witnesseth that THOMAS PEED for sum of one hundred
and thirty pounds, eighteen shillings and four pence current money of Virginia to him
in hand paid by THOMAS JETT, by these presents doth bargain and sell unto THOMAS

JETT and his heirs all that tract of land situate in County of King George containing 100 acres and all houses and underwoods thereunto belonging together with the two following slaves, Moll & Jack, also seven head of Cattle, a bay Mare & 2 feather beds and furniture; To have and to hold the tract of land & premises together with the two slaves 7 head of cattle, 1 bay mare & 2 feather beds & furntire unto THOMAS JETT his heirs, Provided always and it is hereby agreed between the parties to these presents that if THOMAS PEED doth pay THOMAS JETT his heirs the full sum of one hundred and thirty two pounds, eighteen shillings & five pence current money on or before the 20th day of June next coming with lawfull Interest thereon from these presents that then and in such case THOMAS JETT hereby covenants and promises to deliver up and convey unto THOMAS PEED the before mentioned tract of land &c., In Witness whereof the said THOMAS PEED hath hereunto set his hand and seal the day and year first before written Sealed & Delivered in the presence of

REUBIN BRISCOE,   THOMAS PEAD
JN: PAYTON, GEO: CHARMICHAEL,
BENJA: DAY

Received 18th June from THOMAS JETT the sum of One hundred and thirty two pounds, eighteen shillings & five pence current money, being the consideration mentioned in this Indenture to be by the said THOMAS JETT paid to
Witness REUBIN BRISCOE,   THOMAS PEED
JN: PAYTON, GEO: CARMICHAEL,
BENJAMIN DAY

At a Court held for King George County the 7th day of Apl. 1774
An Indented Deed of Mortgage from THOMAS PEAD to THOMAS JETT further proved by BENJAMIN DAY and admitted to Record

pp.   THIS INDENTURE made this 3d. day of July one thousand seven hundred and
1055-   seventy three Between JACOB RAMEY of Parish of Hanover in County of King
1057   George of one part and THOMAS JETT of same County and Parish of other part;
          Witnesseth that JACOB RAMEY for sum of Sixty one pounds, seven shillings & three pence current money of Virginia to him in hand paid by THOMAS JETT   by these presents doth bargain and sell unto THOMAS JETT and his heirs one forth part of a Negro man named David in the possession of DOCTR: WILLIAMS, one black Mare, saddle and bridle, one bed and furniture, 2 chests and one pewter dish, 2 basons, 6 plates, 6 knives and forks, one iron pott & pott hooks, 1 Ladle & flesh fork, 2 gunns, 1 broad axe & weeding hoe, 3 augurs, 2 chissells, carpenters adze, 2 punch bowles, 1 pint mugg, 6 pewter teaspoons, 1 sett shoemakers tools; To have and to hold the aforesaid unto THOMAS JETT his heirs provided always and it is hereby agreed by and between the parties to these presents that if JACOB RAMEY shall pay unto THOMAS JETT his heirs the full sum of sixty one pounds, seven shillings & three pence current money on or before the fifth day of July next coming with lawfull Interest thereon from the date of these presents, then and in such case THOMAS JETT hereby covenants & promises to deliver up & reconvey unto JACOB RAMEY or to his heirs the beforementioned; In Witness whereof the sd. JACOB RAMEY hath hereunto set his hand and seal the day and year first before written
Sealed & Delivered in the presence of
BENJAMIN DAY, REUBEN BRISCOE,   JACOB RAMEY
JOHN WROE, GEO: CARMICHAEL

Received third July 1773 from THOMAS JETT the sum of sixty one pounds, seven shillings and three pence current money being the consideration mentioned in the

Indenture to be by the said THOMAS JETT paid to
Witness BENJAMIN DAY, REUBIN BRISCOE,   JACOB RAMEY
      JOHN WROE, GEO: CHARMICHAEL
   Ballace of J. RAMEYs Acct. on T. M. J. Books. L. 61...7...3.
   At a Court held for King George County the 7th day of April 1774
An Indented Deed of Mortgage from JACOB RAMEY to THOMAS JETT further proved by
BENJAMIN DAY and admitted to Record

pp.   THIS INDENTURE made this 28th day of December in year of our Lord one thou-
1057-   sand seven hundred and seventy two Between ARTHUR MORSON of FALMOUTH,
1062   Merchant, of one part and WILLIAM GRAVES of STAFFORD County, Planter, of
         other part; Witnesseth that ARTHUR MORSON in consideration of the Rents,
duties, reservations & covenants herein after reserved and mentioned on part and behalf of WILLIAM GRAVES his heirs to be paid done and performed; hath granted and to
farm let unto WILLIAM GRAVES his heirs a certain tract of land in tenure & occupation
of said WILLIAM GRAVES now containing one hundred and forty four acres be the same
more or less lying in Brunswick Parish and County of King George and bounded;
Be0gining at two red Oaks and one Hicory Saplin by a Branch of the HORSEPEN and
corner to Land late the property of WILLIAM FRISTO and in HANCOCK LEEs Line, thence
along the said LEEs line S. 50 W. about 90 poles to another corner, thence N. 54 W. about
60 poles to another corner, thence S. 17 W. about 65 poles to BROWNEs Corner, thence
along with BROWNs line about a N. W. course 130 poles to a white Oak, thence about a N.
E., course 170 poles, thence S. E. 160 poles to the begining; together with all profits
commodities and appurtenances belonging; To have and to hold the parcel of one
hundred and forty four acres of land unto WILLIAM GRAVES his heirs from the day of
the date hereof during the natural lives of him the said WILLIAM GRAVES, MARGARET
GRAVES his Wife & THOMAS GRAVES his Son and the longest liver of them, paying unto
ARTHUR MORSON his heirs yearly the rent of seven pounds, four shillings currt. money
and the Quitrents on the first day of January annually; In Witness whereof the said
parties have hereunto interchangably set their hands and affixed their seals the day
month and year first above written
Signed Sealed & Delivered in presence of
      JAMES JEFFRIES,   ARTHUR MORSON
      WILLIAM JFEFRIES, JOHN UHQUHART   WILLIAM GRAVES
   No Rent to be paid for the within mentioned premises except the Quitrents for the
years one thousand seven hundred & seventy three & one thousand seven hundred and
seventy four; Witness my hand this 28th December 1772
                                                   ARTHUR MORSON
   At a Court held for King George County the 4th dy of November 1773
ARTHUR MORSON acknowledges this his Lease for Lives to WILLIAM GRAVES and on the
motion of the said GRAVES is admitted to Record

pp.   KNOW ALL MEN by these presences that I FRANCIS DAY of County of King
1062-   George, Planter, for the sum of One hundred and seventy pounds, five shillings
1063   & nine pence current money of Virginia due by me to Messrs. ANDREW COCK-
         RANE, WILLIAM CUNNINGHAM & COMPANY of the City of GLASGOW, by these
presents do brgain and sell unto Messrs. ANDREW COCKRANE, WILLIAM CUNNINGHAM &
COMPANY their certain factor and attorney their heirs six Negro slaves consisting of
four males, viz. Anthony, George, Harry & Moses & two females, Beck and Bett., together
with the future increase of the said Negroes Bett & Beck; To have and to hold the said

slaves and increase to Messr. ANDREW COCKRANE, WILLIAM CUNNINGHAM & COMPY.
their heirs and I the said FRANCIS DAY do warrant and defend the said hereby sold
slaves; Provided nevertheless and this Bill of Sale is upon this express condition tht if
FRANCIS DAY his heirs shall pay unto ANDREW COCKRANE, WILLIAM CUNNINGHAM &
COMPANY or their certain Factor or Attorney the sum of One hundred seventy pounds,
five shillings and nine pence current money of Virginia with Interest from this date
on or before the first day of January seventeen hundred and seventy four then this
Obligation shall be void & of no effect; In Witness whereof the said FRANCIS DAY hath
hereunto put his hand and seal this Eighteenth day of September one thousand seven
hundred & seventy three
Sealed and Delivered in the presence of
    ADAM NEWALL,   FRANCIS DAY
    WILLIAM McMILLIAN
    At a Court held for King George County the 4th day of November 1773
FRANCIS DAY acknowledged his Bill of Sale & Mortgage to ANDREW COCKRANE & COMPY.
which is admitted to Record Teste JOS: ROBINSON, Cl KGC

pp.   THIS INDENTURE made the Seventh day of July in year of our Lord one thou-
1064- sand seven hundred and seventy three Between JAMES LAVERTY of County of
1065   King George of one part and JOHN BLAND, Mercht., of other part; Witnesseth
      that JAMES LAVERTY for sum of Forty seven pounds, ten shillings and four
pence farthing current money to him in hand paid by JOHN BLAND, by these presents
doth bargain and sell unto JOHN BLAND and his heirs one Negro man, Daniel, about
thirty years of age, one grey mare four years old branded T., on the near buttock, and
on the near buttock J., two cows redish cold. & brindled and two yearlings & one bay
Horse about twelve years old, one feather bed and furniture, one Chest of drawers,
thirteen hoggs marked with a crop in the left ear and a half crop in the right & six
chairs; also all the right and title and Interest of JAMES LAVERTY his heirs in the said
goods & chattles hereby conveyed to JOHN BLAND his heirs; To have & to hold the goods
& chattles unto JOHN BLAND his heirs in Trust for the following uses, that is to say, in
Trust and for the use of JAMES LAVERTY untill the 25th day of December 1774 and afterwards to and for the use of JAMES LAVERTY his heirs forever Provided said JAMES
LAVERTY shall well and truly pay to JOHN BLAND his certain Attorney, his heirs the
sum of forty seven pounds, ten shillings and four pence farthing on or before the 25th
day of December 1774 with lawfull Interest from the date hereof till paid, In Witness
whereof the said JAMES LAVERTY hath hereunto set his hand and seal the day and year
first above mentioned
Signed Sealed and Delivered in presence of
    DAVID BRIGGS,   JAMES LAVERTY
    CHARLES ASHLEY, LA: MACKINTOSH,
    THOMAS BALLARD
    At a Court held for King George County the 4th day of November 1773
JAMES LAVERTY acknowledges this his Mortgage to the Trustees of Mr. JOHN BLAND & IS
admitted to Record   Test JOS: ROBINSON, Cl. KGC

pp.   THIS INDENTURE made this twentieth dy of September one thousand seven hun-
1066- dred and seventy three Between ARTHUR MORSON, Merchant in FALMOUTH, of
1067   one part and PETER HORD of King George County, Planter, of other part; Wit-
      nesseth that ARTHUR MORSON for sum of Ninety seven pounds & four shillings
current money in hand paid doth by these presents bargain and sell unto PETER HORD

his heirs a certain parcel of land situate in King George County on RICHLAND RUN and
containing by estimation one hundred & sixty two acres be the same more or less; and
bounded, Begining at A., an old marked red Oak hard by MOUNTAGUEs Land, upon East
side of RICHLAND RUN on the side of a Knowl & extending thence S. 29 E. 20 poles to
another old marked tree, thence S. 37 E. 16 poles to C., a white and red Oak in MOUNTA-
GUEs Line, thence South 60 E. 48 poles to D., a white Oak saplin, thence N. 82 E. 67 poles to
E., thence No. 43 E. 110 poles to F., thence No. 40 W. 134 po. to G., the mouth of the ( ) in
RICHLAND RUN, thence down said Run N. 49 W. 26 poles (series of distances and directions)
a corner upon RICHLAND RUN, then S. 29 E. 32 poles to the begining; Together with all
houses and appurtenances; To have and to hold the hereby granted land and premises
unto PETER HORD his heirs clear from all incumbrances except the Quitrents, and
ARTHUR MORSON his heirs will at all times hereafter warrant the same against the
claim of all persons; In Testimony of which the said ARTHUR MORSON hath hereunto
set his hand and seal the day month and year first above written
Signed Sealed & Acknowledged in the presence of
    DAVID BRIGGS, A. BUCHANAN,   ARTHUR MORSON
    THOMAS HORD, JOHN ROBERTSON
  At a Court held for King George County the 4th day of November 1773
ARTHUR MORSON acknowledges this his Indented Deed of Feoffment to PETER HORD & it
is admitted to Record

pp.   THIS INDENTURE made the Twelfth day of June in the year of our Lord one
1067-   thousand seven hundred and seventy three Between COLLIN REDDOCK of County
1068   of King George of one part and THOMAS OSWALD of same County of other part;
      Witnesseth that COLLIN REDDOCK for sum of six hundred pounds Sterling to him
in hand paid by these presents doth bargain and sell unto THOMAS OSWALD his heirs all
that tract of land whereon sd. COLLIN REDDOCK resides containing Four hundred and
fifty acres or thereabouts together with all its rights members & appurtenances to
THOMAS OSWALD his heirs, Provided always & these presents are upon this condition
that if COLLIN REDDOCK his heirs shall pay unto THOMAS OSWALD his heirs the just sum
of six hundred pounds Sterling with interest thereon at the rate of four per centum per
annum from the first day of March last past the following proportions, that is to say,
two hundred pounds Sterling on the first day of March next ensuing, other two
hundred pounds Sterling on the first day of March next thereafter and the remaining
two hundred pounds Sterling on the first day of March next following with Interest to
be computed as afsd., Then these presents and every thing therein contained to cease
determine & be utterly void; In Witness whereof the said COLLIN REDDOCK hath hereunto set his hand & seal the day and year aforesaid
Signed Sealed & Acknowledged in presence of
    THOS: JETT, REUBIN BRISCOE   COLLIN REDDOCK
    RICHARD PAYNE, GEO: CARMICHAEL
  Received the within consideration witness my hand
Witness THOS: JETT, RICHARD PAYNE,   COLLIN REDDOCK
    GEO: CARMICHAEL, REUBIN BRISCOE
  At a Court held for King George County the 4th day of November 1773
COLLIN REDDOCKs Indented Deed of Bargain and Sale to THOMAS OSWALD, Gent., proved
by three witnesses & ordered to be recorded
              Test JOS: ROBINSON, Cl, KGC

pp.
1069-
1070

THIS INDENTURE made the Thirtieth day of November in the year of our Lord one thousand seven hundred and seventy three Between WILLIAM LOVE of Town of FALMOUTH, Merchant, of one part and ANDREW BUCHANAN, of the same place, Attorney at Law, of other part; Witnesseth that WM: LOVE for sum of twenty pounds current money to him in hand paid doth by these presents bargain and sell unto ANDREW BUCHANAN (in his actual posssession now being) and to his heirs two lotts of ground in Town of FALMOUTH known in the plan of said Town by the Lots numbers forty six and fifty two; which lots were conveyed to WILLIAM LOVE by Deed from the Trustees of said Town recording in the County of King George, together with all houses profits & appurtenances belonging; To have and to hold the lots & premises unto ANDREW BUCHANAN his heirs; and WILLIAM LOVE his heirs the lots and premises unto ANDREW BUCHANAN his heirs from the claim & demand of every person claiming under him shall warrant and forever defend by these presents;
Sealed and Delivered in the presence of

ROBT. LAWSON,   ALEXR: HANSFORD,   WILLIAM LOVE
DAVID BRIGGS,   ROBT. INNIS,
JOHN ROBERTSON

At a Court held for King George County the 2d. day of December 1773
WILLIAM LOVEs Indented Deed of Bargain & Sale to ANDREW BUCHANAN, Gent., proved by the Oaths of ROBERT LAWSON, ALEXR: HANSFORD & JOHN ROBERTSON & admitted to Record

pp.
1071-
1072

THIS INDENTURE made the Thirtieth day of November in year of our Lord one thousand seven hundred & seventy three Between MOOR of Town of FALMOUTH, Merchant, of one part and WILLIAM LOVE of the same place, Mercht., of the other part; Witnesseth that EDWARD MOOR for sum of fifteen pounds to him in hand paid doth bargain & sell unto WILLIAM LOVE (now in possession thereof) and to his heirs two lotts of ground in Town of FALMOUTH each containing one half acre & known in the plan of sd. Town by the Lots numbers thirty eight & thirty nine, which lotts were conveyed to EDWARD MOOR by the Trustees of said Town by Deed recorded in the County of King George, together with all houses profits & heriditaments belonging; To have and to hold the lots & premises unto WILLIAM LOVE his heirs; And EDWARD MOOR & his heirs the bargained and sold premises from the claim & demand of every person claiming under him shall warrant and forever defend by these presents; In Witness whereof the said EDWARD MOOR hath hereunto set his hand and seal the day & year first above written
Sealed and delivered in presence of

ROBT. LAWSON,   JOHN ROBERTSON,   EDWARD MOOR
ALEXR: HANSFORD,   DAVID BRIGGS,
ROBT. INNIS,   A. BUCHANAN

At a Court held for King George County the 2d. day of December 1773
EDWARD MOORs Indented Deed of Bargain and Sale to WILLIAM LOVE proved by the Oaths of ROBERT LAWSON, ALEXANDER HANSFORD & JOHN ROBERTSON, & admitted to Record

pp.
1072-
1074

THIS INDENTURE made the twenty second day of May MDCCLXXIII Between RICHARD GARNER of County of King George of one part & JAMES BOWIE JR. of County of CAROLINE of other part; Witnesseth that said RICHARD for sum of Fifty eight pounds, six shillings and nine pence half penny for which sum said RICHARD is indebted to said JAMES said RICHARD having received the value thereof from said JAMES by these presents doth bargain and sell unto JAMES BOWIE his heirs a Negro girl named Lett & two beds and furniture; To have and hold the said slave, beds and furniture unto said JAMES his heirs, Provided nevertheless that if said RICHARD his heirs do pay to said JAMES his heirs the full sum of fifty eight pounds, six shillings and nine pence half penny with interest from the date hereof on or before the 22d. day of November next, then this Indenture to be void otherwise to remain in full force and virtue and the said RICHARD for himself his heirs the slave and other the premises gainst all persons shall warrant and forever defend by these presents; In Witness whereof I have hereunto set my hand and affixed my seal the day & year first above written

Signed sealed and delivered in presence of

JOS: TIMBERLAKE JUNR.,   RICHARD GARNER
JAMES KEMP, GEORGE CATLET

Received from JAMES BOWIE JR. fifty eight pounds, six shillings and nine pence, half penny, the consideration afsd.   RICHARD GARNER

Memorandum: RICHD: GARNERs. Rect. against JAMES BOWIE of L. 11...11...3 is to be discounted out of the above

At a Court held for King George County the 2d. day of December 1773

RICHARD GARNERs Indented Deed of Mortgage to JAMES BOWIE JUNR. proved by the Oaths of JOS: TIMBERLAKE & GEORGE CATLET and on the motion of the said BOWIE is admitted to Record

pp. 1074-1075   THIS INDENTURE made the Fifth day of June in the year of our Lord one thousand seven hundred and seventy three Between the Reverend JOHN DIXON, Clerk, of the one part and JOHN DAY of County of King George and Town of FALMOUTH, Tailor, of the other part; Witnesseth that JOHN DIXON hath this day bargained and sold unto JOHN DAY his heirs a lot of land adjoining the Town of FALMOUTH containing half an acre or thereabouts & bounded, Begining at a Stake corner to a Lot sold by said DIXON to GEORGE STRINGFELLOW and runing thence with CAMBRIDGE STREET in the Town of FALMOUTH No. 27 Et. 117 feet to another Stake on said Street, thence No. 63 W. 136 feet to another Stake by the side of the FALLS RUN, thence down the Run S. 27 W. 117 feet to another Stake, corner of STRINGFELLOW, thence S. 63 E. 136 feet to the begining, with the appurtenances there-unto belonging; together with all houses profits and easements belonging and the rents issues and profits unto JOHN DAY his heirs clear from JOHN DIXON his heirs which lot of ground JOHN DIXON hath for the sum of Thirty pounds current money of Virginia bargained and sold unto JOHN DAY his heirs forever; To have and to hold clear from all claims or demands of any person unto JOHN DAY his heirs said JOHN DIXON warranting and for ever defending the same unto JOHN DAY his heirs from all persons; In Witness whereof the said JOHN DIXON have hereunto set his hand and seal the day and year first above written

Signed Sealed and Delivered in the presence of

THOMAS VOWLES, (name in German),   JOHN DIXON
CHARLES WALDEN

Received of JOHN DAY the sum of (blank) current money of Virginia, the consideration within mentioned as witness my hand this (blank) day of June 1773

                        (no witnesses or signature recorded)

At a Court held for King George County the 2d. day of December 1773

JOHN DIXONs Indented Deed of Feoffment to JOHN DAY proved by three witnesses & admitted to Record   Teste JOS: ROBINSON, Cl. KGCo.

pp.   INQUISITION Indented taken in County of King George the 17th day of Novem-
1076-   ber 1773 by virtue of an Order of King George County Court bearing date the 5th
1077   day of November 1773 to the Sheriff of King George County have caused twelve
        good & lawfull Freeholders of my Bailiwick to meet at the place in the said Order
directed and to value one acre of land requested by WILLIAM CHAMPE to be annexed to
the Mill petitioned for by said WILLIAM and to report what the Land may be effected or
laid under water by his doing such Mill or Mills together with the Timber and other
conveniences thereon as in said Order I am commanded. In Compliance therewith, the
said Jury (to wit) JOSEPH JONES, JOHN TALIAFERRO, JOHN POLLARD JUNR., WM. BROWN,
REUBEN OWENS, WM. GRANT, WM. HARRISON, WILLIAM PECK, WM. GRIGSBY, THOMAS
JORDAN, WM. PRICE and ANDREW HARRISON being first legally sworn proceeded in
company with JOHN TRIPLETT, Surveyor of said County, to lay of the acre afsd. now
requesting by the said WM. CHAMPE, as follows; Begining at a Stake in the edge of
POPLAR SWAMP runing thence South 39 1/4 West 22 poles to another Stake, thence No.
32 3/4 W. 10 poles to another Stake, thence to the begining, concluding 105 poles as by
the land survey thereof found by the said JOHN TRIPLETT hereunto annexed will more
fully appear; and the Jurors afsd. on our Oaths do say that the said part of an acre of
Land is of the value of one pound, ten shillings current money of Virginia and no more
and we also adjudge that the damages by overflowing the Land is of the value of thirty
pounds current money which part of an acre of land and the land that appears to us
that may be overflowed is now held by JOHN CHAMPE, Gent., and it doth appear to us that
any other person will be prejudiced thereby. In Testimony whereof as well, I WILLIAM
BOON, Deputy Sheriff for THOS: BERRY, Sheriff of said County, as the Jurors aforesaid
have hereunto set our hands & seals the day and year first above written
        WILLIAM BOON, Deputy Sheriff for THOS: BERRY, Sheriff
        JOS: JONES   JOHN TALIAFERRO   JOHN POLLARD JUNR.
        WM. BROWN   REUBEN OWENS   WM; GRANT,
        WM: HARRISON   WM: PECK   WM; GRIGSBY
        THOMAS JORDAN,   WM. PRICE   ANDW: HARRISON
    At a Court held for King George County the 2d. day of December 1773
This Inquisition returned and ordered to be recorded

pp.   AN INQUISITION Indented taking on the County of King George this twenty
1077   fourth day of September one thousand seven hundred and seventy two by the
1078   virtue of an Order of King George County Court bearing date Sept. 1772 to the
        Sheriff of the said County directed THOS: BERRY, Sheriff of the County afsd. have
caused twelve good and lawfull Freeholders of my Bailiwick to meet at the place in the
said Order directed and to value one acre of Land or such part thereof as may be
requested by JAMES CRAPP to be annexed to a Mill petitioned for by the said JAMES
CRAPP and to report what other lands may be affected or laid under water by building
such Mill together with the Timber and other conveniences thereon as in the said
Order I am commanded. In Compliance therewith, the said Jury, to wit, HANCOCK LEE,
JAMES HORD SENR. TAVERNER BRANHAM, JAMES DRAKE, CHARLES BENSON, ANDREW
SUITER, DANIEL MONROE, JESSE HORD, WILLIAM WOOD, JAMES TURNER, JOHN SMITH &
EVAN JONES, being first legally sworne proceeded in company with JOHN TRIPLETT,
Surveyor of said County, to lay of the acre aforesaid now requested by the said JAMES
CRAPP as follows, Begining at a Beach Tree at the edge of the Run, runing N. 18 E. 6
pole, thence N. 77 E. 26 pole, then So 2d. 30m. W. 14 pole, thence So. 14d. 30 m,. E. 4 pole,
then along the meanders of the Run to the begining including one acre of Land and
survey thereof made by said JOHN TRIPLETT hereunto annexed will more fully appear;

and the Jurors aforesaid on our Oaths do say that the said acre of Land is of the value of Ten shillgs, current money of Virginia and no more and as to any other prejudice erecting a Mill at the place aforesaid may be to any other person as the Jurors afsd. on our Oath aforesaid do further say that we cannot at this time ascertain that it doth not appear that it will be of any immediate prejudice to any person whatsoever; In Testimony whereof aswell I THOAMS BERRY, Sheriff aforesaid, as the Jurors aforesd. have hereunto set our hands & seals the day month and year first above written

THOMAS BERRY Sheriff

DANL: MONROE	JAMES HORD	WILLIAM WOOD
JAMES TURNER	JOHN SMITH	EVAN JONES
HANCOCK LEE	JAMES HORD	TAVERNER BRANHAM
JAMES DRAKE	CHS. BENSON,	ANDW. SUITER

September 24th 1772

Pursuant to an Order of King George County, September Court, 1772, I have laid off an acre of land petitioned for by JAMES CRAPP for the use of a Mill (bounds and distances as above are repeated); including one acre of land

(A small sketch appears on page 1078).   JOHN TRIPLETT, C.S.

At a Court held for King George County the 2d. day of December 1773 This Inquisition returned and admitted to Record

p.   GEORGE the Third by the grace of God of Great Britain France & Ireland, King
1079   Defender of the faith &c., to HORATIO DADE, WILLIAM THORNTON & JOHN SKINKER
        Gentlemen, Justices of King George County, Greeting. Whereas GEORGE ARNOLD and SARAH his Wife by their certain Deed of Bargain and Sale bearing date the 9th day of December 1772 have conveyed the fee simple Estate of one tract of land containing ninety acres be the same more or less with the appurtenances lying in County of King George, And whereas the said SARAH cannot conveniently travel to our said County Court of King George to make her acknowledgement of the said conveyance; Therefore we do assign and give unto you or any two or more of you full power and authority to receive the acknowledgemt. which the said SARAH shall be willing to make before you (the Commission for the privy examination of SARAH, the Wife of GEORGE ARNOLD); Witness JOS: ROBINSON, Clerk of our said Court this 7th day of Decr. 1772 in the thirteenth year of our Reign

Test JOS: ROBINSON C.K G.C

By virtue of the within Commission to us directed, we did personally go to the within named SARAH ARNOLD who the 9th day of December 1772 after being privily examined apart from her Husband, GEORGE ARNOLD did freely and voluntarily acknowledged her consent to the passing the land in the Deeds hereunto annexed and the relinquishment of her right thereto with this Writ as to us directed. Given under our hands and sals this 9th day of Decr. 1772.

Test JOS: ROBINSON, C.K.G.C.

p.   THIS INDENTURE made the seventh day of July one thousand seven hundred
1080   and seventy three Between JOHN COCKSHUTT and others, Trustees of Mr. JOHN
        BLAND of LONDON, Mercht. of the one part and GEORGE PAYNE of King George County of other part; Witnesseth that GEORGE PAYNE for sum of four pounds, nine shillings & seven pence three farthings current money to him in hand paid by JOHN COCKSHUTT & others, Trustees of Mr. JOHN BLAND of LONDON, Merchant, doth bargain and sell unto JOHN COCKSHUTT (&c.) the following goods and chattles, viz. two feather beds & furniture, two cows brindled, one black cow, one yearling and two calves, one black

mare branded H., To have and to hold the goods & chattles unto said JOHN COCKSHUTT (&c.) Provided however that if GEORGE PAYNE shall pay JOHN COCKSHUTT (&c.) the sum of Four pounds, nine shillings and seven pence three farthings curt. money with Interest that this Instrument of Writing to be void otherwise to remain in full force; In Witness whereof the said GEORGE PAYNE hath hereunto set his hand and seal the day and year above written

Signed sealed and delivered in presence of
        DAVID BRIGGS,   GEORGE PAYNE
        CHARLES ASHLEY,   LAUCHN. MACKINTOSH
   At a Court held for King George County the 3d. day of March 1774
GEORGE PAYNEs Mortgage to JOHN COCKSHUTT &c., Trustees of Mr. JOHN BLAND, proved by two witnesses and admitted to Record

p.   THIS INDENTURE made the second day of July one thousand seven hundred and
1081   seventy three Between JOHN COCKSHUTT and others, Trustees of Mr. JOHN BLAND,
        of LONDON, Merchant, of one part and JOHN SWETNAM of STAFFORD County of the other part; Witnesseth that JOHN SWETNAM for sum of twenty one pounds, six shillings and four pence half penny to him in hand paid by JOHN COCKSHUTT and others, Trustees of JOHN BLAND, doth bargain and sell unto JOHN COCKSHUTT (&c.) three feather beds and furniture, a brindled Cow and Calfe, a crop in the left Ear and under and over keel in the right, ten sheep some markt. To have and to hold the goods and creatures unto JOHN COCKSHUTT (&c.) Provided nevertheless that if JOHN SWETNAM shall pay unto JOHN COCKSHUTT (&c.) the aforesaid Debt and Interest from the date hereof then this Instrument of Writing to be void, otherwise to remain in force. In Witness whereof the said JOHN SWETNAM hath hereunto set his hand and seal the day and year above written
Signed Sealed and Delivered in presence of
        DAVID BRIGGS,   JOHN SWETNAM
        LAUCHN: MACKINTOSH,   WILLIAM REVELEY
   At a Court held for King George County the 3rd. day of March 1774
The aforegoing Deed of Mortgage from JOHN SWETNAM to JOHN COCKSHUTT and others, Trustees of JOHN BLAND, was proved by the Oath of LAUCHN. MACKINTOSH and ordered to be recorded

P.   THIS INDENTURE made the twenty first day of August one thousand seven hun-
1082   dred and seventy three Between JOHN COCKSHUTT and others, Trustees of Mr.
        JOHN BLAND of LONDON, Merchant, of one part and ZACHARIAH UNDERWOOD of King George County of other part; Witnesseth that ZACHARIAH UNDERWOOD for sum of Eleven pounds, thirteen shillings and nine pence three farthings currency to him in hand paid by DAVID BRIGGS, doth bargain and sell unto JOHN COCKSHUTT (&c.) two feather beds and all the furniture belonging thereto, twenty two pewters and three pewter dishes, three iron potts, one frying pann, one large and one small leather Trunk, one chest, one Poplar Table, three large earthen potts and the whole of the earthen ware now in my possession; one tinn Buckett nd two tin panns, sundry wooden vessells and one Walnut box; To have and to hold the said goods and chattles unto JOHN COCK-SHUTT (&c.) Provided however that if ZACHARIAH UNDERWOOD shall pay unto JOHN COCKSHUTT (&c)., the aforesd. Debt and interest from date; Then this Instrument of Writing to be void, otherwise to remain in full force. In Witness whereof the said ZACHY: UNDERWOOD hath hereunto set his hand and seal the day and year above written
Signed Sealed and Delivered in presence of
        DAVID BRIGGS,   ZACHARIAH his mark X UNDERWOOD
        CHARLES ASHLEY,   LAUCHN: MACKINTOSH

At a Court held for King George County the 3d. day of March 1774
ZACHARIAH UNDERWOODs Mortgage to JOHN COCKSHUTT, Trustees of Mr. JOHN BLAND,
proved by the witnesses thereto subscribed and admitted to Record

pp.   THIS INDENTURE made the Seventh day of July one thousand seven hundred
1083-   and seventy three Between JOHN MAZARETT of Parish of Hanover in County of
1084   King George of one part and THOMAS JETT of same County and Parish of other
        part; Witnesseth that JOHN MAZARETT for sum of two hundred and thirty one
pounds, four shillings & 3/4 current money of Virginia to him in hand paid by THOMAS
JETT, by these presents doth bargain and sell unto THOMAS JETT and to his heirs 1 grey
Horse & bay Mare and 2 bay Colts, 1 working stear, 1 yearling, 2 sows, 9 shoats, 2 feather
beds bedsteads & furniture, 1 Coat, 2 matted bottom'd chairs, 1 table, 3 trunks & 2 chests,
2 standing and 3 three hand vices, 2 anvils, 2 screw plates, 2 pair bellows, sundry
hammers, files, rasps & other Smith utensils, also 1 cart. To have and to hold the aforesaid unto THOMAS JETT his heirs, Provided always and it is agreed by and between the
parties to these presents that if JOHN MAZARETT shall pay unto THOMAS JETT his heirs
the full sum aforesaid with lawfull Interest from the date of these presents, In Witness
whereof the said JOHN MAZARETT hath hereunto set his hand and seal the day and year
first before written
Sealed and Delivered in the presence of
        BENJAMIN DAY,   GEO: CARMICHAEL,   JOHN MAZARETT
        REUBIN BRISCOE, DANIEL BRISCOE
    Reced. July 7th 1773, from THOMAS JETT the sum of Two hundred and twenty one
pounds, four shillings & 3/4 current money being the consideration mentioned in this
Indenture to be by the said THOMAS JETT paid to
Witness (Same four as above)   JOHN MAZARETT
    At a Court held for King George County the 7th day of Apl. 1774
An Indented Mortgage from JOHN MAZARETT to THOMAS JETT proved by GEO: CAR-
MICHAEL, REUBIN BRISCOE & BENJAMIN DAY, & on motion of the said JETT is admitted to
Record

p.   THIS INDENTURE made this twenty second day of July one thousand seven hun-
1084-   dred and seventy three Between JOHN COCKSHUTT & others, Trustees of Mr. JOHN
1085   BLAND of LONDON, Merchant, of one part and JAMES BROWN of King George Coun-
        ty of other part; Witnesseth that JAMES BROWN for sum of six pounds, three
shillings six pence half penny current money to him in hand paid doth bargain and
sell unto JOHN COCKSHUTT & others, Trustees of JOHN BLAND, of LONDON, Merchant, their
heirs 1 dark bay Mare about twelve years old, twelve hands high and branded on near
buttock with a Stirrup Iron and dark bay Colt, 1 cow and calf marked with a swallow
fork in each ear; To have and to hold the mare colt cow and calf unto JOHN COCKSHUTT
(&c.) Provided however that if JAMES BROWN shall pay JOHN COCKSHUTT (&c.) the aforesaid Debt with Interest from the date hereof, Then this Instrument of Writing to be void
otherwise to remain in force; In Witness whereof the said JAMES BROWN hath hereunto set his hand & seal the day and year above written
Signed sealed and delivered in presence of
        DAVID BRIGGS,   JAMES BROWN
        ALEXR: HANSFORD, CHARLES ASHLEY
    At a Court held for King George County the 7th day of April 1774
JAMES BROWNs Indented Mortgage to JOHN BLAND proved by the oathes of witnesses
thereto subscribed & admitted to Record

p.   THIS INDENTURE made the forth day of May one thousand seven hundred and
1085-   seventy two Between JOHN BLAND of LONDON, Merchant, of one part and AN-
1086   THONY STROTHER of King George County of other part; Witnesseth that ANTHO-
        NY STROTHER for sum of thirty two pounds, eight shillings and three pence one
farthing doth bargain and sell unto JOHN BLAND one Negro woman named Sue about
the age of sixteen or seventeen years and her Child named Sary; To have and to hold
the said Negro woman & Child unto JOHN BLAND his heirs; Provided nevertheless that if
ANTHONY STROTHER shall pay unto JOHN BLAND the aforesaid sum & Interest; Then this
Instrument of Writing to be void, otherwise to remain in force. In Witness whereof the
said ANTHONY STROTHER hath hereunto set his hand & seal the day and year above
written
Sign'd sealed and delivered in presence of
        DAVID BRIGGS,   ANTHO: STROTHER
        CHARLES ASHLEY,   JOHN ROBERTSON
    At a Court held for King George County the 7th day of April 1774
An Indented Deed of Mortgage from ANTHO: STROTHER to JOHN BLAND proved by the
witnesses thereto subscribed and admitted to Record

pp.   THIS INDENTURE made the Twenty seventh day of July one thousand seven
1086-   hundred and seventy three Between JOHN COCKSHUTT & others, Trustees of Mr.
1087   JOHN BLAND of LONDON, Merchant, of one part and WM: ROSE of King George
        County of other part; Witnesseth that WILLIAM ROSE for sum of Twenty five
pounds, two shillings & three pence to him in handpaid by DAVID BRIGGS, doth bargain and sell unto JOHN COCKSHUTT & others, Trustees of Mr. JOHN BLAND of LONDON,
Merchant, one Chesnut Bay Horse no brand, fourteen hands high & about eleven years
old, one Bay mare Colt two years old last June not branded, and twelve head of hoggs
marked with a crop & hole and underkeel in the right ear and a crop and overkeel in
the left ear, three feather beds & furniture & three Poplar bedsteads, one Pine Cupboard
one Cherry Tree table and one Pine table, half a dozen chairs, two iron potts, one iron
kettle, half dozen pewter plates & a pewter dish; To have and to hold the goods & chattles unto JOHN COCKSHUTT (&c.) Provided however that if WILLIAM ROSE shall pay unto
JOHN COCKSHUTT (&c.) the aforesaid sum & Interest from the fourth day of July one
thousand seven hundred and seventy two then this Instrument of Writing to be void,
otherwise to remain in force; In Witness whereof the said WILLIAM ROSE hath hereunto set his hand and seal the day and year above written
Signed sealed and delivered in presence of
        DAVID BRIGGS,   WILLIAM his mark ⊗ ROSE
        CHARLES ASHLEY,   JOHN ROBERTSON
    At a Court held for King George County the 7th day of April 1774
An Indented Deed of Mortgage from WILLIAM ROSE to JOHN BLAND proved by the oaths
of witnesses thereto subscribed & admitted to Record

pp.   THIS INDENTURE made the eight day of July one thousand seven hundred and
1087-   seventy three Between JOHN DICKIE of Parish of Hanover in County of King
1088   George of one part and THOMAS JETT of same County and Parish of other part;
        Witnesseth that JOHN DICKIE for sum of one hundred & fifty seven pounds, thir-
teen shillings & ten pence 1/4 current money of Virginia to him in hand paid by THO-
MAS JETT, by these presents doth bargain and sell unto THOMAS JETT and his heirs those
two lotts lying in LEEDS TOWN numbered 85 & 86, together with all houses gardens &
appurtenances; To have and to hold the two lotts numbered 85 & 86 to THOMAS JETT his

heirs, Provided always and it is agreed by the parties to these presents that if JOHN
DICKIE shall pay unto THOMAS JETT his heirs the full sum of one hundred & fifty seven
pounds, thirteen shillings & ten pence farthing current money on or before the ninth
day of July next coming with lawfull Interest thereon from the date of these presents;
that then and in such case THOMAS JETT hereby covenants to deliver & reconvey unto
JOHN DICKIE or to his heirs the two lotts; In Witness whereof the said JOHN DICKIE hath
hereunto set his hand and seal the day and year first before written
Sealed and Delivered in the presence of
    BENJAMIN DAY, JN: PAYTON,   JOHN DICKIE
    REUBIN BRISCOE, GEORGE CARMICHAEL
    Received July 8th 1773 from THOMAS JETT one hundred and fifty seven pounds,
thirteen shillings and ten pence 1/4 current money being the consideration mentioned
in this Indenture
Witness (Same four witnesses)   JOHN DICKIE
    At a Court held for King George County the 7th day of Apl. 1774
An Indented Deed of Mortgage from JOHN DICKIE to THOMAS JETT proved by the witnesses thereto subscribed & ordered to be recorded

pp.   TO ALL TO WHOM these presents shall come, HENRY HOLLAND of Half Moon
1089-   Street in the County of Middlesex, Builder, and WILLIAM POWELL and CORDALL
1093   POWELL of Piccadilly in said County, Iron Mongers, & Copartners send Greeting;
        Whereas by Indenture dated the first day of this Instant July made between
WILLIAM PERKINS, THOMAS BUCHANAN & WILLIAM BROWN of London, Merchants and
Copartners, of the one part and HENRY HOLLAND, WILLIAM POWELL and CORDALL
POWELL of the other part, that HENRY HOLLAND did on or about the ninth day of March
last become bound for WILLIAM PERKINS, THOMAS BUCHANAN and WM: BROWN to his
Majesty for payment of eighty four pounds on the eighteenth day of February thousand
seven hundred and seventy four and for payment of the further sum of six thousand
one hundred and twenty pounds, four shillings & four pence on the second day of July
one thousand seven hundred and seventy four and for payment of the farther sum of
eight hundred and forty pounds, And on the eleventh day of July said HENRY HOLLAND
did become jointly & severally bound with ANDREW BARLOW to his Majesty for payment
of the further sum of seven hundred and seventy four making together the sum of
eleven thousand pounds and eleven pence being the amount of certain duties payable
in tobacco imported by WM. PERKINS, THOMAS BUCHANAN & WM: BROWN in the ships
and vessells called "The Two Sisters," "The Lord of Baltimore," and "The Industry," from
Virginia, and that WM: & CORDALL POWELL did on or about the seventh day of January
last at the request of WILLIAM PERKINS, THOMAS BUCHANAN and WILLIAM BROWN deliver to them or one of them a Promisory Note drawn by them to WILLIAM PERKINS,
ANDREW BUCHANAN and WILLIAM BROWN payable seven months after the date of them
the said WILLIAM AND CORDALL POWELL or order for two thousand pounds which said
Note they the said WILLIAM & CORDALL POWELL indorsed to accomodate and serve the
said WILLIAM PERKINS, THOMAS BUCHANAN and WILLIAM BROWN without receiving
any value or consideration for the same; NOW KNOW ALL MEN by these Presents that
HENRY HOLLAND, WILLIAM POWELL and CORDALL POWELL for the especial Trust which
they repose in RICHARD HOLLAND of Piccadilly, Gentleman, and for divers other causes
and consideration by these presents do appoint RICHARD HOLLAND their true & lawfull
Attorney to recover from the Executors of JOHN MORTON GORDON, deceased the sum of
twelve thousand and twenty five pounds, seven shillings and seven pence: In Witness
whereof the said HENRY HOLLAND, WILLIAM POWELL and CORDALL POWELL have

hereunto set their hands & seals this sixteenth day of July in the thirteenth year of the reign of our Sovereign Lord George the Third by the grace of God of Great Britain, France & Ireland, King, Defender of the faith &c., and in the year of our Lord one thousand seven hundred & seventy three

Sealed & Delivered being first duly stampt., in the presence of

       RT. CRACRAFT   HENRY HOLLAND

       FRANS: DAVIS, Clk. to Mr. CRACRAFT   WILLIAM POWELL

                                                CORDALL POWELL

     At a Court held for King George County the 7th day of July 1774

An Assignment from WILLIAM PERKINS, THOMAS BUCHANAN by WILLIAM BROWN his partner and Atto: & the said WILLIAM BROWN to HENRY HOLLAND, admitted into Court and ordered to be recorded

                  Test JOS: ROBINSON, C. K. G. C.

pp.
1093-
1099

    THIS INDENTURE made the first day of July in the year of our Lord in the thirteenth year of the Reign of our Sovereign Lord George the Third by the Grace of God of Great Britain France & Ireland, King, Defender of the Faith &c. and in the year of our Lord one thousand seven hundred and seventy three, Between WILLIAM PERKINS, THOMAS BUCHANAN and WILLIAM BROWN of LONDON, Merchants and Copartners, of one part and HENRY HOLLAND of HALFERSON STREET, Piccadilly, Builder, and WILLIAM POWELL and CORDALL POWELL of Piccadilly, Iron Mongers, of other part. Whereas HENRY HOLLAND and WILLIAM POWELL did on or about the ninth day of March last become bound for WILLIAM PERKINS, THOMAS BUCHANAN and WILLIAM BROWN to our Sovereign Lord the King for the payment of the sum of Eighty four pounds on the eighteenth day of February which will be in the year of our Lord one thousand seven hundred and (left out) (this Indenture continues repeating what was in the foregoing Power of Attorney respecting the debt); NOW THIS INDENTURE WITNESSETH that in consideration aforesaid and also for sum of ten shillings of lawfull money of Great Britain to them the said WILLIAM PERKINS, THOMAS BUCHANAN and WILLIAM BROWN in hand paid by HENRY HOLLAND, WILLIAM POWELL and CORDALL POWELL, by these presents doth transfer and set over unto HENRY HOLLAND, WILLIAM POWELL & CORDALL POWELL their and eiach of their assigns the sum of twelve thousand seven hundred and twenty five pounds seven shillings and seven pence so due to them from the Estate of JOHN MORTON GORDON as aforesaid; In Witness whereof the said parties to these presents have hereunto set their hands and seals the day and year above written

Sealed and Delivered by the within named THOMAS BUCHANAN by WM: BROWN his Attorney, the said WM: BROWN and HENRY HOLLAND, being first duly stampt. in the presence of and also by WILLIAM POWELL & CORDALL POWELL

       RT. CRACRAFT   WILLIAM PERKINS   THOMAS BUCHANAN

       FRANCIS DAVIS Clk. to Mr.   by WILLM. BROWN, Attorney

          Cracraft   WILLIAM BROWN   HENRY HOLLAND

                                       WM: POWELL   CORDALL POWELL

     At a Court held for King George County the 7th day of July 1774

An Indented Assignment by way of Mortgage from WILLIAM PERKINS, THOMAS BUCHANAN & WILLIAM BROWN his Attorney & Partner & the said WILLIAM BROWN to HENRY HOLLAND, WILLIAM POWELL and CORDALL POWELL admitted to Record and ordered to be recorded

pp.   (Page 1100-1107 contain much of the same material as in the two foregoing entries,
1100- as well as an account of payments signed by WILLIAM PERKINS, WILLIAM BROWN,
1107   ANDREW BARLOW, JOHN WIGGINTON and WILLIAM FRANCIS)
       At a Court held for King George County the 7th day of July 1774
A Deed Poll from WILLIAM PERKINS & WILLIAM BROWN to ANDREW BARLOW, JOHN
WIGGINTON and WILLIAM FRANCIS, admitted into Court and ordered to be recorded
                    Teste JOS: ROBINSON, C. K. G. C.

pp.   (Pages 1108-1111 contain much of the material in the foregoing entries, this entry
1108- being a Power of Attorney from WILLIAM FRANCIS of LONDON, ANDREW BARLOW and
1111   JOHN BARLOW to JOSEPH SMITH.
       At a Court held for King George County the 7th day of July 1774
A Power of Attorney from ANDREW BARLOW, JOHN WIGGINTON & WILLIAM FRANCIS to
JOS: SMITH admitted to Record and ordered to be recorded
                    Teste JOS: ROBINSON, C. K. G. C.

p.   THIS INDENTURE made the thirtieth day of July one thousand seven hundred
1112   and seventy three Between JOHN COCKSHUTT & others, Trustees of Mr. JOHN
       BLAND, of LONDON, Merchant, of one part and JOHN ARMSTRONG of County of
       King George of other part; Witnesseth that JOHN ARMSTRONG for sum of nine-
teen pounds, three shillings and eleven pence half penny to him in hand paid by
DAVID BRIGGS doth bargain and sell unto JOHN COCKSHUTT & others, Trustees of Mr.
JOHN BLAND, the following goods & chattles viz., two brown Cows, one red Heifer, one
red Bull, horned Steer marked with two crops and an overkeel in each ear, one sorrel
Horse branded on the near buttock P., two beds & furniture, one Gun, four Chairs, one
doz: pewter plates, three pewter dishes, one Chest, one Pine Table, one black Walnut
Table & ten head of hoggs; To have and to hold the goods and chattles unto JOHN COCK-
SHUTT & others, Trustees of Mr. JOHN BLAND, their heirs; Provided however that if JOHN
ARMSTRONG shall pay unto JOHN COCKSHUTT (&c,) the aforesaid Debt and Interest from
the date hereof then this Instrument of Writing shall be void otherwise to remain in
force; In Witness whereof the said JOHN ARMSTRONG hath hereunto set his hand and
seal the day & year above written
Signed Sealed & Delivered in presence of
       DAVID BRIGGS, ALEXR: HANSFORD,   JOHN ARMSTRONG
       CHARLES ASHLEY, JOHN ROBERTSON
   At a Court held for King George County the 7th day of July 1774
JOHN ARMSTRONGs Indented Mortgage to JOHN BLAND proved by the witnesses thereto
subscribed and admitted to Record

p.   TO ALL WHOM IT MAY CONCERN and these presents come Greeting. Know ye
1113   that I RICHARD LEWIS of County of King George for sum of five shillings cur-
       rent money to me in hand paid but more especailly for the natural love and
affection I said RICHARD LEWIS hath & do bare unto my beloved Daughter, ELIZABETH
LEWIS, give and confirm unto ELIZABETH LEWIS and her heirs one Negro Girl called
and known by the name of Lucy, together with her increase; In Testimony whereof I
said RICHARD LEWIS hath this day caused delivery of said Negro Lucy unto sd. LEWIS
with her increase as her lawfull right and property; In Witness whereof I said
RICHARD LEWIS hath hereunto set my hand & seal this 24th day of Jany: 1774

Sealed Signed & Acknowledged in the presence of
  THOS: HARWOOD his mark ✕ JUNR.   RICHD: LEWIS
  JOHN HARWOOD, JOHN MINTON
At a Court held for King George County the 7th day of Apl. 1774
RICHARD LEWIS 's Deed of Gift to ELIZABETH LEWIS acknowledged by the said LEWIS
proved by the witnesses & admitted to Record

pp. TO ALL TO WHOM IT MAY CONCERN and these presents come, Greeting. Know ye
1113- that I RICHARD LEWIS of County of King George for the sum of five shillings
1114 currt. money to RICHARD LEWIS in hand paid but more especially for the
    natural love and effection he hath and beareth unto his beloved Daughter,
MARY LEWIS, do hereby give and confirm unto MARY LEWIS one Negro Girl called &
known by the name of Winny, which Negro Girl with her increase unto MARY LEWIS
her heirs RICHARD LEWIS doth warrant forever. In Testimony whereof RICHARD
LEWIS hath this day cause a delivery of the within named Negro Girl Winny unto MARY
LEWIS as her lawfull just right & property; In Witness whereof RICHD: LEWIS hath
hereunto set his hand & seal this twenty sixth day of Feby: 1774
Sealed & Delivered in presence of
  JOHN EUSTACE,   RICHD: LEWIS
  WILLIAM LEE, THOMAS JAMES
At a Court held for King George County the 7th day of Apl. 1774
RICHD: LEWIS acknowledges this his Deed of Gift to MARY LEWIS and is admitted to
Record

pp. THIS INDENTURE made the Thirteenth day of May one thousand seven hundred
114- & seventy three Between JOHN COCKSHUTT & others, Trustees of Mr. JOHN BLAND
1115 of LONDON, of one part & BLACKLEY GRAVES of King George County of other
    part; Witnesseth that BLACKLEY GRAVES for sum of Twenty pounds, nineteen
shillings and eight pence three farthings Virginia currency doth bargain and sell
unto JOHN COCKSHUTT & others, Trustees of Mr. JOHN BLAND of LONDON, one bay Horse,
thirteen hands and a half high or thereabouts branded on near buttock, H F., two cows
and four calves marked with two underkeeles and a hole through each ear, twenty two
hogs with two underkeels and a hole through each Ear, two feather beds & furniture,
six chairs, three pewter dishes, three pewter basons & one doz. pewter plates, three iron
potts, one small old Desk, two Chests, one weavers loom & tackling & one smooth board
Gun; To have & to hold the goods & chattles unto JOHN COCKSHUTT (&c.) Provided nevertheless that if BLACKLEY GRAVES shall pay unto JOHN COCKSHUTT (&c.), the aforesaid
Debt & Interest from the ninth day of September one thousand seven hundred and
seventy one then this Instrument of Writing to be void, otherwise to remain in force,
In Witness whereof the said BLACKLEY GRAVES hath hereunto set his hand & seal the
day & year above written
Sign'd Sealed & Delivered in presence of
  ANDW: BUCHANAN   BLACKLEY GRAVES
  JOHN ROBERTSON, CHARLES ASHLEY
 Reced. of DAVID BRIGGS twenty pounds, nineteen shillings & eight pence three far-
things in consideration for the above
Test JOHN ROBERTSON   BLACKLEY GRAVES
 At a Court held for King George County the 7th day of Apl. 1774
BLACKLEY GRAVES Mortgage to JOHN BLAND proved by ANDREW BUCHANAN & JOHN
ROBERTSON & further proved by CHARLES ASHLEY and admitted to Record

pp.   THIS INDENTURE made the fourth day of December in year of our Lord one
1115-   thousand seven hundred & seventy three Between the Reverend JOHN DIXON,
1117   Clerk and Professor of Divinity in the COLLEDGE of WILLIAM & MARY of one part
        and DOCTOR CHARLES MORTIMER of the Town of FREDERICKSBURG of the other
part, Witnesseth that JOHN DIXON hath in consideration of eight hundred pounds current money of Virginia to him in hand paid, by these presents doth bargain and sell
unto CHARLES MORTIMER his heirs all that tract of land lying in County of King George
above the Town of FALMOUTH known by the name and called DIXONS STAND containing
Eighty six acres more or less being part of a tract of land which JOHN DIXON the Elder,
Father to the said JOHN DIXON, purchased of (   ) TODD, and dying devised to said JOHN
DIXON his Son, as by his Will in Writing duly proved and recorded may more fully appear; Also all that tract of land near to and adjoining the Town of FALMOUTH whereon
said JOHN DIXON erected a Mill & begining at a Beach Tree and extending thence South
five degrees West three poles nine feet & two inches to a Walnut Tree, thence South five
degrees West two poles seven feet & two inches to a Stake, thence South twenty two degrees East nine poles three feet & three inches to a Stake in the line of CARTERs STREET
thence with the said Street to the RUN RAPPAHANNOCK, thence up said River to the lot
of ground which said DIXON sold to ADAM STEWART above the Mill Taile Race and along
STEWARTs line to the corner of it at the Mill Waste, thence along said line to the Old Mill
Dam together with the said Mill Pond, Mill Run & Mill Waste, and all the benefits profits
& immunities of every kind belonging; Also all that tract or lot of ground between the
lot known by the name of BOWER BAKERs Lot and the Mill Pond so along the Mill Pond
and waste to the upper corner of a lot or parcel of ground known by the name of
FROGGETTS TENEMENT, also the said Tenement called FROGGETTS, which he now lives on
being the waste coming from the Mill Dam, Also a piece of land taken from KING STREET
between DIXONs Warehouse Lot and the River about one hundred and thirty two feet in
length and about twenty feet in width, another piece of land forming Lot No. 4. as by
their record & Deed may fully appear; Together with the freeuse of the passage from
the Hill up to the Tobo: Warehouses along the Mill Pond to the Street going over the
Bridge and full liberty to convey the run that crosses the FORGE ROAD by Canal or
otherwise for the purpose of bringing the water to his Mill Pond but so as to leave the
land uninjured; To have and to hold the lands hereby sold with appurtenances to sd.
MORTIMER and his heirs; In Witness whereof the said JOHN DIXON has set his hand and
affixed his seal the day & date first above written
Signed sealed and delivered in the presence of
          HENRY MITCHELL,   JAMES ROBINSON   JOHN DIXON
          WM: ALLASON,   THO: HORD
          A. BUCHANAN,   ARTHUR MORSON
          LACKLAND CAMPBELL   DAVID BRIGGS
          DAVID BLAIR
    At a Court held for King George County the 1st day of September 1774
JOHN DIXONs Indented Deed of Bargain and Sale to CHARLES MORTIMER proved by
ANDREW BUCHANAN & DAVID BRIGGS, & further proved by ARTHUR MORSON & is
admitted to Record & is truly recorded
                    Teste JOSEPH ROBINSON, C. K. G. C.

p.   THIS INDENTURE made this 6th day of Apl. 1774 Between Sarah, a Free Negro
1117   woman of the Parish of Hanover in the County of King George of one part and
        THOMAS DOUGLASS of the same Parish & County of other part; Witnesseth that
Negro Sarah in consideration of the covenants hereafter mentioned by THOS: DOUGLASS

to be done and performed, by these presents doth put and bind her Son, Robert, to the
sd. THOMAS untill he shall arrive to the age of twenty one years, the said Robert being
now about 14 years old during which time said ROBERT shall behave himself in every
respect as a Servant and THOMAS DOUGLASS doth covenant with said Sarah that he will
at all times during said Roberts Servitude find and provide for him good and sufficient
meat cloathg. and lodging at also at the expiration of his Servitude give him lawfull
Freedom Dues; In Witness whereof the said Negro Sarah and THOMAS DOUGLASS have
hereunto set their hands and seals
Sealed and Delivered in the presence of
          DAN: RICHARDSON,   SARAH WARE
          JOHN SHARPLES   THOS: DOUGLAS
     (No recording appears for this entry although space remains on pages 1117 and 1118).

pp.   THIS INDENTURE made this twelfth day of Apl. in the year of our Lord one
1118-   thousand seven hundred and seventy four Between CHARLES VIVION and ELIZA-
1120   BETH his Wife of County of CAROLINE of one part and WILLIAM ROBINSON of
          County of King George of other part; Witnesseth that CHARLES VIVION and
ELIZABETH his Wife for sum of one thousand pounds current money of Virginia to
CHARLES VIVION in hand paid, by these presents do bargain and sell unto WILLIAM
ROBINSON his heirs all that tract of land situate in County of King George whereon
CHARLES VIVION lately resided, containing three hundred and twenty acres by estimation bounded Northerly by the Plantation of said WILLIAM ROBINSON; Westerly by
RAPPAHANNOCK RIVER, Southerly by the lands of JOHN WASHINGTON and Easterly by a
tract of land belonging to MRS. GARRETT; together with all houses orchards & advantages belonging, To have and to hold the tract of land and premises with the appurtenances unto said ROBINSON his heirs; And CHARLES VIVION and his heirs the tract of
land and premises against all persons shall warrant and forever defend by these presents; In Witness whereof the said CHARLES VIVION and ELIZABETH his Wife have set
their hands & seals the day and year before written
Signed Sealed and Acknowledged in presence of
          ROBT. LOVELL,   JOHN WASHINTON   CHARLES VIVION
          CHARLES DEANE, THOS: JETT,   ELIZA: VIVION
          THOS: HODGE,   MUNGO ROY
     Reced. of the within named WILLIAM ROBINSON the sum of One thousand pounds cur-
rent money, being the consideration within mentioned; Witness my hand the day and
year within written
Witness JOHN WASHINGTON   CHARLES VIVION
          CHARLES DEANE,   THOS: JETT,
          THOS: HODGE,   MUNGO ROY
     At a Court held for King George County the 5th day of May 1774
CHARLES VIVION and ELIZA: his Wife (she being first privately examined by virtue of a
Commission) Deed Indented to WILLIAM ROBINSON, Gent., proved by THOS: JETT, THOS:
HODGE & MUNGO ROY, which is admitted to Record and is truly recorded

          George the Third by the grace of God of Great Brittain, France and Ireland,
King, Defender of the faith &c., to THOS: JETT, THOS: HODGE and B. DAVENPORT, Gent.,
Justices of King George County, Greeting. Whereas CHARLES VIVION and ELIZABETH his
Wife, by their certain Deed of Bargain and Sale (the Commission for the privy examination of
ELIZABETH, the Wife of CHARLES VIVION). Witness JOS: ROBINSON, Clerk of our said Court
this 1st day of Apl. 1774 in the 14th year of our Reign
                                        JOSEPH ROBINSON, C. K. G. C.

King George County, Sct. Pursuant to the within Commission to us directed, we the subscribers personally went to the within named ELIZABETH VIVION, Wife of the within named CHARLES VIVION, and received her acknowledgment (the return of the execution of the privy examination of ELIZABETH VIVION). Given under our hands and seals this 13th day of Apl. 1774   THOS: JETT
                                                      THOS: HODGE

(On margin. Delivered to Mr. WM. ROBINSON).

pp.   THIS INDENTURE made the twenty fifth day of October one thousand seven hun-
1121- dred and seventy three Between MARTIN WELCH of County of King George of one
1122   part and DAVID BRIGGS of same County of other part; Witnesseth that MARTIN
       WELCH for sum of fifteen pounds, eight shillings and five pence half penny to
him in hand paid by DAVID BRIGGS, doth bargain and sell unto DAVID BRIGGS his heirs
two feather beds and furniture, 4 cat tailed beds & furniture, 1 Roan Horse about fourteen hands high eight years old branded on the near buttock C. C., on the near shoulder C paces, one dark Bay paceing Horse 10 hands high nine years old branded R. on
the near buttock, a bay Horse eight years old fourteen hands high or near it; a Roan
mare two years old 12 hands high branded on the near buttock something like two C C.,
on the near shoulder one C., a dray Cart and a common Cart, one dozen flag chairs, two
square Pine tables and an Oval black Walnut table, one brindled heifer marked two
holes & a crop in right ear, two brown cows one of which I bought of ANDREW
BUCHANAN, and the other at ONEALs Sale, one brown Heifer I bought of RICHARD
PAYNE, one pyed Heifer I bought of Mr. ANDREW BUCHANAN, a young Steer, three
Chests, one Trunk and all the Kitchen Furniture, one nine hhd. Flatt & a Fowling Peice;
To have and to hold the goods & chattles unto DAVID BRIGGS his heirs, Provided however that if MARTIN WELCH shall pay unto DAVID BRIGGS the aforesaid Debt and In-
terest from the date hereof then this Instrument of Writing to be void, otherwise to re-
main in force; In Witness whereof the said MARTIN WELCH hath hereunto sett his hand
and seal the day and year above written
Signed Sealed & Delivered in presence of
    LA: MACKINTOSH,   MARTIN his mark /M| WELCH
    CHARLES ASHLEY,   DANL: McDONALD
    At a Court held for King George County the 5th day of May 1774
MARTIN WELCHs Mortgage to DAVID BRIGGS proved by CHS: ASHLEY & further proved
by DANL. McDONALD & is admitted to Record

pp.   THIS INDENTURE made this Seventh day of February one thousand seven hun-
1122- dred and seventy four Between PATRICK KENDRICK of King George County of
1123   one part and NEIL JAMISON and COMPANY of other part; Witnesseth that
       PATRICK KENDRICK for sum of eighty seven pounds, four shillings and ten
pence half penny current money of Virginia to him in hand paid by NEIL JAMISON and
COMPANY, by these presents doth bargain and sell unto NEIL JAMISON and COMPANY
their heirs all that tract of Land containing one hundred and seventy acres be the same
more or less situate in County of King George and STAFFORD upon the Branches of
(   ) and is the tract of land conveyed by GEORGE WASHINGTON to the said PATRICK
KENDRICK by Deeds recorded in the General Court; also eight head of Cattle and the crop
of tobo: made by PATRICK KENDRICK last year and the crop of Wheat now upon the
ground on the said Land; To have and to hold the tract of land and premises and also the
cattle, tobacco and Wheat with the appurtenances unto NEIL JAMISON and COMPANY
their heirs, Provided always nevertheless and it is the true intent and meaning of these

presents, that if PATRICK KENDRICK his heirs shall pay NEIL JAMISON nd COMPANY
their heirs the aforesaid sum on or before the first day of October next ensuing with
lawfull Interest on the same from the date hereof, That then this present writing to be
void and of none effect, otherwise to be and remain in full force and virtue
Signed Sealed and Acknowledged by the said PATRICK KENDRICK
as his act and deed in presence of
   THOMAS HORD   PATRICK KENDRICK
   JOHN ROBERTSON, JOHN POLLARD,
   ARTHUR MORSON, JAMES CLELAND
 At a Court held for King George County the 5th day of May 1774
PATRICK KENDRICKs Indented Deed of Mortgage to NEIL JAMISON & COMPY., further
proved by JAMES CLELAND and being first proved by two other witnesses is admitted to
Record   Teste JOS: ROBINSON, C. K. G. C/

pp. THIS INDENTURE made the fourth day of May in the year of our Lord one thou-
1124- sand seven hundred and seventy four Between WILLIAM BOON of County of King
1125 George and KERRIAH his Wife of one part and SAMUEL KENDALL of the same
   County of other part; Whereas by Deed of Bargain and Sale made the (blank) day
of September in the year of our Lord 1771, the said SAMUEL KENDALL and ELIZABETH
his Wife for the consideration therein mentioned conveyed unto WILLIAM BOON about
fifty acres of land in the said County; And Whereas SAML. KENDALL hath since contracted with WILLIAM BOON for the purchase thereof for the sum of Eighty one pounds
NOW THIS INDENTURE Witnesseth that the said WILLIAM BOON and his Wife for the sum
of eighty one pounds to them in hand paid by SAMUEL KENDALL by these presents doth
bargain and sell unto SAMUEL KENDALL and his heirs all that tract of land whereon
SAML: KENDALL lived and now liveth containing one hundred and two acres be the
same more or less and which was given ELIZA:, the Wife of sd. SAML. in tail, together
with the buildings & improvements thereon and the rights members and appurtenances belonging; To have and to hold the tract of land and premises with appurtenances unto SAMUEL KENDALL his heirs and WILLIAM BOON and KERRIAH for themselves their heirs shall when required make such further Deeds & Conveyances as may
be necessary for the sure making of said tract of land unto SAML: KENDALL his heirs;
In Witness whereof the said WM: BOON hath hereunto set his hand and seal this day &
year first above written
Sealed & Delivered in the presence of
   GEORGE his mark ⅄ JOHNSTON   WILLIAM BOON
   JNO: BODINGTON,   KERRIAH BOON
   JOHN his mark ✗ RANKINS
 Received of SAMUEL KENDALL the sum of eighty one pounds, the consideration
money within mentioned this 4th day of May 1774
   JOHN BODINGTON   WILLIAM BOON
   JNO. his mark ✗ RANKINS
   GEORGE his mark ✗ JOHNSON
 At a Court held for King George County the 5th day of May 1774
WM: BOON & KERRIAH his Wifes Indented Deed of Mortgage to SAML. KENDALL, said
KERRIAH being first privately examined, it is acknowledged & admitted to Record

pp. THIS INDENTURE made the Second day of June in year of our Lord one thousand
1125- seven hundred and seventy four Between JOSEPH JONES of County of King
1126 George of one part and JAMES ALLEN, FIELDING LEWIS, CHARLES DICK, LEWIS
   WILLIS, CHARLES WASHINGTON, JOHN THORNTON & JAMES MERCER, Trustees for

the Town of FREDERICKSBURG in County of SPOTSYLVANIA of other part; Whereas (blank) McPHERSON of County of SPOTSYLVANIA by his Last Will and Testament in Writing bequeathed all his Estate unto ye Trustees of FREDERICKSBURG and their successors for the purpose in the said Will mentioned as said Will of Records in Court of SPOTSYLVANIA may appear; And Whereas the Trustees having agreed to dispose of the said Estate at Publick Sale upon seven years Credit paying Interest from the date upon real security, the said JOS: JONES became purchaser of two slaves, Dick & Clio for the price of one hundred & sixty pounds; THIS INDENTURE WITNESSETH that JOS: JONES in consideration of the two slaves, Dick & Clio, delivered him by said Trustees at and before the sealing hereof by these presents do bargain and sell unto ye sd. Trustees and their Successor Trustees for the Town of FREDERICKSBURG all that tract of land called SEALS scituate in County of King George containing one hundred acres being part of ye tract where said JOS: JONES now lives; To have and to hold the tract of land with appurtenances unto said Trustees & their Successors UPON CONDITION that in case JOS: JONES his heirs shall pay unto said Trustees and their Successors the sum of One hundred & sixty pounds at or upon ye first day of March in ye year one thousand & Eighty with lawfull Interest to be paid annually that then these presents to be void otherwise to be & remain in full virtue; In Witness whreof JOS: JONES hath hereunto set his hand & seal the day & year above written
Sealed and Delivered in presence of
(no witnesses recorded)   JOS: JONES
At a Court held for King George County the 2d. day of June 1774
JOS. JONES acknowledged this his Indented Deed of Bargain and Sale to the Trustees of FREDERICKSBURG & is admitted to Record

pp.   THIS INDENTURE made the xxiv day of January in year of our Lord 1774 Be-
1127-   tween JOHN ALEXANDER of County of STAFFORD, Gent., and LUCY ALEXANDER,
1129   Daughter of said JOHN ALEXANDER, of the first part and JOHN TALIFERRO of
         County of King George of second part and SEMOUR HOOE of County of STAFFORD
of the third part. Whereas MARY DONNE, Widow, late of County of King George by her Last Will and Testament in Writing bearing date the 20th dy of June 1769, among other things devised unto LUCY ALEXANDER, her Grand Daughter, one half of her tract of land in County of CULPEPER in fee simple and also sundry slaves by name, Jupiter, Jane, Jupiter, Violet the younger, Peter, Lett, John, Will, Judy the younger, Bob, Tom, Lett, Bess, Bristol, Nelly & young Philis, likewise one half of her stocks of cattle hoggs horses & sheep as by the sai Will of Record in County Court of King George will appear; And Whereas a Marriage is intended by the permission of God to be shortly had and solemnized between the said JOHN TALIAFERRO and LUCY ALEXANDER; NOW THIS INDENTURE WITNESSETH that in consideration of the intended Marriage taking effect and of the land, slaves & stocks herein before mentioned being delivered to said JOHN TALIAFERRO at or before the solemnization of the Marriage and in farther consideration of the sum of ten shillings paid unto SEMOUR HOOE said JOHN TALIAFERRO shall within six months from the date transfer at any time after the solemnization of said Marriage when thereto required, good and sufficient Deeds in the Law, settle convey and assure all that Plantation tract of land and premises whereupon the said JOHN TALIAFERRO lately lived scituate on the RIVER RAPPAHANNOCK in County of King George, also that moiety or one half of the land in CULPEPER County devised ye sd. LUCY ALEXANDER as aforesaid; likewise the Negroes herein before mentioned by name with their Increase as well as those hereafter to be born as those which already have been born since the decease of the said MARY DONNE, together with the several Stocks before

mentioned to such uses intents and purposes as herein after expressed concerning the
same, that is to say, the tract of Land scituate on RAPPAHANNOCK RIVER, the one half of
the said tract of land in CULPEPER County with the slaves and their increase together
with ye several stocks to the use of SEMOUR HOOE and his heirs to support the uses and
limitations herein after expressed from being disipated or destroyed and in the first
place to permit and suffer sd. JOHN TALIAFERRO to take possess and enjoy the rents
issue & profits of the lands, slaves and stocks together with their respective increase
during the term of his natural life and from & after the decease of JOHN TALIAFERRO
then to the use of said SEYMOUR HOOE In Trust and for benefit of LUCY ALEXANDER in
case she should survive and out live JOHN TALIAFERRO during her natural life in full
satisfaction & lieu of Dower and after the decease of JOHN TALIAFERRO and LUCY
ALEXANDER then to the use of such Child or Children of JOHN TALIAFERRO and LUCY
ALEXANDER, the issue of such Marriage, as shall be then living or if dead the legal
representatives and their heirs excepting the tract of land on RAPPAHANNOCK RIVER
which is to decend and pass after the death of LUCY ALEXANDER to such person or persons as JOHN TALIAFERRO shall direct and appoint and in default of such appointment to
the right heirs of JOHN TALIAFERRO; In Witness whereof the parties hereunto have
mutually set their hands and seals the day and year above written
Sealed & Deliverd in presence of
      RD: BROOKE,   JNO: ALEXANDER
      LAWN: TALIAFERRO,   LUCY ALEXANDER
      GEORGE THORNTON,   JOHN TALIAFERRO
                                    SEMOUR HOOE
   These words as well those hereafter to be born as those which have already been
born since the decease of the aforesaid MARY DONNE inserted between the third and
fourth lines of the second page of this Indenture before the signing and delivery of the
same; Witness our hands   RD: BROOKE
                                     LAWN: TALIAFERRO
                                     GEORGE THORNTON
   At a Court held for King George County the 2d. day of June 1774
JOHN TALIAFERRO acknowledged these his Marriage Articles with his Wife, LUCY, and
SEMOUR HOOE also acknowledged his executing the said Deed which is ordered to be
recorded

pp.   ARTICLES of AGREEMENT made executed entered into & agreed upon this 18th
1129- day of March 1773 Between WILLIAM ROWLEY of County of King George and
1130   ANN GRIGSBY of County of STAFFORD as followeth, to wit, Whereas there is an
          intended Marriage to be solemnized between WILLIAM ROWLEY and ANN GRIGS-
BY; Therefore if the Marriage shall take place and be actually solemnized between the
said parties, It is concluded covenanted and agreed between that in the first place that
in case WILLIAM ROWLEY shall be the longest survivor, he shall enjoy the Estate of
ANN GRIGSBY is at present possessed of to him and his heirs & that it shall be in his
power to give devise and bequeath the same either to his relations or to the relations of
ANN GRIGSBY or to whomsoever he shall think the most deserving; And in the next
place it is agreed that in case ANN GRIGSBY shall be the longest liver that she shall
enjoy no part of the Estate of WILLIAM ROWLEY after his death but shall retire to that
place where she now lives which she shall enjoy during her natural life, it still being
in the power of WILLIAM ROWLEY to receive and apply the profits of the same during
coverture as he shall think fit still reserving power and authority to WILLIAM ROWLEY
to give whatever part of his present Estate he pleases at his death to ANN GRIGSBY for

and during her natural life but after her death to whomsoever WILLIAM ROWLEY shall
give the same and no waste to be committed by ANN GRIGSBY her representatives or
immediatge forfeiture to be incurred and that ANN GRIGSBY freely and voluntarily
relinquishes all claim to Dower from the Estate of WILLIAM ROWLEY in case the
nuptials shall be compleated and she to abide by the Marriage Contract in lieu thereof;
Moreover it is the true meaning of this Contract that in case ANN GRIGSBY shall out live
WILLIAM ROWLEY her whole Estate which she now before marriage enjoys shall be
entirely at her own disposal and in case ANN GRIGSBY shall depart this life before
WILLIAM ROWLEY, he shall enjoy her whole Estate both real & personal during his
natural life; In Witness whereof the parties have hereunto set their hands and seals
the day of date above written
Signed sealed and acknowledged in presence of
    RICHARD TAYLOR,   WILLIAM ROWLEY
    JOHN WISHART   ANN GRIGSBY
   At a Court held for King George County the 2d. day of June 1774
WILLIAM ROWLEY & ANN GRIGSBYs Marriage Contract presented into Court was proved
by JOHN WISHART & RICHARD TAYLOR & is admitted to Record

pp.   THIS INDENTURE made the first day of September in year of our Lord one thou-
1131- sand seven hundred and seventy four Between JOS: JONES of County of King
1132   George of one part and JAMES WENT JUNIOR of same County of other part;
    Whereas JOSEPH JONES hath agreed to sell unto JAMES WENT part of the tract of
land purchased by JOS: JONES of JAMES HUBBARD for the price of twenty shillings p.
acre; NOW THIS INDENTURE WITNESSETH that JOS: JONES for sum of one hundred and
five pounds, fiveteen shillings in hand paid by JAMES WENT by these presents doth
bargain sell and make over unto JAMES WENT & his heirs all that tract of land containing one hundred and five acres and those part of an acre begining at a marked white
Oak a line tree between the said tract of land and the land of Mr. WILLIAM FITZHUGH,
the same being a corner to PAYNE & BROWNs Lotts, Tenants to FITZHUGH, runing thence
along HANSFORDs line So. 30 Et. 94 po. to a Stake near to an Oak marked as a corner,
thence So. 44d. 15 Wt. 180 po. to a Stake, some red Oaks & white Oaks marked round the
corner, thence No. 30d Wt. 94 po. to a Stake in the deviding line between FITZHUGH &
land of HUBBARD, thence along the deviding line No. 44d. 15' Et. 184 poles to the begining, Together with all rights members and appurtenances belonging; To have and
to hold the land and premises with appurtenances unto JAMES WENT JUNIOR his heirs
and JOS: JONES for himself his heirs the tract of land and premises to the use of JAMES
WENT JUNIOR his heirs against the claim of all persons shall warrant and for ever
defend; In Witness whereof JOS: JONES hath hereunto set his hand & seal the day and
year first above written
Sealed & Delivered in the presence of
     (no witnesses recorded)   JOS: JONES
   At a Court held for King George County 1st day of Septr. 1774
JOS: JONES, Esqr., ackd. this his Indented Deed of Bargain and Sale to JAMES WENT
JUNIOR and is admitted to Record

p.   KNOW ALL MEN by these presents that I WILLIAM WEEKS of County of King
1132 George for divers good causes me thereunto moving but more especially for the
     love & affection I bear my Son, JAMES WEEKS, have given and confirmed to my
Son, JAMES, a Negro girl named Fan aged about seven or eight years with all her
increase to him & his heirs lawfully begotten and I do hereby warrant the sd. Negro to

my Son from the claim of any person for the consideration before mentioned and the
further consideration of five shillings to me in hand paid, the receipt whereof is here-
by ackd. In Witness whereof I have hereunto set my hand & seal this 22d. day of Feby:
1771
Signed Sealed & Delivered in presence of
     DAVID BRIGGS,   WILL: WEEKS
     AL: WODROW, GAWIN LAWSON
     ARTHUR MORSON, ANDW: BUCHANAN
   At a Court held for King George County the 2d. day of May 1771
WILLIAM WEEKS Deed of Gift to his Son, JAS: WEEKS, was proved by the Oaths of DAVID
BRIGGS & ANDW: BUCHANAN, witnesses thereto, and admitted to Record
         Test JOS: ROBINSON, C. K. G. C.

pp.   THIS INDENTURE made the twenty sixth day of April in year of our Lord one
1133- thousand seven hundred and seventy four Between JOHN TRIPLETT of County of
1136   King George and Parish of Hanover and MARTHA his Wife of one part and
       ALEXANDER SPARK of County of WESTMORELAND and Parish of COPLE of other
part; Witnesseth that for sum of One hundred and eight pounds, fifteen shillings lawfull money of Virginia to JOHN TRIPLETT in hand paid by ALEXANDER SPARK, by these
presents do bargain and sell unto ALEXANDER SPARK his heirs all that tract of land
lying in County of King George and Parish of Hanover, Begining at a white Oak
standing by the side of the REEDY SWAMP RUN and runing from thence along the
several meanders of the said Run to the OLD ROAD and from thence continuing to run
along the line of JOSEPH MURDOCK, deced., to the River, and from thence along the
River side to the line which formerly belong'd to THOMAS UNDERWOOD and now in the
possession of said ALEXANDER SPARK, from thence along the said line to the line of
WILLIAM TRIPLETT & continuing along the said line to a Hicory standing at the head of
a Valey & at the point of stand of Woods belonging to WM: TRIPLETT, and standing near
the Road and from thence to the begining; containing according to survey made by
JOHN TRIPLETT, Two hundred and seventeen acres and one half acre; And all houses orchards profits and appurtenances belonging; To have and to hold the land hereby
conveyed unto ALEXANDER SPARK and his heirs free and clear from all Incumbrances
(the Quit Rents hereafter to grow due and payable to our Sovereign Lord the King his
heirs and Successors for and in respect of the premises only excepted and foreprized);
And JOHN TRIPLETT and MARTHA his Wife the premises with the appurtenances unto
ALEXANDER SPARK and his heirs against all persons shall warrant and forever defend
by these presents; In Witness whereof the parties to these presents have hereunto set
their hands and seals the day and year first above written
Signed Sealed and Delivered in presence of us
     AUGUTINE MOXLEY,   JOHN TRIPLETT
     JOHN PERKINS,   MARTHA TRIPLETT
     WILLIAM DEACONS, WILLIAM PORTER
   Received the day of the date of the within Indenture of the within named ALEXANDER
SPARK the sum of one hundred and eight pounds, fifteen shillings, lawfully currency
of Virginia being in full of the consideration money mentioned to be paid by him to me
according to the said Indenture
        (same four witnesses)   JOHN TRIPLETT
   At a Court held for King George County the 1st day of September 1774
JOHN TRIPLETT and MARTHA his Wife, she being first privately examined by a Commission, acknowledged there Deed & Receipt to ALEXANDER SPARK and ordered to be recorded

George the Third by the grace of God of Great Brittain, France and Ireland, King, Defender of the faith &c., to THOMAS JETT, WILLIAM ROBINSON and WILLIAM THORNTON Gentlemen, Greeting. Whereas JOHN TRIPLETT and MARTHA his Wife by their certain Indenture of Bargain and Sale bearing date the 21st day of April 1774, have conveyed the fee simple Estate of one tract of land containing Two hundred and seventeen acres & half be the same more or less (the Commission for the privy examination of MARTHA, the Wife of JOHN TRIPLETT); Witness JOSEPH ROBINSON, Clerk of our said Court, this 25th day of April 1774, in the fourteenth year of our Reign

JOS: ROBINSON, C. K. G. C.

King George County Sct. Pursuant to the within Commission to us directed, we the Subscribers personally went to the within named MARTHA TRIPLETT and received her acknowledgment (the return of the execution of the privy examination of MARTHA TRIPLETT); Given under our hands this 27th April 1774   WILLIAM ROBINSON
                                                                          WILLIAM THORNTON

pp.   THIS INDENTURE made this first day of Octr. in year of our Lord one thousand
1137-   seven hundred and seventy four Between DOCTR: COLLIN RIDDOCK of HANOVER
1138   County and JANE his Wife of one part and THOMAS HODGE of King George County
          Merchant, of other part; Witnesseth that COLIN REDDOCK and JANE his Wife for
sum of six hundred pounds current money of Virginia to them in hand paid by THOMAS
HODGE by these presents do bargain and sell unto THOMAS HODGE his heirs all that Plantation and tract of land with all rights members and appurtenances thereof scituate in
County of King George & WESTMORELAND containing by estimation about four hundred
acres more or less & purchased by COLIN REDDOCK of Colonel THOMAS OSWALD and by
him of JOHN ORR, as by the respective conveyances recorded in the Office of King
George County may fully appear; To have and to hold the plantation and tract of land
unto THOMAS HODGE his heirs; And COLIN RIDDOCK for himself his heirs doth covenant
and agree with THOMAS HODGE to warrant and defend the plantation and tract of land
with the appurtenances against the claims of all persons; In Testimony whereof the sd.
COLLIN RIDDOCK & JANE his Wife have hereunto set their hands and seals the day and
year above written
Signed Sealed Acknowledged and Delivered in presence of
          DANIEL RICHARDSON   COLLIN RIDDOCK
          ANDREW CRAWFORD, REUBEN BULLARD
          THOS: JETT
Received the first day of October in the year 1774 from THOMAS HODGE the sum of six
hundred pounds current money, being the consideration within mentioned
          (same four witnesses)   COLLIN RIDDOCK
At a Court held for King George County the 2d. day of March 1775
COLLIN RIDDOCKs Deed of Bargain & Sale to THOMAS HODGE proved by ANDREW CRAW-
FORD, REUBIN BULLARD & THOS: JETT & is admitted to Record
                              Teste JOS: ROBINSON, C. K. G. C.

pp.   THIS INDENTURE made the twenty first day of October in the year of our Lord
1139-   one thousand seven hundred & seventy four Between THOMAS TURNER of County
1142   of King George, Esqr., and JANE his Wife of one part and THOMAS HODGE of the
          same County, Merchant, of other part; Witnesseth that THOMAS TURNER and
JANE his Wife for sum of Six hundred pounds current money of Virginia to them in
hand paid by THOMAS HODGE by these presents do bargain and sell unto THOMAS HODGE
his heirs all that Plantation and tract of land with all rights members and appurte-

nances lying adjacent to and in the neighbourhood of the Town of LEEDS in sd. County, containing by estimation about Two hundred and thirty acres more or less, one part of sd. Land having been purchased by HARRY TURNER, Father of the sd. THOMAS, from JOSEPH MORTON & by him, the sd. JOS: MORTON purchased of DANIEL WHITE, and the other part of said land was purchased by THOMAS TURNER of WM: BROCKENBROUGH, Esqr., as by the respective conveyances recorded in the Office of the County may fully appear; To have and to hold the Plantation and tract of land with appurtenances unto THOMAS HODGE his heirs; And THOMAS TURNER for himself his heirs doth covenant and agree with THOMAS HODGE his heirs to warrant & defend the plantation and tract of land against the claim of all persons; In Testimony whereof the sd. THOMAS TURNER & JANE his Wife have hereunto put their hands and seals the day & year above written Signed Sealed acknowledged and delivered in presents of

WILL: ROBINSON,   T: TURNER
BIRKETT DAVENPORT,   JANE TURNER
AUSTIN BROCKENBROUGH

Received the twenty 1st day of Octr. in the year one thousand seven hundred and seventy four from THOMAS HODGE the sum of six hundred pounds current money being the consideration with mentioned
Witness (same three witnesses)   T: TURNER

At a Court held for King George County the 2d. day of Feby. 1775 THOMAS TURNER & JANE his Wife, she being first privately examined by virtue of a Commission, ackd. their Deed of Bargain & Sale to THOMAS HODGE & is admitted to Record
Teste JOS: ROBINSON, C. K. G. C.

George the Third by the grace of God of Great Brittain, France & Ireland, King, Defender of the faith, &c. to WILLIAM ROBINSON, BIRKETT DAVENPORT and WM: THORNTON of County of King George, Gentlemen, Greeting; Whereas THOMAS TURNER and JANE his Wife of ye sd. County by their certain Deed of bargain and sale (the Commission for the privy examination of JANE, the Wife of THOMAS TURNER); Witness JOS: ROBINSON, Clerk of our said County Court of King George this twenty second day of Octr: in the (blank) year of our reign   JOS: ROBINSON, C. K. G. C.

King George sct. Pursuant to the within Commission to us directed, we the Subscribers went to JANE TURNER, Wife of the within mentioned THOMAS TURNER and received her acknowledgmt. (the return of the execution of the privy examination of JANE TURNER); Given under our hands and seals this 22d. day of October 1774
WILL: ROBINSON
BIRKETT DAVENPORT

pp.   THIS INDENTURE made the 6th day of April in year of our Lord one thousand
1142-   seven hundred and seventy five Between WILLIAM THORNTON and SARAH his
1144   Wife of the Parish of Brunswick in the County of King George of one part and
JOHN WASHINGTON of Hanover Parish in the same County of other part; Witnesseth that WM: THORNTON for sum of three hundred pounds current money to him in hand paid by JOHN WASHINGTON, by these presents doth bargain and sell unto JOHN WASHINGTON his heirs a certain tract of land scituate in Parish of Hanover containing Two hundred acres and bounded Northerly by a tract of land belonging to the said JOHN WASHINGTON, Easterly by a tract of land purchased by THOMAS HODGE from THOMAS TURNER, and Southerly by lands in ye possession of THOMAS DOAKE, together with all houses profits and advantages belonging; To have and to hold the tract of land with all its rights members and appurtenances unto JOHN WASHINGTON his heirs; And WILLIAM THORNTON the tract of land against all persons shall warrant and forever defend by

by these presents; In Witness said WILL: THORNTON and SARAH his Wife have hereunto
set their hands and seals the day and year above written
Signed, Sealed & Delivered in presence of
      BECKWITH BUTLER,   WILL: THORNTON
      WM: FITZHUGH,   JNO: SKINKER
  Received of the within named JOHN WASHINGTON the consideration within mentioned
Witness my hand
Witness WILLIAM FITZHUGH,   WILL: THORNTON
      BECKWITH BUTLER
  At a Court held for King George County the 6th day of Apl. 1775
WILL: THORNTON acknowledges this his Indented Deed and Receipt of Bargain and Sale
annexed with a Bond to JOHN WASHINGTON and is admitted to Record
            Teste JOS: ROBINSON, C.K.G.C.
  KNOW ALL MEN by these presents that I WM: THORNTON of Parish of Brunswick am
held and firmly bound unto JOHN WASHINTON of County of King George in the penal
sum of five hundred pounds current money to the which payment well and truly to be
made I bind myself my heirs firmly by these presents; In Witness whereof I have
hereunto set my hand and seal this 6th day of Apl. one thousand seven hundred and
seventy five
  WHEREAS the said WM: THORNTON by one Indenture of Bargain and Sale of the same
date with these presents hath conveyed unto JOHN WASHINTON in fee simple a certain
tract of land therein mentioned with general warranty; And whereas SARAH, the Wife
of sd. WILLIAM THORNTON will upon his demise be intitled to Dower therein and cannot
at this time on Acct. of her Infancy return the dame, The Condition of the above obligation is that when the said SARAH shall arrive to full age shall relinquish her Down in
the sd. Tract of Land to JOHN WASHINTON his heirs or that he or they shall be indemni-
fied against her claim of Dower therein, Then the above obligation to be void, otherwise
to remain in full force and virtue
Signed Sealed & Acknowledged in presence of
      WILL: FITZHUGH,   WILL: THORNTON
      BECKWITH BUTLER

p.   THIS INDENTURE made the Third day of November in the year of our Lord one
1144   thousand seven hundred and seventy four Between JOSEPH HARRISON and
       PEGGY his Wife of County of King George one part and JOHN SKINKER of said
County of other part; Witnesseth that JOSEPH HARRISON in consideration of the sum of
Six hundred pounds current money to him in hand paid, the said JOSEPH HARRISON and
PEGGY his Wife by these presents do bargain and sell unto JOHN SKINKER his heirs a
certain tract of land situate in County of King George and containing Nine hundred
acres, together with all houses orchards profits and hereditaments; To have and to hold
the parcel of land with appurtenances unto JOHN SKINKER his heirs and JOSEPH HAR-
RISON and PEGGY his Wife for themselves and their heirs against all persons to JOHN
SKINKER his heirs shall warrant and for ever defend by these presents; In Witness
whereof they the said JOSEPH HARRISON and PEGGY his Wife have set their hands and
seals the day and year first above written
    (no witnesses recorded)   JOSEPH HARRISON
                                   PEGGY HARRISON
  At a Court held for King George County the 3d. day of November 1774
JOSEPH HARRISON and PEGGY his Wife, she being first privately examined, acknowledged their Deed to JOHN SKINKER, Gent., and ordered to be recorded

pp.   THIS INDENTURE made this Twenty third day of September one thousand seven
1145-   hundred and seventy four Between DANIEL RICHARDSON of LEEDS TOWN in
1146   County of King George of one part and WILLIAM ROBINSON of said County of
         other part; Witnesseth tht DANIEL RICHARDSON for sum of two hundred pounds
current money of Virginia to him in hand paid by these presents doth bargain and sell
unto WILLIAM ROBINSON and his heirs the lott or half acres of Land lying in the Town
of LEEDS whereon DANIEL RICHARDSON now lives together with all the houses gardens
and advantages to the same belonging; To have and to hold the lott or half acre of land
with the appurtenances unto WILLIAM ROBINSON his heirs; And DANIEL RICHARDSON
doth for himself lhis heirs covenant with WILLIAM ROBINSON his heirs that he shall
warrant and forever defend by these presents the lott or half acres of land against
every person; In Witness whereof the said DANIEL RICHARDSON hath hereunto set his
hand and seal the day and ayear above written
Signed Sealed and Delivered in the presence of
         THOMAS JETT, THOMAS DRAKE   DANIEL RICHARDSON
         CHARLES DEANE JUNR.   ANDREW CRAWFORD
     Received of the within named WILLIAM ROBINSON the sum of two hundred pounds
being the consideration within mentioned; Witness my hand this 23d. of September
1774
Witness (the same four witnesses recorded)   DANIEL RICHARDSON

         KNOW ALL MEN by these presents that I DANIEL RICHARDSON of LEEDS TOWN in
County of King George am held and firmly bound unto WILLIAM ROBINSON of the same
County in the penal sum of two hundred pounds current money to Virginia to which
payment well and truly to be made I bind myself my heirs firmly by these presents;
Sealed with my seal and Dated this 23d. day of September 1774
     WHEREAS the above bound DANIEL RICHARDSON hath by his Deed of Bargain and Sale
bearing date with these presents sold and conveyed to WILLIAM ROBINSON the lott or
half acre of Land lying in the Town of LEEDS whereon DANIEL RICHARDSON now lives;
And Whereas NANCY the Wife of DANIEL RICHARDSON is an Infant and therefore cant
make proper and legal acknowledgment of the said lott and premises; THE CONDITION of
the above obligation is such that if the said NANCY shall when she comes to lawfull age
sign seal and acknowledge a proper Deed to WILLIAM ROBINSON for a release of her
Dower in said Lott and premises, Then the above obligation to be void, otherwise to
remain in full force power and virtue
Sealed & Delivered in presence of
         THOMAS JETT, THOMAS DRAKE,   DANIEL RICHARDSON
         CHARLES DEANE JUNR., ANDREW CRAWFORD
     At a Court held for King George County the 3d. day of November 1774
DANIEL RICHARDSONs Deed, Bond and Receipt to WILLIAM ROBINSON proved by THOMAS
JETT, THOMAS DRAKE and CHARLES DEANE JUNR., and ordered to be recorded

pp.   THIS INDENTURE made the Third day of March in year of our Lord one thousand
1146-   seven hundred and seventy five Between JOHN WHARTON of County of GLOU-
1147   CESTER of one part and JOHN THORNLEY of County of King George of other part;
         Witnesseth that JOHN WHARTON for sum of thirty pounds current money to him
well and truly paid by these presents doth bargain and sell unto JOHN THORNLEY his
heirs a certain tract of land lying in County of King George and containing Sixty acres
which tract of land was purchased by ZACHEUS WHARTON, Father of said JOHN WHAR-
TON, of WILLIAM and JAMES WREN, and descended from said ZACHEUS to the said JOHN as

his Heir at Law, together with all houses orchards profits and hereditaments
belonging; To have and to hold the parcel of land unto JOHN THORNLEY his heirs; And
JOHN WHARTON and his heirs the tract of land and premises against every person to
JOHN THORNLEY his heirs shall warrant and forever defend by these presents; In
Witness whereof the said JOHN WHARTON hath set his hand and seal the day and year
first above written
Witness   JOHN SKINKER,
         AARON THORNLEY, WILLIAM ROBINSON   JOHN his mark+ WHARTON
     At a Court held for King George County the 3rd day of November 1774
JOHN WHARTON acknowledged his Deed to JOHN THORNLEY and rodered to be recorded

pp.,   THIS INDENTURE made the Fifteenth day of April in year of our Lord one thou-
1147-   sand seven hundred and seventy four Between WILLIAM JACOBS of County of
1150   King George of one part and MESSRS. HASLOP and BLAIR of County of SPOTSYL-
         VANIA of other part; Witnesseth that WILLIAM JACOBS for sum of Eighty nine
pounds, four shillings and nine pence current money of Virginia to said WILLIAM
JACOBS in hand paid by HASLOP and BLAIR, by these presents doth bargain and sell
unto HASLOP & BLAIR their heirs three Negroes, viz., Liverpool aged about twenty two
years; a wench named Betty about twenty six years of age, a Negro girl named Mary
about eight years of age and their future increase; To have and to hold the Negro man
named Liverpool, the wench named Betty and girl named Mary unto HASLOP & BLAIR
their heirs, Provided always and upon condition that if WILLIAM JACOBS his heirs shall
well and truly pay HASLOP & BLAIR their heirs the sum of Eighty nine pounds, four
shillings and nine pence current money of Virginia on or before the first day of
October next which shall be in the year of our Lord one thousand seven hundred and
seventy four together with lawfull Interest thereon from the date of these presents;
Then from thenceforth these presents shall cease determine and be void; In Witness
whereof the parties to these presents have interchangeably set their hands and affixed
their seals the day and year aforewritten
Signed Sealed and Delivered in presence of
         JAMES MARSHALL,   WILLIAM JACOBS
         JAMES BLAIR,   JOHN HARDIN
     Received of HASLOP & BLAIR the sum of Eighty nine pounds, four shillings and nine
pence being the consideration within mentioned this 15th day of April 1774
Test   JOHN HARDIN,   WILLIAM JACOBS
         JAMES BLAIR, JAMES MARSHALL
     At a Court held for King George County the 3d. day of November 1774
WILLIAM JACOBS Mortgage to HASLOP and BLAIR proved by the Oaths of JAMES MAR-
SHALL and JOHN HARDIN, who swore they see JAMES BLAIR sign the same as witness
and that the said BLAIR is out of the Colony and ordered to be recorded

pp.   THIS INDENTURE made the Tenth day of November in year of our Lord one
1151-   thousand seven hundred and seventy four Between WILLIAM PANNILL and
1154   ANN his Wife of County of ORANGE of one part and CHARLES DEAN SENR. of
         County of King George of other part; Witnesseth that WILLIAM PANNILL and
ANN his Wife for sum of five shillings current money to him in hand paid, do by these
presents bargain and sell unto CHARLES DEANE a certain tract of land lying in Parish of
Hanover and County of King George containing Eighty three acres more or less and is
bounded, Begining on East side of the MAIN COUNTY ROAD and extedning thence with a
line of marked trees which divides this land from the land of THOMAS TURNER, to the

East Branch of THATCHERS CREEK, thence up the several courses of the Branch dividing the land from the land of THOMAS DRAKE to a marked white Oak, the reputed corner of the said Land, thence to two Locusts and a Cedar standing on or near the line as marked and agreed to be the dividing line between SHORT now THOMAS and said land to the MAIN COUNTY ROAD, thence down the Road to the begining; which tract of land was sold by MAXIMILIAN ROBINSON to the said SHORT and by JOHN SHORT and WINIFERD his Wife sold and conveyed by Deed dated the twenty eighth day of July in the year of our Lord one thousand seven hundred and sixty six to DAVID PANNILL from whom it descended to WILLIAM PANNILL his Nephew and Heir at Law, who sold the same to the said SHORT but never made him a Deed for it, and the said SHORT has agreed to sell the same and that said PANNILL shall execute Deeds to him for the same; together with all houses profits and heredtitaments to the same belonging; To have and to hold the tract of land and premises to CHARLES DEANE and assigns during the term of one full year paying one eare of Indian Corn on the Feast of Christmas if demanded to the intent that by virtue of these presents and of the Statute for transferring uses into possession, said CHARLES DEANE may be in the actual possession of the premises and thereby enabled to accept a release of the reversion and Inheritance thereof; In Witness whereof the said WILLIAM PANNILL and ANN his Wife have hereunto set their hands and seals the day and year first above written

Witness   JOSEPH SPENCER,   WILLIAM PANNILL
          ANDREW SHEPARD, FRANCIS MOORE,   ANN PANNILL
          URIEL MALLORY, JOHN COOKE,
          W. D. STROTHER, CALEB BAKER

THIS INDENTURE made the Eleventh day of November in year of our Lord one thousand seven hundred and seventy four Between WILLIAM PANNILL and ANN his Wife of County of King George and CHARLES DEANE SENR. of King George County of other part; Witnesseth that WILLIAM PANNILL and ANN his Wi_____ of Fifty pounds current money of Virginia to them in hand paid and by these presents do bargain and sell unto CHARLES DEANE in his actuall possession now being by virtue of a bargain and sale to him made for one year and by force of the Statute for transferring uses into possession a certain tract of land lying in Parish of Hanover and County of King George containing Eighty three acres more or less and bounded (the description of the boundss repeated as in the Lease above); To have and to hold the tract of land and premises unto CHARLES DEANE his heirs and WILLIAM PANNILL and his heirs the land and premises unto CHARLES DEANE his heirs shall warrant and forever defend by these presents; In Witness whereof the said WILLIAM PANNILL and ANN his Wife have hereunto set their hands and seals the day and year first above written

Sealed and Delivered in presence of
          JOSEPH SPENCER,   WILLIAM PANNILL
          ANDREW SHEPARD, FRANCIS MOORE   ANN PANNILL
          URIEL MALLORY, JOHN COOKE,
          W. D. STROTHER, CALEB BAKER
     1774 November. Received of CHARLES DEANE the sum of Fifty pounds current money of Virginia being the consideration within mentioned; Witness my hand the day and year above written
Test (same seven witnesses)   WILLIAM PANNILL

George the Third by the grace of God of Great Britain France & Ireland, King, Defender of the faith &c., to FRANCIS MOORE and ANDREW SHEPARD, Gentlemen,

Justices of ORANGE County, Greeting; Whereas WILLIAM PANNILL and ANN his Wife of
the County of ORANGE by their certain Deeds of Lease and Release (the Commission for the
privy examination of ANN, the Wife of WILLIAM PANNILL); Witness JOSEPH ROBINSON, Clerk of
our said Court the 4th day of November 1774, in the fifteenth year of our Reign
   King George County to wit. Pursuant to the within Commission we went to the within
named ANN PANNILL and examined her agreeable thereto (the return of the execution of
the privy exmaination of ANN PANNILL); Given under our hands and seals this 13th day of
December 1774   FRANCIS MOORE
                                                   ANDREW SHEPARD
   At a Court held for King George County the 4th day of May 1774
WILLIAM PANNILL and ANN PANNILL acknowledged their Deeds of Lease and Release
and proved by some witnesses, JOHN COOKE, W. D. STROTHER and CALEB BAKER and
ordered to be recorded and Commission returned

p.   Dr. Sir. My Grandson, JOHN COMBS informs me he has proposed to you a Match
1155   betwixt Miss Sukey and himself which you have consented to provided I will
          give him what I have promised and what I shall give him after my death is as
follows, the tract of Land that I now possess containing 401 acres, Negroes Phill, Luse,
Thomas, Simon, Roos, and some household furniture. I shall be glad to know what you
will give your Daughter.   GEORGE RIDING
To Mr. WM: THORNTON   January the 8th 1777

   At a Court held for King George County the 3d. day of December 1778
This Letter from GEORGE RIDING to WILLIAM THORNTON proved by JOHN SKINKER,
FRANCIS THORNTON and JOHN LOVELL, Gent., and ordered to be recorded
               Test JOS: ROBINSON, C. K. G. C.
   (The remainder of this page is blank.)

pp.   THIS INDENTURE made the 31st day of March in year of our Lord one thousand
1156-   seven hundred and seventy four Between WILLIAM CHAMPE of Parish of Bruns-
1159   wick and County of King George & MARY his Wife of one part and JOHN CHAMPE,
          Gent., of same Parish and County of other part; Witnesseth that WILLIAM
CHAMPE for sum of five shillings current money of Virginia to him in hand paid by
JOHN CHAMPE, by these presents doth bargain and sell unto JOHN CHAMPE one certain
tract of land containing by estimation Ninety three and three quarters acres more or
less situate in County of King George and bounded; Begining at a large white Oak, corner tree of the land of DANIEL GRANTs Orphans and side line of said JOHN CHAMPE, So.
75 Et. 128 1/2 poles, thence N. 56 1/2 E. 54 poles to three marked saplins joining the land
of said CHAMPE, thence No. 26 1/2 W. 170 poles joining the land of DANIEL GRANTs
Orphans to the begining; and all houses orchards profits and appurtenances belonging;
To have and to hold the land hereby conveyed unto JOHN CHAMPE and assigns during
the full time of one whole year paying therefore the Rent of one Pepper Corn on Lady
Day next if demanded to the intent that by virtue of these presents and of the Statute for
transferring uses into possession, JOHN CHAMPE may be in the actual possession of the
premises and be thereby enabled to accept a release of the reversion and inheritance
thereof; In Witness whereof the said WILLIAM CHAMPE hath hereunto set his hand and
seal the say and year first above written
Sealed & Deliverd in presence of
     JOHN TALIAFERRO.   WILLIAM CHAMPE
     FRANCIS TALIAFERRO, ANDREW WOODROW   MARY CHAMPE

THIS INDENTURE made the 31st day of March in year of our Lord one thousand
seven hundred and seventy four Between WILLIAM CHAMPE of Parish of Brunswick
and County of King George and MARY his Wife of one part and JOHN CHAMPE, Gent., of
same Parish and County of other part; Witnesseth that for sum of Two hundred and
fifty pounds current money of Virginia to WILLIAM CHAMPE in hand paid by JOHN
CHAMPE, by these presents doth bargain and sell unto JOHN CHAMPE his heirs in his
actual possession now being by virtue of a bargain and sale to him thereof made for
one year and by force of the Statute for transferring uses into possession, one certain
tract of land containing by estimation Ninety three and three quarters acres more or
less situate in County of King George and bounded, Begining (the description of the bounds
of the land repeated as in the Lease above); To have and to hold the lands hereby conveyed
and other the premises with appurtenances unto JOHN CHAMPE and his heirs; And
WILLIAM CHAMPE and his heirs unto JOHN CHAMPE his heirs shall warrant and forever
defend by these presents; In Witness whereof the sd. WM: CHAMPE hath set his hand
and seal the day & year first above written
Sealed & delivered in Presence of
FRANCIS TALIAFERRO,   WILLIAM CHAMPE
ANDREW WOODROW, JOHN TALIAFERRO   MARY CHAMPE
Received the day and year within written of the within named JOHN CHAMPE, the
consideration money within mentioned. L. 250...0.
Witness FRANCIS TALIAFERRO,   WILLIAM CHAMPE
ANDREW WOODROW, JOHN TALIAFERRO
George the Third by the grace of God of Great Britain France and Ireland, King, De-
fender of the faith &c., to ANTHONY STROTHER, JOHN TALIAERRO and HORATIO DADE, of
County of King George, Gent., Greeting; Whereas WILLIAM CHAMPE and MARY his Wife
by their certain Deed of Lease and Release (the Commission for the privy examination of
MARY, the Wife of WILLIAM CHAMPE). Witness JOS: ROBINSON, Clerk of our said Court of
King George aforesaid this 2d. day of May 1774 in the fourteenth of our Reign
In Obedience to the within Commission we met and examined the said MARY CHAMPE,
Wife of WILLIAM CHAMPE, privately and apart from her said Husband (the return of the
execution of the privy examination of MARY CHAMPE); Given under our hands this 8th day of
August 1774   ANTHONY STROTHER
                                          JOHN TALIAFERRO

pp.   THIS INDENTURE made the Eighteenth day of March in year of our Lord one
1160-   thousand seven hundred and seventy four Between DAVID BRIGGS of Town of
1162   FALMOUTH and County of King George of one part and THOMAS HUNT of said
         County of other part; Witnesseth that DAVID BRIGGS in consideration of the
Rents, Reservations and Covenants herein after reserved and mentioned on part of
DAVID BRIGGS his heirs to be paid and performed, hath demised and to farm let unto
THOMAS HUNT his heirs a certain parcel of land in the Town of FALMOUTH known by
the number Twenty four, the property of the said DAVID BRIGGS and bounded; Begining at the corner to Lot No. 20 belonging to CHARLES CARTER, Esqr., and running
along said lot half the length Easterly about 82 1/2 feet, then into said Lot. No. 24 forty
eight feet Northerly, then About 82 1/2 feet Westerly, then forty eight feet to the begining; together with the profits commodities and appurtenances to the same
belonging; To have and to hold the parcel of an acre of land with the appurtenances
unto THOMAS HUNT his heirs during the term of Twenty years, paying ten pounds current money on the last day of every year; In Witness whereof the parties have hereunto interchangeably set their hands and affixed their seals the day month & year
above written

Signed Sealed and Deld. in presence of
      CHARLES ASHLEY,   DAVID BRIGGS
      GEORGE LOBB, ARTHUR MORSON   THOMAS HUNT
      (No recording shown for this Lease.)

p.   THIS INDENTURE made the 21 day of January in year of our Lord one thousand
1162   seven hundred and seventy five Between WILLIAM ROBINSON of King George
        County of one part and DANIEL BRISCOE and DANIEL RICHARDSON of other part.
Witnesseth that WILLIAM ROBINSON in consideration of Two hundred pounds current
money of Virginia to him in hand paid sold unto DANIEL BRISCOE and DANIEL RICHARD-
SON one half acre or lott of land lying in Town of LEEDS which said ROBINSION bought
of DANIEL RICHARDSON with all the houses gardens and appurtenances belonging; To
have and to hold the half acre or lott of land with appurtenances unto DANIEL BRISCOE
and DANIEL RICHARDSON their heirs; In Witness whereof I have hereunto set my hand
and seal the day and year above written
      ANDREW CRAWFORD,   JNO: DICKIE,   WILLIAM ROBINSON
      RICHARD PAYNE, REUBEN BRISCOE
      (No recording shown for this Indenture of Bargain and Sale.)

pp.   THIS INDENTURE made the 8th day of July in year of our Lord one thousand
1162-   seven hundred and seventy four Between JNO: GLENDENING, Eldest Son and Heir
1164   of JAMES GLENDENING, late of County of King George, deceased, and MARGARET
        his Wife of one part and JOSEPH JONES of same County of other part; Whereas
JAMES GLENDENING being seized in fee simple of a certain piece of land whereon said
JAMES GLENDENING lived situate in sd. County on MUDDY CREEK, by his Last Will and
Testament bearing date the 21st of October in the year 1776, demised the same unto his
Son, JAMES GLENDENING in tail and default of issue of his body unto his Sons, JNO:
GLENDENING and GEORGE GLENDENING and their heirs; equally to be divided; And
Whereas sd. JAMES GLENDENING, the Son, having departed this life without Issue, the
Land has been vested in sd. JNO: AND GEORGE, and said GEORGE being an Infant under
the age of twenty one hath by his Guardian, JNO: COX, agreed to make partition of said
land agreeable to a Survey thereof by JAMES TAYLOR, Gent., allotting unto JOHN GLEN-
DENING that part of the land adjoining to the land whereon JAMES DAVIS now live; And
whereas said JNO: GLENDENING hath agreed to sell his moeity of the land unto JOS:
JONES; This Indenture Witnesseth that JNO: GLENDENING and MARGARET his Wife for
sum of Twenty six shiillings per acre for JNO: GLENDENINGs share of the land in hand
paid by JOS: JONES by these presents do bargain sell and make over unto JOS: JONES his
heirs all that the sd. JNO: GLENDENINGs share or moiety of the tract of land lfeft by his
Father unto him and his Brother, GEORGE GLENDENING; containing by estimation one
hundred and fifty acres be the same more or less and divided in manner herein before
recited, the tract being bounded and abutting on the land of JNO: TALIAFERRO,
MUDDY CREEK, the land JOS: JONES bought of JAS: HUBARD, the land of JAMES DAVIS and
the land of sd. JOSEPH JONES bought of JNO: SEAL, together with all buildings rights
members and appurtenances belonging; To have and to hold to JOS: JONES his heirs and
JNO: GLENDENING and MARGARET his Wife & all persons shall warrant and forever defend; In Witness whereof the sd. JNO: GLENDENING & MARGARET his Wife have hereunto set their hands and seals the day and year above written
Sealed & Delivered in the presence of
      ANTHONY STROTHER,   JOHN GLENDENING
      JOHN TALIAFERRO, JAMES DAVIS   MARGARET GLENDENING
      (No recording shown for this Indenture of Bargain and Sale.)

George the Third by the grace of God of Great Britain France and Ireland, King, Defender of the faith &c., to ANTHONY STROTHER and JNO: TALIAFERRO, of County of King
George, Gent., Greeting; Whereas JNO: GLENDENING and MARGARET his Wife of your
said County by their certain Deed of Bargain & Sale (the Commission for the privy examination of MARGARET, the Wife of JOHN GLENDENING); Witness JOS: ROBINSON, Clerk of our sd.
County Court this 8th day of July 1774. in the 14th year of our Reign
                                                JOS: ROBINSON, C. K. G. C.
    By virtue of the Commission to us directed, we have examined the within named
MARGARET GLENDENING privately & apart from her Husband, JNO: GLENDENING; (the
return of the privy examination of MARGARET GLENDENING); Given under our hands this 8th
day of July 1774   ANTHONY STROTHER
                                                JOHN TALIAFERRO

pp.   THIS INDENTURE made the 13th day of January in year of our Lord one thou-
1164-   sand seven hundred and seventy five Between DAVID BRIGGS of Town of FAL-
1166   MOUTH in the County of King George of one part and THOMAS BROWN of said
        Town and County of other part; Witnesseth that DAVID BRIGGS in consideration
of the Rents, Reservations and Covenants herein after reserved and mentioned on part
of DAVID BRIGGS his heirs to be paid done & performed, hath demised & to farm let unto
THOMAS BROWN his heirs a certain parcel of land in the tenure & occupation of sd.
THOMAS BROWN now being containing part of a lot of land in Town of FALMOUTH
known by the number Twenty Four 24 the property of DAVID BRIGGS bounded, Begining at the corner of that ground leased to THOMAS HUNT in CARTERs line, then running along that line about 82 1/2 feet Easterly to Mr. VOWLES corner, thence forty eight
feet along said VOWLES line Northerly, then 82 1/2 feet or thereabouts to another corner of the ground leased to THOMAS HUNT, then along sd. HUNTs back line to the
begining, Also another parcel of land on sd. Lot No. 24 begining at Mr. RICHARD LEWIS
East corner on CAROLINE STREET & running 22 feet or thereabouts alaong sd. Street to
Mr. VOWLES Corner, thence 24 feet along sd. VOWLESs West line & sd. lot No. 24, then
about 32 1/2 feet Westerly to another corner of the land leased to RICHARD LEWIS, then
along said North & South back line to the begining; together with the profits, commodities and appurtenances belonging; To have and to hold the parcel of land with the
appurtenances unto THOMAS BROWN his heirs from Twenty eight day of September one
thousand seven hundred and seventy four and during the term of Nineteen years, five
months and twenty days to end the same day with the Lease granted to THOMAS HUNT,
paying to DAVID BRIGGS his heirs yearly the Rent of five pounds current money on the
last day of every year; In Witness whereof the sd. parties have hereunto interchangeably set their hands and affixed their seals the day month and year above written
Signed Sealed and delivered in presence of
    GEORGE LOBB,   DAVID BRIGGS
    WILLIAM WINLOCK, GEORGE GRAVES
    (No recording shown for this Lease.)

pp.   THIS INDENTURE made the 13th day of January in year of our Lord one thou-
1166-   sand seven hundred and seventy five Between DAVID BRIGGS of Town of FAL-
1167   MOUTH and County of King George of one part and JNO: SHARPE JUNR. of the
        same County of other part; Witnesseth that DAVID BRIGGS in consideration of
the Rents, Reservations & Covenants herein after reserved and mentioned on part of
DAVID BRIGGS his heirs to be paid done and performed hath demised and to farm let
unto JNO: SHARPE JUNR. his heirs a certain parcel of land & House thereon in the

tenure and occupation of sd. JNO: SHARPE now being part of a lot of land in Town of
FALMOUTH known by the No. Twenty Four 24 the property of sd. DAVID BRIGGS and
bounded, Begining at Mr. RICHD: LEWIS corner on the West twenty four feet from the
sd. LEWIS corner opposite to Mr. WOODROWs, thence along sd. LEWIS line South eighty
two and a half feet Easterly then along the same course 82 1/2 feet to Mr. VOWLES, (   )
feet on CAROLINE STREET thence Southerly 33 feet along VOWLES line, then one
hundred & sixty five feet (this Deed is too faded to abstract) To have and to hold the parcel
of land unto JNO: SHARPE JUNR. his heirs during the term of fifteen years paying the
rent of ten pounds current money on the last day of each year; In Witness whereof the
sd. parties have hereunto interchangeably set their hands and affixed their seals the
day month and year first above written
Signed Sealed and Delivered in presence of
 GEORGE LOBB,   DAVID BRIGGS
 WILLIAM WINLOCK, GEORGE GRAVES JOHN SHARPE JUNR.
 (No recording for this Lease.)

p. THIS INDENTURE made the 28th day of Feby. in year of our Lord one thousand
1168 seven hundred and seventy five Between DAVID BRIGGS of Town of FALMOUTH
of one part and RICHARD LEWIS of other part; Witnesseth that in consideration
of the Rents and Covenants hereinafter reserved and mentioned DAVID BRIGGS hath
demised and to farm letten to RICHARD LEWIS a certain parcel of land being part of a
lott of land belonging to DAVID BRIGGS situate in Town of FALMOUTH and known by the
number Twenty Four and bounded; Begining at the North West corner of the sd. Lott
and running thence Easterly along CAROLINE STREET the length of the Lot 82 1/2 feet,
thence at right angles into the Lot Southerly seventy four feet, thence making a right
angle Westerly 82 1/2 feet to the Street opposite to the Warehouse, thence along the
Street twenty four feet to the begining; together with all houses and appurtenances
belonging; To have and to hold the part of a lot and premises to RICHARD LEWIS his
heirs from the seventeenth day of March in the year of our Lord one thousand seven
hundred and seventy three during the term of ten years thence next ensuing paying
yearly the Rent of ten pounds current money unto DAVID BRIGGS his heirs; In Witness
whereof the sd. parties have hereunto interchangeably set their hands and affixed
their seals the day and year first above written
Sealed and delivered in presence of
 THOMAS BROWN,   DAVID BRIGGS
 JOHN LEWIS, ALEXANDER WOODROW RICHARD LEWIS
 (No recording shown for this Lease.)

pp. THIS INDENTURE made the 28th day of January in year of our Lord one thou-
1169 sand seven hundred and seventy four Between WALKER TALIAFERRO of County
of CAROLINE of one part and DAVID BRIGGS of County of King George of other
part; Witnesseth that WALKER TALIAFERRO for sum of Four pounds current money to
him in hand paid by DAVID BRIGGS by these presents doth bargain and sell unto DAVID
BRIGGS his heirs one lot or half acre of land lying in Town of FALMOUTH and County of
King George numbered Nineteen conveyed by the Trustees of Town of FALMOUTH to
JOHN WILLIAMS, afterward by the said WILLIAMS to LYONEL LYDE and JOHN TAYLOR,
Esqrs., and others, afterwards to THOMAS TURNER the Younger, from him to WALKER
TALIAFERRO Esqr. party to these presents; in taile by Marriage; To have and to hold
the lot or half acre of land with appurtenances unto DAVID BRIGGS his heirs and WAL-
KER TALIAFERRO his heirs the land and premises unto DAVID BRIGGS his heirs shall

warrant and forever defend by these presents; In Witness whereof the said WALKER
TALIAFERRO hath hereunto set his hand and seal the day and year above written
Signed sealed and delivered in presence of
      BENJAMIN GIVIN   WALKER TALIAFERRO
      LAUCHLIN McINTOSH, CHARLES ASHLEY
    (No recording for this Indenture shown.)

pp.   THIS INDENTURE made this first day of April in the fifteenth year of the Reign
1169- of our Sovereign Lord George one thousand seven hundred and seventy five
1170   Between SARAH McWILLIAM and JOSEPH her Son of Parish of Hanover and
      County of King George of onepart and LAWRENCE BALTHROP, Carpenter and
Joiner, of King George County of other part; Witnesseth that SARAH McWILLIAM and
JOSEPH her Son of their own free will hath put and bound the said JOSEPH McWILLIAM
an Apprentice to the sd. LAWRENCE BALTHROP during the full term of five years from
the date hereof to faithfully serve said LAWRENCE BALTHROP as an Apprentice ought to
do and the said SARAH McWILLIAM doth oblige herself to find her Son clothes, washing
diet and mending and LAWRENCE BALTHROP doth hereby oblige himself to pay unto the
said SARAH McWILLIAM Forty shillings this present year and four pounds during the
term of years and the said LAWRENCE BALTHROP doth oblidge himself to do his true
endeavour to learn the Apprentice, JOSEPH McWILLIAM, the art and trade of a Carpenter and Joiner during the sd. term and at the expiration of the sd. term to pay the sd.
Apprentice the just sum of four pounds, ten shillings; In Testimony whereof the parties to these presents have hereunto set their hands and affixed their seals the day and
year first above written
Signed sealed and delivered in presence of
      (no witnesses recorded)   SARAH McWILLIAM
                              JOSEPH McWILLIAM
                              LAWRENCE BALTHROP
    (No recording shown for this Indenture of Apprenticeship)

p.   THIS INDENTURE made this thirteenth day of February in year of our Lord
1170   one thousand seven hundred and seventy five Between ARTHUR MORSON of
      of King George County, Merchant, of one part and JOSEPH PALMER, Joiner, of
other part; Witnesseth that ARTHUR MORSON for sum of Twenty pounds current money
of Virginia to him in hand paid by these presents doth bargain and sell unto JOSEPH
PALMER his heirs one tract of land containing two half acre lotts in the Town of FAL-
MOUTH distinguished by the Numbers Forty Two and Forty Nine together with the
appurtenances; To have and to hold the two lotts of land unto JOSEPH PALMER his heirs
and ARTHUR MORSON for himself his heirs the lotts of land will warrant and forever
defend by these presents; In Witness whereof the said ARTHUR MORSON hath hereunto
set his hand and seal the day and year first above written
Signed sealed and delivered in the presence of
      WILLIAM BLAIR, EDWARD MOOR,   ARTHUR MORSON
      DAVID BROWN, WILLIAM (faded)
    (No recording shown for this Indenture of Bargain and Sale.)

pp.   KNOW ALL MEN by these presents that I WILLIAM WEEKS of King George Coun-
1170- ty, Planter, for sum of ninety six pounds, three shillings and three pence cur-
1171   rent money of Virginia to me in hand paid by JAMES ROBINSON of Town of FAL-
      MOUTH in sd. County, Mercht., in behalf of MESSRS. WILLIAM CUNNINGHAM and

COMPY., of City of GLASGOW in the Kingdom of Great Britain, Merchants & Partners, by
these presents do bargain and sell him Negro slaves, vizt., Frank and Mymie (two
women), Agg & Tamer (two girls) and Benjamin a boy with the future increase of the
said females; To have and to hold unto JAMES ROBINSON to the proper use of MESSRS.
WILLIAM CUNNINGHAM and COMPANY their heirs; Provided nevertheless and this Bill
of Sale is upon this express condition that if WILLIAM WEEKS his lheirs shall pay
WILLIAM CUNNINGHAM and COMPY. their certain Factors or Attorney the sum of
seventy six pounds, three shillings & three pence current money of Virgini on the first
day of November seventeen hundred and seventy four with lawfull Interest for the
same then this Bill of Sale shall become void and of no effect, But till the default is made
in the payment of the principal sum of seventy six pounds, three shillings and three
pence current money of Virginia and Interest on the day herein before mentioned for
payment thereof, it shall be lawfull for me, the said WILLIAM WEEKS, my heirs to keep
the said slaves; In Witness whereof the sd. WILLIAM WEEKS hath hereunto set his hand
and seal this 5th day of September seventeen hundred and seventy four
Sign'd Seal'd and deliver'd in presence of
    WALTER COLQUHOUN,   WILLIAM WEEKS
    ADAM NEWALL
   (No recording shown for this Bill of Sale and Mortgage.)

p,   FORASMUCH as LETTICE WISHART, Widow and Relict of JNO: WISHART, Clerk,
1171   lately deced., is not satisfied with the provisions made for her by her said late
       Husbands last Will and Testament, the sd. LETTICE WISHART doth declare that she
will not accept receive or take the Legacy or Legacies given or bequeathed unto the sd.
LETTICE WISHART by the Last Will and Testament of JNO: WISHART, her late Husband, or
any part thereof; But doth renounce all benefit and advantage which she might claim
or demand by the sd. Last Will of sd. JNO: WISHART as aforesd. In Witness whereof, the
sd. LETTICE WISHART hath hereunto set her hand and seal this 21st day of April in the
year of our Lord 1775
Signed & sealed in presence of
    THOMAS JETT, JAMES DAVIS,   LETTICE WISHART
    THOMAS HORD, MICHAEL WALLACE
   (No recording shown for this Renouncing of the provisions of the Will of JNO: WISHART, Clerk.)

pp.   THIS INDENTURE made this Ninth day of August one thousand seven hundred
1171- and seventy four Between ROBERT WALKER of the Parish of Hanover and Coun-
1172   ty of King George of one part and THOMAS JETT, Mercht. of the same Parish
       and County of other part; Witnesseth that ROBERT WALKER for sum of One hun-
dred and eleven pounds, seventeen shillings & four pence half penny current money
of Virginia to him in hand paid by these presents doth bargain and sell unto THOMAS
JETT his heirs the following stocks and household furniture, vizt., seventeen head of
Cattle, 2 Mares and young black Gelding, three beds & furniture, one Chest, 2 Cupboards,
1 square Table, eight Chairs, 1 copper Skillet, 1 copper Kettle, & all other the household
& kitchen furniture belonging to sd. ROBERT WALKER unto THOS: JETT his heirs provided always & it is agreed between the parties to these presents that if ROBERT WALKER
his heirs shall pay THOMAS JETT his heirs the full and just sum of One hundred & eleven
pounds, seventeen shillings and four pence half penny on demand with legal Interest
thereon that then sd. THOMAS JETT his heirs shall at the request and charges of ROBERT
WALKER his heirs recovery of the said (the items are listed again) In Witness whereof I
ROBT. WALKER hath hereunto set his hand & seal this the day and year first above
written

Sealed and Delivered in the presence of
        DANL: RICHARDSON, JNO: PAYTON   ROBERT WALKER
        GEORGE CARMICHAEL, ALEXR: ROWE,
        THOMAS GRANT, THS: GOWRY S. TYLER (?)
    Reced. of THS: JETT this 9th day of Augt. 1774. One hundred & Eleven pounds, seven-
teen shillings 4 1/2, it being the consideration mentioned in this Indenture pd. by him
to
Witness: DANIEL RICHARDSON, JNO: PAYTON   ROBERT WALKER
        GEORGE CARMICHAEL, ALEXR> ROWE,
        THS: GOWRY S. TYLER, THOMAS GRANT
    (No recording shown for this Mortgage.)

pp.   THIS INDENTURE made this eighth day of June one thousand seven hundred
1172-   and seventy five Between PATRICK KENDRICK of County of King George, Planter,
1173   of one part and JACOB FOLLIS of County aforesaid, Blacksmith, of other part;
        Witnesseth that PATRICK KENDRICK and JANE his Wife for sum of One hundred
pounds current money by JACOB FOLLIS to PATRICK KENDRICK in hand paid, by these
presents do bargain and sell unto JACOB FOLLIS his heirs one hundred acres of land mor
or less being part of the One hundred and seventy acres lying in County of King George
granted to LAWRENCE WASHINGTON by Patent dated the fourth day of Feby. 1744 and
bounded thus; Begining at a Hickory at or near WILLIAM HORTON corner, S. 87 E. 95
poles to 4 Box Oaks pointers. thence South twenty degrees E. 62 poles to a small box Oak
on the Road side, thence South thirty nine degrees West one hundred & seven poles to a
red Oak, corner to CARTERs, thence with another of sd. CARTERs lines W. 88 poles to a
white Oak, corner to sd. CARTERs on a Hill side and on the West side a (   ) thence North
25 degrees E. 172 poles to the begining from said LAWRENCE WASHINGTON conveyed to
GEORGE WASHINGTON, his Brother, and then conveyed to PATRICK KENDRICK, thence to
JACOB FOLLIS his heirs. and all the houses orchards profits and appurtenances
belonging; To have and to hold the one hundred acres of land and all appurtenances
unto JACOB FOLLIS his heirs; In Witness whereof the sd. PATRICK KENDRICK and JANE
his Wife hath hereunto set their hands & seals the day & year first above written
Signed sealed and delivered in presence of us
        ARTHUR MORSON   PATRICK KENDRICK
                                           JANE her mark X KENDRICK
    Reced. of the above named JACOB FOLLIS the sum of one hundred pounds current
money being the consideration money for the land and premises above expressed, As
Witness my hand this 8th day of June 1775.
Witness: ARTHUR MORSON, DAVID BRIGGS   PATRICK KENDRICK
        WILLIAM NEWTON, GERARD BANKS,
        A. BUCHANAN, HARRIS HOOE
    (No recording shown for this Indenture of Bargain and Sale.)

pp.   THIS INDENTURE made the 25th day of March one thousand seven hundred and
1174-   seventy five Between CHARLES DEANE JUNR. and MARY his Wife of Parish of
1175   Hanover in the County of King George of one part and THOMAS DRAKE of the
         same parish and County of other part; Witnesseth that CHARLES DEANE nd
MARY his Wife for sum of Two hundred and seventy five pounds current money of
Virginia to them in hand paid by these presents do bargain and sell unto THOS, DRAKE
and to his heirs all that tract of land formerly belonging to MARY BROOK deced. situate
in County aforesaid which Land lies on RAPPAHANNOCK RIVER adjoining to the Land of

JNO: WASHINGTON, WILLIAM THORNTON and the sd. THOMAS DRAKE and contains One
hundred acres be the same more or less with all houses profits & advantages; To have
and to hold the tract of land and premises unto THOMAS DRAKE his heirs: In Witness
whereof the said CHARLES DEANE & MARY his Wife have hereunto set their hands and
seals the day and year first above written
Sealed and Delivered in presence of

THOMAS JETT, WILLIAM ROBINSON,	CHARLES DEANE
REUBEN BULLARD	MARY DEANE

Reced. of the within named THOMAS DRAKE the sum of Two hundred and seventy five
pounds, the consideration within mentioned; Witness my hand this 25th day of March
1775

Witness THS: JETT, WILLIAM ROBINSON,   CHS: DEANE
          REUBEN BULLARD, DANL. BRISCOE
    (No recording shown for this Indenture of Bargain and Sale.)

        George the Third by the grace of God of Great Britain, France & Ireland, King,
Defender of the faith &c., to THOS: JETT, WILLIAM ROBINSON and THOS: HODGE, Gent.,
Greeting. Whereas CHARLES DEANE and MARY his Wife by their certain Deed of bar-
gain and sale bearing date the 28th day of March last past have sold and conveyed unto
THOMAS DRAKE the fee simple Estate of one hundred acres of land (the Commission for the
privy examination of MARY, the Wife of CHARLES DEANE); Witness JOS: ROBINSON, Clerk of our
said Court at the Court House this 26th day of March 1775, in the fifteenth year of our
Reign   JOS: ROBINSON
        Pursuant to the within Commission, we the Subscribers personally went to the within
named MARY DEANE, the Wife of CHARLES DEANE within named and reced. her acknowledgment of the Indenture (the return of the execution of the privy examination of MARY
DEANE); Given under our hands & seals at King George County the 26th day of March
1774   THOMAS JETT
                                                         WILLIAM ROBINSON
    At a Court held for King George County the 2d. day of November 1775
The aforegoing Deed being presented in Court and acknowledged by CHARLES DEANE to
be his act & deed and together with the Commission ordered to be recorded
            Test JOS: ROBINSON, C. K. G. C.

pp.   THIS INDENTURE made the 27th day of September one thousand seven hundred
1175-   & seventy five Between JAMES QUISENBERRY & ANN his Wife of Parish of
1176   WASHINGTON in County of WESTMORELAND of one part & CHARLES DEANE of the
          Parish of Hanover in County of King George of other part; Witnesseth that
JAMES QUISENBERRY and ANN his Wife for sum of Fifteen pounds current money of
Virginia & other considerations hereinafter mentioned to be done and performed by
CHARLES DEANE by these presents doth bargain and sell unto CHARLES DEANE his heirs
all that part of a tract of Land situate on RAPPAHANNOCK RIVER in County of King
George containing by estimation Twenty five acres which Land was granted by MARY
BROOK deced. to the said ANN, her Grand Daughter, and is now in the possession of
CHARLES DEANE the Younger by virtue of a Lease from sd. JAMES QUISENBERRY for
some years to come and all houses profits and appurtenances belonging; To have and to
hold the parcel of land unto CHARLES DEANE and his heirs, But is is agreed between the
parties that in case ANN QUISENBERRY should survive the sd. JAMES that in such case
said CHARLES DEANE covenants that he will on the death of JAMES QUISENBERRY make
to the sd. ANN a Lease for the Land for and during her natural life without any

consideration for annual or other Rent; And it is further covenanted by JAMES QUISEN-
BERRY and ANN his Wife that they will when required by CHARLES DEANE his heirs
make or cause to be made such further lawfull act or conveyance to CHARLES DEANE his
heirs; In Witness whereof the sd. JAMES QUISENBERRY and ANN his Wife hath here-
unto set their hands and seals the day month & year before written
Sealed & Delivered in presence of
      REUBEN BRISCOE, ROBERT LOVELL   JAMES QUISENBERRY
      JOHN MAZARET, THOMAS DRAKE   ANN QUISENBERRY
  Reced. from CHARLES DEANE the sum of Fifteen pounds current money being the consideration money mentioned in the Deed
Witness REUBEN BRISCOE, ROBERT LOVELL,   JAMES QUISENBERRY
      JOHN MAZARET, THOMAS DRAKE
   (No recording shown for this Indenture of Bargain and Sale.)

pp.   THIS INDENTURE made the 12th of Feby: one thousand seven hundred and
1176- seventy four Between THOMAS GRIFFIN of King George County of one part and
1177   JNO: COCKSHUTT & others, Trustees of Mr. JNO: BLAND of LONDON, of other part;
      Witnesseth that THOMAS GRIFFIN for sum of twenty eight pounds thirteen shil-
lings and five pence currency to him in hand paid by JNO: COCKSHUTT & others, Trustees of Mr. JOHN BLAND, doth bargain and sell one Negro woman named Judy & her
future increase, a black Horse now three years old I had from JNO: DEARING and a Gray
Mare nine years old about 4 1/2 feet high; To have and to hold the Negro woman Judy
and horses unto JOS: COCKSHUTT & others, Trustees of Mr. JNO: BLAND, provided however
that if THOS: GRIFFIN shall pay or cause to be paid unto JNO: COCKSHUTT & others, Trustees of Mr. JNO: BLAND, the aforesaid sum and Interest from the tenth day of May last,
Then this Instrument of Writing to be void, otherwise to remain in force; In Witness
whereof the sd. THOMAS GRIFFIN hath hereunto set his hand and seal the day and year
above written
Signed, sealed & delivd. in presence of
      DAVID BRIGGS,   THOS: his mark ╈ GRIFFIN
      CHARLES ASHLEY, WM: TEMPLEMAN
   (No recording shown for this Mortgage)

pp.   George the third by the grace of God of Great Britain, France and Ireland, King,
1177- Defender of the faith &c. to JNO: SNELSON, MERIWETHER SHELTON & BENJAMIN
1178   ANDERSON of County of HANOVER, Gentlemen, Greeting. Whereas COLLIN
      RIDDOCK & JANE his Wife by their certain Indenture of Bargain and Sale
bearing date the first day of October one thousand seven hundred & seventy four did
convey unto THOMAS HODGE (the Commission for the privy examination of JANE, the Wife of
COLLIN RIDDOCK); Witness JOS: ROBINSON, Clerk of our said Court of King George aforesaid this 16 day of July 1775   JOS: ROBINSON
   Pursuant to the within Commission to us directed, we the Subscribers went to JANE
RIDDOCK, Wife of the within named COLLIN RIDDOCK, and received her acknowledgment (the return of the execution of the privy examination of JANE RIDDOCK); Given under our
hands and seals this 27th day of July 1775   JOHN SNELSON
                            MERIWETHER SHELTON
   (No recording shown for this Commission and the return thereof.)

p.   BE IT KNOWN to all men by these presents that I ANN ARNOLD, Widow, of the
1178   County of King George, about to enter into the state of Matrimony with JNO:

LOVELL of sd. County and being unwilling that the several Negroes heeafter mentioned should vest in him by virtue thereof, have with the privily consent of sd. JNO. LOVELL & by these presents sell & make over unto WILLIAM BERNARD of County of WESTMORE-LAND his heirs the Negro slaves following, to wit, Theophilus, James, Sarah,& Hannah & the future increase of the sd. Sarah & Hannah for the several uses expressed, that is to say, for the absolute use of ANN ARNOLD until the sd. Marriage takes effect and from and after the solemnization thereof in Trust for the sue of me the sd. ANN ARNOLD during my natural life & after my demise to my Daughter, JUSTITIA, her heirs and for no other use and purpose whatsoever; In Witness whereof I have hereunto set my hand and seal the Fourth day of February one thousand seven hundred & seventy five Signd. seald. & delivd. in presence of

WILLIAM MARSHALL, ANN her mark ✝ ARNOLD
WILLIAM (? BAIRD); JNO: (? BAIRD)
(No recording shown for this Marriage Contract.)

pp. 1179-1182   THIS INDENTURE made this 3d. day of February in the year of our Lord one thousand seven hundred and seventy six Between ARTHUR MORSON of one part and WILLIAM MITCHELL, Planter, of other part; Witnesseth that ARTHUR MORSON in consideration of the Rents, Duties, Reservations & Covenants herein after mentioned on part of WILLIAM MITCHELL his heirs to be paid done and performed, hath demised to WILLIAM MITCHELL his heirs a certain parcel of land in the tenure and occupation of said WILLIAM MITCHELL now being containing One hundred and forty three acres be the same more or less and bounded; Begining at a red Oak on the Ridge, corner to SAMUEL MARTINs Lot, thence S. 10 W. 42 poles to another corner amongst some Pines, thence S.63 E. about 125 poles to HANCOCK LEEs line in an old field, thence S. 20 W. about 34 poles to a corner of HANCOCK LEE, thence S. 20 W. 129 poles to two red Oaks and a Hickory sappling to a Branch, thence N. 42 W. 160 poles to a white Oak, corner to WILLIAM GRAVEs lot, thence about North 45 E. to the begining; together with all the profits and appurtenances to the same belonging; To have and to hold the parcel of one hundred and forty three acres of land with appurtenances unto WILLIAM MITCHELL his heirs from the day of the date hereof during the term of the natural lives of WILLIAM MITCHELL, SUSANNAH MITCHELL his Wife and THOMAS MITCHELL his Son, & the longest liver of them paying unto THOMAS MORSON his heirs yearly the Rent of seven pounds lawfull money of Virginia; In Witness whereof the sd. parties have hereunto interchangeably set their hands and affixed their seals the day month and year first above written
Signed Sealed and Delivered in presence of
Nobody ARTHUR MORSON
WILLIAM MITCHELL

King George County 3d. Feby. 1776. The within named WILLIAM MITCHELL is to have this present year 1776 and the years 1777 & 1778 Rent free excepting the Quit rents which is to be paid annually for the within mentioned premises
ARTHUR MORSON

(No recording is shown for this Lease).

pp. 1182-1183   THIS INDENTURE made this 6th day of November one thousand seven hundred and seventy three Between WILLIAM SULLIVAN of King George County of one part and JOHN COCKSHUTT and others, Trustees of Mr. JOHN BLAND of LONDON, Mercht., of the other part; Witnesseth that WILLIAM SULLIVAN in consideration of the sum of fourteen pounds, thirteen shillings one penny three farthings currency to him in hand paid by JOHN COCKSHUTT and others, Trustees of Mr. JOHN BLAND, doth bargain and sell unto JOHN COCKSHUTT and others, Trustees of Mr. JNO, BLAND of LONDON, Merchant, 6 head of Cattle, vizt. 5 Cowes and 1 Calf marked with a crop in the left ear and a swallow fork in the right ear, a black Horse about 13 hands high, eleven or twelve years old branded on the near shoulder W., and on the near buttock S., two gray Mares 13 hands high 4 years old next Spring and branded on the near buttock S., 6 head of Hoggs mark'd with a crop in the left ear & a swallow fork in the right ear; 1 Oak bedstead, 1 Poplar ditto, 2 feather beds & furniture, 1 Oak Chest, 1 Walnut Table; 5 Chairs, 1 doz. pewter Plates, 2 pewter Dishes & 4 pewter Basons. To have and to hold the Cattle hogs and chattles unto JOHN COCKSHUTT and others, Trustees of Mr. JOHN BLAND of LONDON, Mercht., their heirs; Provided however that if WILLIAM SULLIVAN shall pay or cause to be paid the aforesaid Debt and Interest from date hereof, Then this Instrument of Writing to be void, otherwise to remain in force; In Witness whereof the said WILLIAM SULLIVAN hath hereunto set his hand and seal the day and year above written

Signd. Seald. & delivered in presence of
    CHARLES ASHLEY,   WILLIAM his mark Y SULLIVAN
    LAC: McINTOSH, DAVID BRIGGS
  (No recording is shown for this Mortgage).

p.   THIS INDENTURE made the Nineteenth day of February one thousand seven
1183 hundred and seventy four Between VINCENT COX of County of King George of
      one part and JOHN COCKSHUTT and others, Trustees of Mr. JOHN BLAND of LON-
DON, Mercht., of the other part; Witnesseth that VINCENT COX in consideration of the sum of Fourteen pounds, eighteen shillings and nine pence currency to him in hand paid by JOHN COCKSHUTT and others, Trustees of Mr. JOHN BLAND of LONDON, hath bargained and sold unto JOHN COCKSHUTT and others, Trustees of Mr. JOHN BLAND of LONDON, one bay Mare thirteen hands and an half high six years old, branded on the near buttock T. H., five Cows and three Calves, ten Sheep, each mark'd with a crop and slit in the right ear and a slit in the left ear; seventeen head of Hogs mark'd the same as the Sheep three feather beds and furniture, three tables, eight chairs, three chests, fourteen pewter plates, & 2 dishes, one bay Horse two years old branded T. H., on the near buttock, one bay Mare 13 1/2 hands high eight years old, no brand, To have and to hold the Horses, Cattle & goods & chattles unto JOHN COCKSHUTT and others, Trustees of Mr. JOHN BLAND of LONDON their heirs, Provided however that if VINCENT COX shall pay unto JOHN COCKSHUTT and others, Trustees of Mr. JOHN BLAND of LONDON the aforesaid Debt and Interest from the 24th day of June last, Then this Instrument of Writing to be void, otherwise to remain in force; In Witness whereof the said VINCENT COX hath hereunto set his hand and seal the day and year above written

Signd. seald. and delivd. in presence of
    DAVID BRIGGS,   VINCENT COX
    CHARLES ASHLEY, LAC: McINTOSH
  (No recording shown for this Mortgage.)

p.   THIS INDENTURE made this 27th day of November one thousand seven hundred
1184 and seventy three Between WILLIAM ROSE of County of King George of one part
      and JOHN COCKSHUTT and others, Trustees of Mr. JNO: BLAND of LONDON, Mercht.
of other part; Witnesseth that WILLIAM ROSE for sum of Twenty five pounds, two shillings and three pence to him in hand paid by DAVID BRIGGS, doth bargain and sell unto JOHN COCKSHUTT and other, Trustees of Mr. JOHN BLAND of LONDON, Mercht., their heirs

one gray stone Horse near 15 hands high three years old branded on the near buttock
CB To have and to hold the Horse unto JOHN COCKSHUTT and others, Trustees of Mr.
JOHN BLAND of LONDON their heirs, Provided however that if MARTIN WELSH shall pay
or cause to be paid unto JOHN COCKSHUTT and others, Trustees of Mr. JOHN BLAND of
LONDON their Attorney the sum of twenty pounds with Interest; Then this Instrument
of Writing to be void otherwise to remain in force; In Witness whereof the sd. MARTIN
WELSH hath hereunto set his hand and seal the day and year above written
Signd. seald. & delivd. in presence of
      CHARLES ASHLEY,   MARTIN his mark ⌒ WELSH
      DAVID BRIGGS, ALEXR: HANSFORD
(No recording shown for this Mortgage.)

p.   KNOW ALL MEN by these presents that we WILLIAM HUDSON and ABIGAIL
1185   HUDSON of County of WESTMORELAND are held and firmly bound unto SAMUEL
      KENDALL JUNR. of County of King George in the sum of Fifty pounds current
money of Virginia to the payment well and truly to be made we bind ourselves our
heirs firmly by these presents; Sealed with our seals and dated this sixteenth day of
August one thousand seven hundred and seventy four
   THE CONDITION of the above obligation is such that whereas said SAMUEL KENDALL
hath bargained with WILLIAM HUDSON for a certain tract of land lying in County of
King George whereon said KENDAL now liveth and hath passed his Bond payable to the
said HUDSON for the same, And the Land being intail, the said KENDAL is to pay all
charges towards docking the said intailed land and WILLIAM HUDSON & ABIGAIL HUD-
SON is to make execute and acknowledge any Deed or Deeds to the safe conveyance of
the said Land to SAMUEL KENDAL his heirs at any time when requested by said KENDAL,
Then the above obligation to be void, otherwise to remain in full force and virtue
Sealed and Acknowledg'd in presence of
      ROWLEY MARDERS,   WILLIAM his mark ⊖ HUDSON
      BENJA: MARSHALL,   ABIGAIL her mark ✝ HUDSON
      LAWRENCE BALTHROP
(No recording shown for this Bond.)

pp.   THIS INDENTURE made the Twentieth day of January one thousand seven hun-
1185- dred and seventy four Between THOMAS SHARPE JUNR. of (blank) County of one
1186 part and JOHN COCKSHUTT and others, Trustees of Mr. JOHN BLAND of LONDON of
      the other part; Witensseth that in consideration of the sum of twenty two
pounds, fourteen shillings and ten pence three farthings currency to him in hand paid
doth bargain and sell unto JOHN COCKSHUTT and others, Trustees of Mr. JOHN BLAND of
LONDON, their heirs one certain parcel of land situate in County of King George in the
Parish of Brunswick containing Eighty nine acres more or less and joining THOMAS
BALLARD on the North, HANCOCK LEE on the West of WAUGHs line now in possession of
Mr. JAMES HUNTER on the East, and JOHN SHARPE JUNR. on the South as mentioned
(with the courses) by a Deed from JOHN SHARPE SENR. to THOMAS SHARPE JUNR. now in
King George Office, one sorrel Horse no brand six years old next Spring about fifteen
hands high, one brindled Bull about two years old mark'd with a crop and underkeel in
the left ear and two slits in the right ear, two Sows and 6 Shoats mark'd with a crop and
an underkeel in the right ear & 2 slits in the left year, 1 black Walnut Desk, 2 black
Walnut Oval Tables, 1 painted Buffett, 1 safe painted Pine, ten chairs, 3 Pine Chests, two
Poplar bed steads, 1 Oak do., 3 feather beds and furniture, 2 iron pots, 1 Dutch Oven, 1
frying pan, fire tongs, 1 pr. bellows, 1 Tea Chest and furniture, 1 Weavers Loom, 4 slays

to do., 1 Spinning wheel & 1 Gun; To have and to hold the land goods & chattles & cattle &c. unto JOHN COCKSHUTT and others, Trustees of Mr. JOHN BLAND of LONDON, Provided however that if THOMAS SHARPE shall pay or cause to be paid unto JOHN COCKSHUTT and others, Trustees of Mr. JOHN BLAND of LONDON, the aforesaid Debt with Interest from this date, Then this Instrument of Writing to be void, otherwise to remain in force, In Witness whereof THOMAS SHARPE JUNR. hath hereunto set his hand and seal the day and year above written
Signed Sealed and Delivered in presence of
    DAVID BRIGGS,   THOMAS SHARPE
    CHARLES ASHLEY,   LAC: McINTOSH
  (No recording shown for this Mortgage).

p.   THIS INDENTURE made the Seventeenth day of February one thousand seven
1186   hundred and seventy four Between WILLIAM JETT of County of King George of
      one part and JOHN COCKSHUTT and others, Trustees of Mr. JOHN BLAND of LON-
DON of other part; Witnesseth that WILLIAM JETT in consideration of the sum of Twenty seven pounds, two shillings and eleven pence three farthings currence to him in
hand paid doth bargain and sell unto JOHN COCKSHUTT and others, Trustees of Mr. JOHN
BLAND of LONDON, their heirs one Negro fellow named Charles about 20 years of age, 1
red Cow marked with a crop in each ear, 1 red do. with a crop and slit in each ear, 2
Heifers each having their left ear cut off & with the Cows increase, two old gray Mares
vizt. one branded ‡ on the off buttock about twelve hands high fifteen years old, 1 do.
branded S on the near buttock twelve hands high four years old next Spring, one dark
Bay Colt at present not branded 1 year old next Spring, fifteen head of hogs each mark'd
with a crop and slit on the left ear and a crop and underkeel on the right ear; 2 feather
beds and furniture (dishes, plates and basons, remainder too faded to abstract); To have and to
hold the stock goods and chattles unto JOHN COCKSHUTT and others, Trustees of Mr. JOHN
BLAND of LONDON, their heirs; Provided however that if WILLIAM JETT shall pay or
cause to be paid the aforesaid Debt with Interest , Then this Instrument of Writing to be
void, otherwise to remain in force. In Witness wherof WILLIAM JETT hath hereunto set
his hand and seal the day and year above written
Signd. Seald. & delivd. in presence of
    DAVID BRIGGS,   WILLIAM JETT
    CHARLES ASHLEY, LAC: McINTOSH
  (No recording for this Mortgage.)

p.   THIS INDENTURE made this 16th day of September one thousand seven hundred
1187   and seventy four Between THOMAS TURNER Esqr., of the Parish of Hanover in
      County of King George of one part and STEPHEN TURNBULL of the same Parish
and County of other part; Witnesseth that said THOMAS TURNER in consideration of the
yearly rents and covenants hereinafter mentioned and reserved on part and behalf of
STEPHEN TURNBULL to be paid done and performed, doth demise granted lease sell and
to farm lett unto STEPHEN TURNBULL and to his Wife, CATHARINE TURNBULL, during
their natural lives all that parcel of land lying in Parish of Hanover and County aforesaid containing by Estimation two hundred acres more or less and is the Land whereon
said TURNBULL now lives and rents from THOMAS TURNER, To have and to hold the parcel of land with the appurtenances unto STEPHEN TURNBULL and CATHARINE his Wife
from the 25th day of December next during the terms of the natural lives of STEPHEN
TURNBULL and CATHARINE his Wife and longest liver of them paying yearly unto THO-
MAS TURNER his heirs the rent of One thousand pounds of tobo: and cask; In Witness

whereof the said THOMAS TURNER and STEPHEN TURNBULL hath hereunto set their hands and seals the day and year before written

Signed Sealed & delivd. in presence of

AUSTIN BROCKENBROUGH,	THOMAS TURNER
CHARLES DEANE,	STEPHEN TURNBULL
CHARLES DEANE JUNR.	

    (No recording shown for this Lease for Lives)

pp.   THIS INDENTURE made the 5th day of December in year of our Lord one thou-
1188-   sand seven hundred and seventy eight Between GEORGE RIDING of County of
1189   King George, Gent., of one part and THOMAS SMITH and WINNY SMITH, Daughter
       of the said THOMAS, both of said County, Planter, of other part; Whereas a
Marriage is intended to be had and solemnized between the said GEORGE RIDING and said
WINNY SMITH and said GEORGE in consideration of the said Marriage of the very great
affection for the said WINNY and of the great disparity of years between him and his
intended Wife, has resolved and agreed to make a liberal Settlement of a considerable
part of his Estate in favour of his said intended Wife and the Child or Children of the
Marriage, if any. NOW THIS INDENTURE WITNESSETH that the said GEORGE RIDING in
consideration of the said Marriage & of his singular affection for the said WINNY and of
the sum of Fifty pounds no other or given Marriage Portion being required by him the
said GEORGE RIDING in hand paid by THOMAS SMITH doth bargain and sell unto THOMAS
SMITH his heirs the following slaves (the names of the slaves are too faded to abstract upwards
to fifteen or so, with a proviso that if the Marriage does not occur, the slaves to be returned to
GEORGE RIDING); In Witness whereof the said parties have interchangeably set their
hands & seals the day & year first written

Signed Sealed & acknowledged in presence of

WILLIAM BOON	GEORGE RIDING
THOMAS his mark + WILKERSON, JUNR.	WINNEY SMITH
THOMAS his mark X WILKERSON, SENR.	THOMAS SMITH
MARY her mark + WILKERSON	

    Received the 5th day of December 1778 of THOMAS SMITH the sum of Fifty pounds
current money, it being in full for the consideration mentioned in this Deed

WILLIAM BOON,	
THOMAS his mark + WILKERSON, JUNR.	GEORGE RIDING
THOMAS his mark X WILKERSON, SENR.,	
MARY her mark + WILKERSON	

    (No recording shown for this Marriage Contract.)

p.   THIS INDENTURE made
1189   (This Indenture is too faded to abstract any of it.)

p   THIS INDENTURE made the (   ) day of October in the year of our Lord one
1190   thousand seven hundred and seventy six Between WILLIAM MONDAY of Parish
       of OVERWHARTON in County of STAFFORD of one part and JAMES (P------) of
Parish of Hanover in County of King George of other part; Witnesseth that WILLIAM
MONDAY in consideration of the sum of Two hundred pounds current money to him in
hand paid by JAMES (P------) by these presents doth bargain and sell (another entry too
faded to abstract. No recording is shown for this Indenture of Bargain and Sale).

p. THIS INDENTURE made this xxvi day of September in year of our Lord one
1191 thousand seven hundred and seventy four Between the REVEREND JOHN DIXON,
Clerk, of City of WILLIAMSBURG of one part and JOHN RICHARDS of County of
King George of other part; (another entry too faded to abstract. The witnesses can be made out:
Test JAMES MARSHALL, DAVID BLAIR (The Recording does not appear to be signed)
DANIEL PAYNE, JOHN ROSE
   At a Court held for King George County the 4th day of April 1775
JOHN DIXONs Deed, Receipt and Memo to JOHN RICHARDS was presented into Court,
proved by the Oath of JOHN ROSE, one of the witnesses thereto and ordered to be Certi-
fied; And at another Court held for the same County the 2d. day of May 1775, was
further proved by the Oath of DANIEL PAYNE and DAVID BLAIR and ordered to be
recorded   Test JOS: ROBINSON, C. K. G. C.

pp THIS INDENTURE made the twenty third day of February in the Sixteenth year
1192- of the Reign of our Sovereign Lord George the third of Great Britain France and
1193 Ireland, King, Defender of the faith &c. and in the year of our Lord one thousand seven hundred and seventy six Between JOHN TRIPLETT of Parish of ST.
MARK in County of CULPEPER of one part and WILLIAM TRIPLETT of Hanover Parish in
County of King George of other part; Witnesseth that JOHN TRIPLETT for sum of Eighty
pounds current money of Virginia to him in hand paid by WILLIAM TRIPLETT, by these
presents doth bargain and sell unto WILLIAM TRIPLETT his heirs all that tract of land
containing One hundred and sixty acres situate in Parish of Hanover and County of
King George (then this entry becomes too faded to abstract. The Recording does show the signa-
ture of JOHN TRIPLETT. The witness THOMAS ROBISON and SAMUEL DALE can be made out.)
   Received of the within named WILLIAM TRIPLETT the within mentioned sum of
Eighty pounds current money, being the consideration money mentioned in the within
Deed to be paid by him on the perfection thereof. Witness my hand this Twenty third
day of February one thousand seven hudnred and seventy six
          THOMAS ROBISON,   JOHN TRIPLETT
          SAMUEL DALE
   George the Third by the grace of God of Great Britain, France and Ireland, King, defender of the faith &c., to JOHN SLAUGHTER, JAMES SLAUGHTER and JOSEPH (? ROBINS)
of County of CULPEPER Gentlemen, Greeting. Whereas JOHN TRIPLETT and MARTHA
TRIPLETT his Wife, of your County, by a certain Deed of Feoffment bearing date the 23d
day of February did convey unto WILLIAM TRIPLETT of County of King George the fee
simple Estate of One hundred and sixty acres of land situate in Parish of Hanover and
County of King George, And Whereas the said MARTHA TRIPLETT cannot conveniently
come to our said County Court of King George to make her personal acknowledgment
(the Commission for the privy examination of MARTHA, the Wife of JOHN TRIPLETT); Witness
JOSEPH ROBINSON Clerk of our said County Court of King George aforesaid this Eighth
day of March 1776, in the sixteenth year of our Reign
                                        JOSEPH ROBINSON, C. K. G. C.
   CULPEPER County. Sct. By virtue of the within Commission to us directed, we the subscribers did personally go to the within named MARTHA TRIPLETT and examine her
privately and apart from the said JOHN TRIPLETT, her Husband, touching the acknowledgment of the conveyance annexed and she declares that she is willing that the same
should be recorded in the County Court of King George. Given under our hands and
seals this seventeenth day of June 1776   JOHN SLAUGHTER
                                                 JAMES SLAUGHTER

pp.   THIS INDENTURE made the Eighth day of July in year of our Lord one thousand
1193-   seven hundred and seventy six Between ROBERT MONDAY and CATHRINE his
1194   Wife of FAUQUIER COUNTY of the one part and WILLIAM MONDAY of the same
        County of the other part; Witnesseth that ROBERT MONDAY and CATHRINE his
Wife in consideration of the natural love and affection which they have unto their Son,
WILLIAM MONDAY as also for the consideration of the sum of five shillings to them in
hand paid by these presents do give and confirm unto WILLIAM MONDAY all that tract
of land lying in County of King George and Parish of Hanover containing One hundred
acres be the same more or less with all appurtenances rents and services of the premises; To have and to hold the tract of land unto WILLIAM MONDAY his heirs and
ROBERT MONDAY with CATHRINE his Wife for themselves their heirs doth covenant
with WILLIAM MONDAY his heirs shall lawfully from henceforth occupy possess and
enjoy the premises hereby given free and clear from all Incumbrances suffered by the
said ROBERT MONDAY and CATHRINE his Wife their heirs; In Witness hereunto we have
set our hands & seals the day and year first above mentioned
Done in presence of
    HENRY BERRY,   ROBERT his mark X MONDAY
    WILLIAM OWENS, WILLIAM BERRY,   CATHRINE MONDAY
    JOHN MONDAY, ANN OWENS
   George the Third by the grace of God of Great Brittain France and Ireland, King, Defender of the faith &c. to CHARLES CHINN and HENRY PEYTON, Gentlemen, Greeting;
Whereas ROBERT MONDAY and CATHRINE his Wife of County of FAUQUIER by their
certain Deed of Bargain and Sale bearing date the Eighth day of July one thousand
seven hundred and seventy six (the Commission for the privy examination of CATHRINE, the
Wife of ROBERT MONDAY); Witness JOSEPH ROBINSON, Clerk of our said County Court of
King George this Third day of June one thousand seven hundred and seventy six, in the
sixteenth year of our Reign   JOSEPH ROBINSON, C. K. G. C.
   FAUQUIER County, Sct. We the Commissioners within named, Justices of the Peace in
the said County, repaired to the Residence of CATHRINE MONDAY in this Commission
mentioned, who upon being examined privately and apart from her Husband (the return
of the execution of the privy examination of CATHRINE MONDAY). Given under our hands and
seals this 30th day of August 1776   CHARLES CHINN
                            HENRY PEYTON

    (No recording for this Deed of Gift, nor the Commission.)

pp.   THIS INDENTURE made the Eighteenth day of December in year of our Lord one
1194-   thousand seven hundred and Seventy Between SIMON MILLER JUNR., of County
1194a of CULPEPER of one part and JANE HOARD of County of King George of other part
        Witnesseth that said SIMON MILLER for sum of Sixty pounds current money of
Virginia to him in hand paid by these presents doth bargain and sell unto JANE HORD
and to her heirs all that tract of land now in the actual possession of JANE HORD lying
in County of King George containing by estimation Two hundred acres be the same
more or less and binding as well on the RIVER RAPPAHANNOCK above twelve miles
above the FALLS thereof, the same being conveyed to said SIMON MILLER, party to these
presents, by his Father, SIMON MILLER, of County of CULPEPER and all the houses,
orchards commodities and hereditaments belonging; To have and to hold the tract of
land and premises unto JANE HORD and SIMON MILLER JUNIOR for himself his heirs the
tract of land hereby conveyed unto JANE HORD her heirs against all persons shall warrant and forever defend by these presents; In Witness whereof the said SIMON MILLER
JUNIOR hath set his hand and seal the day month and year above written

Sealed and acknowledged in presence of
      GAVIN LAWSON,   ARTHER MORSON,   SIMON MILLER JUNR.
      WILLIAM NEWTON,   THOMAS HORD   SARAH MILLER
      A. BUSHANAN

p.   KNOW ALL MEN by these presents that I MARY STIGLER, Widow and Relict of
1194a   JAMES STIGLER, late of County of King George, deceased, in consideration of the
           natural love and affection which I have and bear unto my Son, BENJAMIN STIG-
LER as for the further consideration of his supporting me in a decent manner during
my life, by these presents do remise release and quit claim unto BENJAMIN STIGLER and
his heirs the real and personal Estate which was devised to me by the Last Will and
Testament of my Husband, JAMES STIGLER, as will more fully appear by the said Will,
and all the right title claim and demand of me said MARTHA STIGLER in the real and
personal Estate aforesaid so that neither I the said MARTHA STIGLER or assigns or any
of them shall claim or demand the said real and personal Estate; In Witness whereof I
have hereunto set my hand and seal this 19th day of April 1776
Signed Sealed in the presence of
      JEDEDIAH PULLIN,   MARTHA her mark ⫢ STIGLER
      JAMES KAY, JOHN COLHAM
     (No recording of this Deed of Gift is shwon.)

p.   THIS INDENTURE made the Twenty second day of October in year one thousand
1195   seven hundred and seventy nine Between WILLIAM ALLAN and MARY his Wife
           of County of CULPEPER of one part and THOMAS SMITH of County of King George
of other part: Witnesseth that WILLIAM ALLAN and MARY his Wife for sum of Forty
pounds current money of Virginia to them in hand paid by THOMAS SMITH, by these
presents do bargain and sell unto THOMAS SMITH his heirs a certain Plantation, tract of
land in Parish of Hanover and County of King George containing Ninety eight and a
half acres according to survey lately made thereof JOHN TRIPLETT JUNR., Surveyor of
County of King George, which land was given to WILLIAM ALLAN intailed by the Last
Will and Testament of SARAH SETTLE, deceased, dated the nineteen day of December one
thousand seven hundred and fifty four and recorded in County Court of King George
which will more fully appear: which land hereby conveyed or meant to be conveyed by
the same more or less begins according to the Survey at a Maple on the side of a Run,
runing thence No. 34 1/2 W. 19 poles. thence N. 27 W. 26 poles, thence N. 39, W. 10 poles
to SAMUEL KENDALs corner, thence along said KENDALs line N. 26 1/2 E. 8 p;oles to a
white Oak. thence N. 32 1/2 E. 14 poles, thence No. 2 W. 9 1/2 poles near two white Oaks
line tree of Colo. GREENs Land and black Oak corner to the said KENDALs, thence N. 71 E.
56 poles. thence S. 39 E. 16 poles, thence S. 14 E. 20 poles, thence S. 10 1/2 E. 36 poles,
thence S. 26 E. 10 poles, thence S. 1 E. 6 poles, thence S. 11 E. 20 poles to a Run, thence
down said Run to the begining, containing Ninety eight and a half acres of land be the
same more or less, Together with all houses orchards, profits and appurtenances in any
wise belonging: To have and to hold the Plantation and tract of land with appurtenances unto THOMAS SMITH his heirs and WILLIAM ALLEN and his heirs the Plantation
and tract of land against every person shall warrant and forever defend by these presents; In Witness whereof WILLIAM ALLEN and MARY his Wife have hereunto set their
hands and seals the day and year first mentioned
Signed Sealed and acknowledged in presence of
      GEORGE JOHNSON,   WILLIAM ALLAN
      ELISABETH JOHNSON,   MARY ALLAN

WILLIAM BOON, JOHN CLAYTON
GORING WHITE
Received this 22 day of October 1779 the sum of forty pounds current money of the
above named THOMAS SMITH the said sum being the consideration mentioned in this
Deed
Witness WILLIAM BOON,   WILLIAM ALLAN
          JOHN CLAYTON, GORING WHITE
    The Commonwealth of Virginia to NATHANIEL PENDLETON and EDWARD STEVENS,
Gentlemen, Justices of Culpeper County, Gentlemen, Greeting. Whereas WILLIAM
ALLAN and MARY his Wife by their certain Indenture of Bargain and Sale bearing date
the 4th day of November 1770 have conveyed (the Commission for the privy examination of
MARY, the Wife of WILLIAM ALLAN); Witness JOSEPH ROBINSON, Clerk of our said Court the
20th day of October 1779 in the seventeenth year of our Reign
                                            JOSEPH ROBINSON, C. K. G. C.
    CULPEPER County Sct. In Obedience to the within Order we the subscribers have exa-
mined MARY ALLAN, who freely acknowledges the within Deed and that the same
should be recorded. Given under our hands this Twenty second day of October 1779
                                            NATHANIEL PENDLETON
                                            EDWARD STEVENS
(No recording shown for this Indenture of Bargain and Sale)

p.   KNOW ALL MEN by these presents that we RICHARD OWENS, WILLIAM KENTON,
1196   legally (   ) of JEREMIAH OWENS, deceased, AARON OWENS, WILLIAM OWENS,
        SARAH GRIGSBY, MARY BERRY and LETTICE WHITE, are each of us are separate-
ly and severally held and firmly bound unto JOSHUA OWENS of County of PRINCE WIL-
LIAM in the full and penal sum of Two hundred pounds of good and lawfull money of
Virginia; for which payment well and truly to be made we bind our selves our heirs
firmly by these presents; Sealed severally with our seals and dated this Ninth day of
June in the year of our Lord one thousand seven hundred and seventy six;
    THE CONDITION of this obligation is such that if the above bound RICHARD OWENS,
WILLIAM KENTON, AARON OWENS, WILLIAM OWENS, SARAH GRIGSBY, MARY BERRY
and LETTICE WHITE their and each of their heirs do well and truly agreed to and stand to
a certain Division of an Estate this day made of RICHARD OWENS JUNR., deceased, that
then this Bond to be null and void, that there shall be hereafter any confusion, dis-
turbance or Law suit commenced against the said JOSHUA OWENS touching any the
above articles, That then this shall remain in full force and virtue. In Confirmation
whereof the contracting parties have hereunto interchangeably affixed their hands
and seals the day and ate as above mentioned
Signed Sealed & delivered in presence of
        WILLIAM SMITH,   RICHARD his mark ┼ OWENS
        JOEL BERRY   WILLIAM KENTON
                                                AARON OWENS
                                                WILLIAM OWENS
                                                WILLIAM GRIGSBY
                                                GEORGE BERRY
                                                LETTICE her mark ┼ WHITE

(No recording shown for this Bond.)

pp.   THIS INDENTURE made the fourteenth day of February in the year of our Lord
1196-   one thousand seven hundred and seventy six Between ALEXANDER HANSFORD of
1197   the Parish of Brunswick in County of King George and ANNE his Wife of one
        part and STEPHEN HANSFORD, Son of the said ALEXANDER, of the second part; And
ELLENDER WENT, Daughter of JAMES WENT of said Parish and County of the third part,
WHEREAS a Marriage is intended shortly to be had and solemnized between the said
STEPHEN HANSFORD and the said ELLENDER WENT, Now This Indenture Witnesseth that
ALEXANDER HANSFORD as well as in consideration of the natural love which he hath for
his said Son as in consideration of the intented Marriage doth by these presents give
unto STEPHEN HANSFORD and his heirs the following tracts of land, viz. one tract of land
lying in the said Parish and County containing Eighty acres which was conveyed to
ALEXANDER HANSFORD by his Father, STEPHEN HANSFORD, and Wife by Deed recorded in
the said County Court; Another tract of Land adjoining the former containing seventy
acres purchased by ALEXANDER HANSFORD of MOTT DERMITT and Wife on which they
live; and which they are to have the use of during their time; Also about sixty acres of
land being a Neck or Strip of Land part of the tract of land the said ALEXANDER HANS-
FORD lives on and is separated from any other woodland belonging to ALEXANDER
HANSFORD and adjoining JOHN JONES's Plantation on the East side and the land of Mr.
ALEXANDER on the West; And all houses orchards and hereditaments to the same belonging; To have and to hold the tracts of land with the appurtenances unto STEPHEN
HANSFORD and his heirs, Subject nevertheless to the use occupation and possession of
said ELLENDER WENT during her natural life in case the intended Marriage should take
effect and in case she should survive STEPHEN HANSFORD, her intended Husband, and
ALEXANDER HANSFORD for himself and his heirs doth hereby covenant and grant to
and with STEPHEN HANSFORD and his heirs that immediately after the Marriage takes
effect said STEPHEN his heirs &c. shall quietly enter into possession of the premises
without the hindrance or molestation of ALEXANDER HANSFORD or his heirs; And
ALEXANDER HANSFORD for himself his heirs the land and premises in the manner
above limited to STEPHEN HANSFORD and ELLENDER WENT from the claim and demand of
every person shall warrant and for ever defend by these presents; In Witness whereof
the said ALEXANDER HANSFORD and ANNE his Wife have hereunto set their hands and
seals the day and year first above written
Sealed and Delivered in the presence of
        W. BRUCE,   ALEXANDER HANSFORD
        JAMES WENT,   JOHN ARMSTRONG   ANNE HANSFORD
        (No recording shown for this Deed of Gift.)

pp.   THIS INDENTURE made the Twentieth day of September in the first year of the
1197-   Commonwealth of Virginia and in the year of our Lord one thousand seven hun-
1198   dred and seventy six, Between Capt. MOORE FAUNTLEROY of Parish of LUNEN-
        BURG and County of RICHMOND, Gent., of one part and THOMAS PEAD of afore-
said Parish and County, Planter, of other part; Witensseth that MOORE FAUNTLEROY in
consideration of the Rents and Covenants herein after mentioned on part of THOMAS
PEAD to be paid observed and done by these presents do demise lease and to farm let
unto THOMAS PEAD all that tract of land situate in Parish of Hanover and County of King
George containing by estimation One hundred and thirty acres, be the same more or
less and bounded by the Land of Mr. COOK, the said PEAD, JOHN CARTER and JOHN CAR-
PENTER, Together with all houses orchards and appurtenances belonging; To have and
to hold the before granted land & premises with appurtenances unto THOMAS PEAD
during the natural life of said THOMAS PEAD, PHILLIP PEAD,. Son of said THOMAS, and

THOMAS PEAD, Son of said PHILLIP, he or they paying yearly unto MOORE FAUNTLEROY his heirs on the 25th day of December if lawfully demanded, the neat quantity of Four hundred and fifty pounds of sound merchantable tobacco; In Witness whereof the parties within mentioned have hereunto set their hands and seals the day and year first above mentioned
Sealed and Confirmed in presence of
    DANIEL CONNELLES,   MOORE FAUNTLEROY
    RICHARD BENNETT,
    WINEFRED YATEMAN
    I assign all my right and title to this Lease to my Son, PHILLIP PEAD; Witness my hand
                              THOMAS PEAD

(No recording shown for this Lease for Lives).

pp.   THIS INDENTURE made the third day of June in year of our Lord one thousand
1198- seven hundred and seventy eight Between THOMAS BUNBURY JUNR., of County
1199   of King George, Gent., of one part and JOHN HOOE of the County of PRINCE WIL-
        LIAM of other part; Witnesseth that in consideration of Ten shillings current
money to said THOMAS in hand paid by said JOHN, by these presents doth bargain and
sell unto JOHN HOOE and assigns all that parcel of land formerly sold and conveyed to
said THO: BUNBURY by RICHARD FOWKE SENR., now deceased, by Deed bearing date the
fourth day of September in the year of our Lord one thousand seven hundred and
seventy five, duely proved and recorded in STAFFORD County (the said Land then lying
in that Coun-ty) at present situate in County of King George on POTOWMACK RIVER and
bounded; Begining at a Stake on the bank of POTOWMACK RIVER being a corner
between this land and the land of CHANDLER FOWKE SENR., thence up the River to the
Corner of the GLEBE, thence with the GLEBE Line So. 2 1/2 E. three hundred and twenty
four poles to a white Oak, thence with another line of the GLEBE Land So. 89d. W. one
hundred and seventy six poles to a Stake at the Roots of a white Oak Stump by the Main
Branch of PASBITANAY, thence So. forty six poles to a Locust Post, the begining of
HUMPHREYs Patent, thence binding with said Patent and the land of FITZHUGH, N. 88d.
E. to a Stake being another corner between this land and the land of CHANDLER FOWKE,
thence along the division of the last named tracts of land to the begining as by a Survey and Division made between RICHARD FOWKE and CHANDLER FOWKE by JOHN MAUZY
on the 10th of May 1750 may appear, the tract of land containing Five hundred acres
more or less and all houses swamps marshes and sunken grounds and fisheries; To have
and to hold the tract of land and premises with appurtenances unto JOHN HOOE and
assigns paying the said THOMAS his heirs one Pepper Corn if the same shall be lawfully
demanded; to the intent that by virtue of these presents and of the Statute for transferring uses into possession the said JOHN HOOE may be in the actual possession of the
hereby bargained and sold premises and enabled to accept a Release of the reversion
and inheritance thereof; In Witness whereof the said parties have hereunto set their
hands and seals the day and year first before written
Signed Sealed delivered and acknowledged before
    JOHN BURTON   THOMAS BUNBURY
    WILLIAM HOOE, THOMAS MASSEY,
    HOWSON HOOE, WILLIAM STEWARD
  At a Court held for King George County the 4th day of June 1778
(This recording of the above Lease not completed).

THIS INDENTURE made the fourth day of June in year of our Lord one thousand seven hundred and seventy eight Between THOMAS BUNBURY of County of King George, Gent., of one part and JOHN HOOE of County of PRINCE WILLIAM, Gent., of other part; Witnesseth that for sum of Two thousand six hundred pounds current money to THOMAS BUNBURY in hand paid by JOHN HOOE by these presents doth bargain and sell unto JOHN HOOE (in his actual possession now being by virtue of a bargain and sale to him thereof made for one year and by force of the Statute for transferring uses into possession) and to his heirs all that tract of land containing Five hundred acres more or less situate on POTOMACK RIVER in County of King George, having been formerly sold and conveyed to THOMAS BUNBURY in fee by RICHARD FOWKE being bounded as particularly specified in the said Indenture of Lease; To have and to hold the tract of land and premises with appurtenances unto JOHN HOOE his heirs, the said THOMAS BUNBURY his heirs the five hundred acres of land bounded as aforesaid and all other the premises with appurtenances unto JOHN HOOE his heirs against every person shall warrant and forever defend by these presents; In Witness whereof the said THOMAS BUNBURY hath hereunto set his hand and seal the day and year first before written
Signed Sealed and acknowledged in presence of
JOHN BURTON,   THOMAS BUNBURY
WILLIAM HOOE, THOMAS MASSEY,
HOWSON HOOE, WILLIAM STEWARD
Received from JOHN HOOE Two thousand six hundred pounds current money, the consideration in this Deed mentioned. 4th June 1778
Witness JOHN BURTON,   THOMAS BUNBURY
WILLIAM HOOE, THOMAS MASSEY,
HOWSON HOOE, WILLIAM STEWARD
At a Court held for King George County the 4th day of June 1778
The foregoing Deeds of Lease and Release from under the hand and seal of THOMAS BUNBURY was proved by three witnesses & ordered to be recorded
Test JOS: ROBINSON, C. K. G. C.

p.   THIS INDENTURE made the 27th day of July in year of our Lord one thousand
1200   seven hundred and seventy nine Between WILLIAM FITZHUGH and ANN his Wife
        of Parish of Brunswick and County of STAFFORD of one part and WILLIAM HOOE of Parish of Saint Paul and County of King George of other part; Witnesseth that WILLIAM FITZHUGH for sum of One thousand and twenty five pounds, three shillings current money of Virginia to him in hand paid by WILLIAM HOOE, doth by these presents bargain and sell unto WILLIAM HOOE and his heirs a certain tract of land lying in Parish of Saint Paul and County of King George containing Two hundred and three acres and is bounded; Beginning at a Stump in the line of CLIFTONs Land, and corner to this Land and the Land of WILLIAMSONs, extending thence in the line of CLIFTON S. 40d. E. 160 poles to a small Branch, thence down the meanders of the Branch to the mouth thereof, thence down the dam N. 6d. W. 30 poles to the mouth of another small Branch, thence up the meanders of said Branch to the head thereof, thence N. 79d. W. 106 poles to a Stake in a Corn Field, thence N. 20d. W. 10 pole to another Stake, thence N. 5d. W. 12 pole to a place near the Road where formerly stood a Crooked Hiccory, corner to this Land, PRATTs Land, WILLIAMSONs Land and a small tract of land sold and conveyed to GEORGE MIFLIN by Deed bearing date with these presents from said FITZHUGH, thence binding on said WILLIAMSONs Land S. W. 94 poles to the begining; Together with all houses and appurtenances to the same belonging; To have and to hold the land and premises unto WILLIAM HOOE his heirs; And WILLIAM FITZHUGH and his heirs the land and

premises unto WILLIAM HOOE his heirs from the claim and demand of every person shall warrant and forever defend by these presents; In Witness whereof the said WILLIAM FITZHUGH and ANN his Wife hath hereunto set their hands and affixed their seals the day and year first above written
Sealed and delivered in presence of

PETER HANSBROUGH   WILLIAM FITZHUGH
DANIEL FITZHUGH, ENOCH MEHOMER   ANN FITZHUGH

Received of WILLIAM HOOE one thousand and twenty five pounds and three shillings current money, it being the consideration mentioned
Witness   PETER HANSBROUGH,   WILLIAM FITZHUGH
DANIEL FITZHUGH, ENOCH MEHOMER
(No recording shown for this Indenture of Bargain and Sale)

p. 1201   THIS INDENTURE made the 27th day of July in year of our Lord one thousand seven hundred and seventy nine Between WILLIAM FITZHUGH and ANN his Wife of Parish of Brunswick and County of STAFFORD of one part and GEORGE MIFLIN of Parish of Saint Paul and County of King George of other part; Witnesseth that WILLIAM FITZHUGH and ANN his Wife in consideration of the sum of Three hundred and fifty eight pounds, eleven shillings current money of Virginia to them in hand paid by GEORGE MIFLIN, doth by these presents bargain and sell unto GEORGE MIFLIN and his heirs a certain tract of land lying in Parish of Saint Paul and County of King George containing Seventy one acres and is bounded; Beginning at a Oak standing a little below Mr. FITZHUGH Mill, running down the dam to an Ash standing on the side of the Dam near the mouth of a small Branch, thence leaving the dam and running up the Branch and binding on PRATTs line to a place near the Road where formerly stood a crooked Hiccory, corner to this Land, the Land of said PRATT, WILLIAMSONs Land and tract of land sold and conveyed by said FITZHUGH to WILLIAM HOOE by Deed bearing equal date with these presents; thence with WILLIAMSONs line N. 11 1/2d. W. 86 pole, thence to the beginning, Together with all houses and appurtenances to the same belonging; To have and to hold the land and premises unto GEORGE MIFLIN his heirs and WILLIAM FITZHUGH and his heirs the above bargained and sold land and premises unto GEORGE MIFLIN his heirs against the claim and demand of every person shall warrant and forever defend by these presents; In Witness whereof, the said WILLIAM FITZHUGH and ANN his Wife hath hereunto set their hands and affixed their seals the day & year first above written
Sealed and Delivered in presence of

PETER HANSBROUGH,   WILLIAM FITZHUGH
DANIEL FITZHUGH,   ANN FITZHUGH
ENOCH MEHOMER, WILLIAM HOOE

Received of GEORGE MIFLIN Three hundred and fifty eight pounds and eleven shillings Virginia currency, it being the consideration mentioned in the within Deed
Witness   PETER HANSBROUGH,   WILLIAM FITZHUGH
DANIEL FITZHUGH, ENOCH MEHOMER
WILLIAM HOOE
(No recording shown for this Indenture of Bargain and Sale.)

p. 1202   THIS INDENTURE mde on the first day of July in year of our Lord one thousand seven hundred and seventy eight Between THOMAS MANN RANDOLPH and ANN his Wife of County of GOOCHLAND of one part and THOMAS TURNER of County of WESTMORELAND of other part; Witnesseth that THOMAS MANN and ANN his Wife in

consideration of the sum of Six thousand six hundred pounds to him in hand paid by
these presents do bargain and sell unto said THOMAS one certain tract of land in County
of King George known by the name of HANGALLIES containing by estimation Two thousand two hundred acres and bounding on the Lands of said THOMAS TURNER, JOSEPH
MURDOCK, JOHN PITMAN and FRANCIS THORNTON together with all appurtenances to
him the said THOMAS TURNER to have and to hold the tract of land with its appurtenances unto said THOMAS TURNER and his heirs and the said THOMAS for himself his
heirs doth covenant with the said THOMAS TURNER his heirs that he shall warrant and
forever defend by these presents; In Witness whereof the said THOMAS MANN and
ANNE have hereto subscribed their names and affixed their seals on the day and year
within written
Delivered by said THOMAS MANN and ANNE as
their act and deed in presence of
                WILLIAM BOON,   THOMAS M. RANDOLPH
                WILLIAM GREEN & SAMUEL WHARTON   ANN RANDOLPH
    Received the first day of July 1778 of the within named THOMAS TURNER six thousand
six hundred pounds in full of the consideration for this Deed
Witness WILLIAM BOON,   THOMAS MANN RANDOLPH
                WILLIAM GREEN & SAMUEL WHARTON
    The Commonwealth of Virginia &c. to JOHN WOODSON and STEPHEN SAMPSON, Gentle-
men, Justices of GOOCHLAND County, Greeting; Whereas THOMAS MANN RANDOLPH and
ANNE his Wife by their certain Deed of bargain and sale (the Commission for the privy examination of ANNE, the Wife of THOMAS MANN); Witness JOSEPH ROBINSON, Clerk of our said
Court this first day of July 1778 in the Second year of the Commonwealth
                                                JOSEPH ROBINSON, C. K. G. C.
    GOOCHLAND County Sct. In pursuance of the Commission hereto annexed, we have
personally gone to the said ANNE herein named and examined her privily and apart
from the said THOMAS her Husband and have received her acknowledgment (the return
of the execution of the privy examination of ANNE RANDOLPH); Certified under our hands and
seals this first day of July in the year of our Lord one thousand seven hundred and
seventy eight   JOHN WOODSON
                                                STEPHEN SAMPSON
    (No recording shown for this Indenture of Bargain and Sale, nor the Commission and return.)

p.   THIS INDENTURE made the Ninth day of December in year One thousand seven
1203   hundred and seventy six Between THOMAS TURNER and JANE his Wife of County
        of King George of one part and WILLIAM BOON of the same County of the other
part; Witnesseth that THOMAS TURNER and JANE his Wife in consideration of the sum of
One hundred and sixty nine pounds current money of Virginia to them in hand paid by
WILLIAM BOON, by these presents do bargain and sell unto WILLIAM BOON and his heirs
a certain Plantation, tract of land situate in Parish of Hanover and County aforesaid
containing by estimation One hundred and thirty acres, Begining at a Box Oak in CON-
WAYs Line, formerly called GIBSONs, opposite the Southwest corner of ISAAC ARNOLD
SENR., deced., Land, thence along a line of marked trees to the said Southwest corner of
the said ARNOLDs Land to a Hiccory tree, corner to said ARNOLD, thence along another
line to a small Branch at the North corner of the said ARNOLDs Land, thence down the
said Branch to BALTHROPs line, thence a South East course along BALTHROPs line to two
corner white Oaks as the South East corner of the said ISAAC ARNOLDs Land, thence
along a line of marked trees to a red Oak in THORNLEYs Line (bought of BOWLS BAL-
THROPE) thence along said line to GINGOTEAGUE SWAMP, thence up the several mean-

ders of said Swamp to the land of said BOON purchased of GEORGE ARNOLD, thence along the said line to a corner in BALTHROPEs Land a little below WILLIAM BOON's House, thence along the said line formerly called BALTHROPEs to a North Branch of GINGO-TEAGUE, thence up the several meanders of the said Branch to CONWAYs line (formerly called GIBSONs), thence along CONWAYs Line to the begining, containing by estimation One hundred and thirty acres be the same more or less, Together with all houses orchards profits and emoluments o the said Land belonging; To have and to hold the Plantation and tract of land unto WILLIAM BOON his heirs and THOMAS TURNER his heirs the Plantation and tract of land with the appurtenances and all other premises unto said WILLIAM BOON his heirs against all persons shall warrant and forever defend by these presents; In Witness whereof the said THOMAS TURNER and JANE his Wife have hereunto put their hands and seals the day and year first mentioned
Signed Sealed and acknowledged in presence of
    (no witnesses recorded)   THOMAS TURNER
  Received this Ninth day of December 1776 the sum of One hundred and sixty nine pounds current money of the within named WILLIAM BOON, the said sum being the consideration mentioned in this Deed
                              THOMAS TURNER
  At a Court held for King George County the 2d. day of Jany: 1777
This aforegoing Indented Deed of Bargain & Sale with the Receipt thereon endorsed from under the hand and seal of THOMAS TURNER to WILLIAM BOON (being then presented into Court) was acknowledged by the said THOMAS as his proper act and deed and ordered to be recorded

p.   THIS INDENTURE made the third day of March one thousand seven hundred
1204   and seventy seven Between ELIZABETH ARNOLD of County of King George of
       one part and WILLIAM BOON of the same County of the other part; Witnesseth
that ELIZABETH ARNOLD in consideration of the sum of Thirteen pounds current money to her in hand paid by WILLIAM BOON, by these presents do bargain and sell unto WILLIAM BOON his heirs a certain Plantation and tract of land situate in Parish of Hanover and County aforesaid containing by estimation about four acres which lands was given by MARY ARNOLD, deceased, to ELIZABETH ARNOLD by Deed of Gift recorded in King George County Court will more fully appear; which land hereby conveyed or meant to be conveyed begins at the MAPLE BRANCH in CONWAYs Line, formerly called GIBSONs, runing straight down the said Branch to a crooked white Oak near a Sasafras tree by a North Branch of GINGOTEAGUE, thence down the several meanders of the said North Branch to the Lands of WILLIAM BOON purchased of Col. THOMAS TURNER, thence along the said BOONs land to CONWAYs line, thence along CONWAYs line to the begining, containing by estimation four acres of land more or less together with all houses orchards profits and appurtenances belonging; To have and to hold the Plantation and tract of land unto WILLIAM BOON his heirs and ELIZABETH ARNOLD doth hereby grant for herself and her heirs that the Plantation and tract of land and all other the premises unto WILLIAM BOON and his heirs agaisnt every person shall warrant and forever defend by these presents; In Witness whereof the said ELIZABETH ARNOLD have hereunto put her hand and seal the day and year first mentioned
Sealed and acknowledged in presence of
    THOMAS SMITH   ELIZABETH her mark ✝ ARNOLD
    PHILLIP PEED, WILLIAM GREEN
  Received this third day of March 1777 the sum of thirteen pounds current money of Virginia of WILLIAM BOON, the said sum being the consideration mentioned in this Deed

Witness THOMAS SMITH,   ELIZABETH her mark ✝ ARNOLD
     PHILLIP PEED & WILLIAM GREEN
     At a Court held for King George County the 3d. day of April 1777
This Indented Deed of Bargain & Sale with the Receipt thereon endorsed from under the
hand and seal of ELIZABETH ARNOLD to WM. BOON being presented into Court was proved
by the Oaths of the witnesses thereto subscribed and ordered to be recorded

p.   THIS INDENTURE made the Third day of March in year of our Lord one thousand
1205   seven hundred and Eighty one Between JAMES HANSBROUGH and LETTICE his
            Wife of County of STAFFORD of one part and PETER HANSBROUGH JUNR.of County
of King George, and Son of said JAMES and LETTICE, of other part; Witnesseth that
JAMES HANSBROUGH for sum of Three hundred pounds to him in hand paid by PETER
HANSBROUGH doth by these presents bargain and sell unto PETER HANSBROUGH his
heirs a certain tract of land lying in County of King George containing Two hundred
and Sixty three acres be the same more or less, lying on the Branches of POTOMACK &
PASPATANZY CREEKs, it being part of a Tract granted to WILLIAM WHITBEY for eighteen hundred acres bearing date the Thirteenth day of July one thousand seven hundred and Fifty three, and afterwards escheated by JOSEPH SUMNER and after divided
between his three Daughters, and is now the Dwelling Plantation of PETER HANS-
BROUGH, and is now bounded by the lines of the Lands of the Heirs of JOHN WAUGH,
WILLIAM MURPHY, JOHN MERCER, WILLIAM SMALLWOOD & MOTT DONIPHAN; Together
with all houses profits and hereditaments belonging; To have and to hld the tract of
land and premises unto PETER HANSBROUGH his heirs; And JAMES HANSBROUGH &
LETTICE HANSBROUGH & their heirs the premises & land unto PETER HANSBROUGH his
heirs against the claim & demand of every person shall warrant and forever defend by
these presents; In Witness whereof the said JAMES HANSBROUGH & LETTICE HANS-
BROUGH his Wife have hereunto set their hands and seals the day & year above written
Sealed and Delivered in presence of
           WILLIAM ANDERSON   JAMES HANSBROUGH
           JEMIMAH her mark ✕ ANDERSON   LETTICE her mark ✕ HANSBROUGH
           ANN her mark ✕ ANDERSON
     At a Court held for King George County the 5th day of July 1781
This Indented Deed of Bargain and Sale from under the hands and seals of JAMES HANS-
BROUGH & LETTICE HANSBROUGH his Wife to PETER HANSBROUGH was presented into
Court by the said PETER & proved by the Oaths of WILLIAM ANDERSON, JEMIMA ANDER-
SON & ANN ANDERSON, the witnesses thereto subscribed, which on the motion of the
said PETER HANSBROUGH JUNR. was ordered to be recorded

p.   THIS INDENTURE made the Eight day of November in year of our Lord one
1206   thousand seven hundred and seventy seven Between WILLIAM CHAMPE Esqr.,
            on the one part and WILLIAM BRUCE SENR. on the other part; Witnesseth that
WILLIAM CHAMPE in consideration of the rents & covenants hereafter mentioned on
part of WILLIAM BRUCE to be paid & performed, by these presents doth demise grant &
to farm let unto WILLIAM BRUCE One hundred and fifty acres of Land with the appurtenances lying in Parish of Brunswick in County of King George being a part of the Land
that descended to me by my Father & is joining to the land of ELIZABETH HANSFORD,
JOHN JONES, (   ) TRACT now in the possession of MRS. LUCY ALEXANDER and JOHN
TALIAFERRO SENR., Gent., To have and to hold the land & premises unto WILLIAM BRUCE
& his assigns during the term of his life, of his Wife ELIZABETH BRUCE & his Son,
GEORGE BRUCE, paying therefore yearly during the life of WM. CHAMPE SENR. one year

of Indian Corn and afterwards five hundred & thirty pounds of tobacco; In Witness whereof the said WILLIAM CHAMPE & the said WILLIAM BRUCE have hereunto inter-changably set their hands & seals the day and year first above written
Seald. 1& Deliver'd in the presence of

WILLIAM WATKINS,	WILLIAM CHAMPE
JOS: ROBINSON,	WILLIAM BRUCE
JOHN TALIAFERRO,	
JOHN TALIAFERRO JUNR.	

(No recording shown for this Lease for Lives)

pp.
1206-
1208

THIS INDENTURE made the Fourth day of August in the year of our Lord one thousand seven hundred and seventy eight Between MICHAEL WALLACE and LETTIS his Wife of County of King George and RICHARD TAYLOR of County of CAROLINE, Gentlemen, and CATHARINE his Wife of the one part & JAMES DAVIS of County of King George of other part; Whereas WILLIAM ROWLEY lately deceased in his lifetime purchased of MADGELAIN DONIPHAN eighty acres of Land in the County of STAFFORD for the consideration of Eighty pounds and had the fee simple Estate in the said Land conveyed unto him and her heirs by Deeds of Lease and Release bearing date the thirteenth and fourteenth days of September in the year of our Lord one thousand seven hundred & Sixty two as by the said Deeds of Record in the County Court of STAF-FORD may appear; And Whereas the said WILLIAM ROWLEY being seized in fee of the said Land departed this life on or about the (blank) day of (blank) 1774 (according to the Will Book, 11th of May 1774) having first made his Last Will and Testament in writing where-by he gave all the rest of his Estate real and personal (after sundry Legacies and Be-quests before given) unto the said LETTIS WALLACE, then LETTIS WISHART, the Wife of the Reverend JOHN WISHART, since deceased, and to CATHARINE TAYLOR, Wife of the said RICHARD TAYLOR and their heirs as by the said Will of Record in the County of King George may appear; And whereas the said MICHAEL WALLACE and LETTIS his Wife and RICHARD TAYLOR and CATHARINE his Wife have agreed to sell the tract of land unto JAMES DAVIS for the consideration herein after mentioned; THIS INDENTURE WITNES-SETH that MICHAEL WALLACE and LETTIS his Wife and RICHARD TAYLOR and CATHA-RINE his Wife for sum of Forty pounds to them in hand paid by JAMES DAVIS by these presents do bargain and sell unto JAMES DAVIS and his heirs all that tract of land situate in County of King George, formerly STAFFORD, containing Eighty acres, Be-gining at a read Oak corner to CATHERINE HOLEBROOKs Land, thence dividing this from her Land N. N. E. 116 po. to a Stake in an Old Field, thence dividing this Land from NATHANIEL JEFFERIES Et. S. Et. 110 poles to a Hickory, thence dividing this land from BRYANT FOLIEs South South West 116 po. to a read Oak, finally Wt. N. Wt. 110 poles to the begining, being part of Three hundred and fifty five acres of Land the back part of a Patent of Eight hundred acres granted to DAVID ANDERSON SENR. by Patent dated the 27 day of April 1668, Together with all houses rights members and appurtenances to the same belonging; To have and to hold the tract of land and premises with appurte-nances unto JAMES DAVIS his heirs; and MICHAEL WALLACE and LETTIS his Wife and RICHARD TAYLOR and CATHARINE his Wife for themselves their heirs the tract of Land & premises unto JAMES DAVIS his heirs against the claim of every person shall war-rant and forever defend; In Witness whereof the said MICHAEL WALLACE and LETTIS his Wife and RICHARD TAYLOR and CATHARINE his Wife have hereunto set their hands and seals the day & year above written

Sealed and Delivered in presence of
          JOSEPH JONES to R.T. & C.T.   MICHAEL WALLACE
          JOHN TALIAFERRO   LETTIS WALLACE
          JOHN TALIAFERRO   RICHARD TAYLOR
                                                         CATHARINE TAYLOR

     Received the day & year within written of and from the within named JAMES DAVIS
the sum of Forty pounds the whole consideration money within mentioned
Witness   JOHN TALIAFERRO   MICHAEL WALLACE
                 JOHN TALIAFERRO   RICHARD TAYLOR
     In the name of the Commonwealth to JOHN TALIAFERRO JUNR. JOHN TALIAFERRO
SENR. & JOHN POLLARD, Gent. of County of King George, Greeting; Whereas MICHAEL
WALLACE and LETTIS his Wife and RICHARD TAYLOR and CATHARINE his Wife of ye sd.
County by their certain Deed of Bargain and Sale (the Commission for the privy examinations
of LETTIS, Wife of MICHAEL WALLACE and CATHARINE, Wife of RICHARD TAYLOR); Witness JOS:
ROBINSON Clerk of our sd. Court of King George at the Court House aforesaid this 4th day
of August 1778 in the third year of the Commonwealth
                                                    JOS: ROBINSON, C. K. G. C.
     King George Sct. We do hereby certify that we did this day examine the above men-
tion'd LETTIS WALLACE and CATHARINE TAYLOR privily and apart from their respective
Husbands agreeable to the Injunction of the above Writ (the return of the execution of the
privy examination of LETTIS WALLACE and CATHARINE TAYLOR); Given under our hands and
seals this 6th day of August A. Dom: 1778   JOHN TALIAFERRO JUNR.
                                                     JOHN TALIAFERRO
     At a Court held for King George County the 6th day of August 1778
This Indented Deed of Bargain and Sale from under the hands and seals of MICHAEL
WALLACE & LETTIS his Wife and RICHARD TAYLOR & CATHARINE his Wife was presented
into Court by JAMES DAVIS & proved by the witnesses thereto & the said LETTIS &
CATHARINE being first privately examined by Commission and on motion of the said
DAVIS was ordered to be recorded

pp.   THIS INDENTURE made the Nineteenth day of September in year of our Lord
1208-   MDCCLXXVII Between JOSEPH WINLOCK of County of STAFFORD, Planter, and
1209   MARGARET his Wife of the first part, RICHARD TODD and ELIZABETH his Wife
           of Parish of Brunswick of second part and JAMES DAVIS of Parish of Brunswick
aforesaid and County of King George of third part; Whereas THOMAS HARRISON formerly of OVERWHARTON Parish in STAFFORD County by his Last Will and Testament
dated the xth day of November 1725 proved at the Court of the said County at the suc-
ceeding Court did among other devices give unto his Daughter, CATHARINE HARRISON
Eighty acres of Land then joining on Mr. RICHARD FOWLEY to her & her heirs and if in
case she died without any heirs then to fall to the next heir; And Whereas the said
CATHARINE died without issue whereupon the title to the land vested in the heirs of
those Sisters of said CATHARINE who are likewise mentioned in the said Will, to wit,
JANE, FRANCES and ANN; And Whereas the said FRANCES died intestate leaving SAMUEL
DAVIS her Son and heir, who likewise died intestate leaving issue Daughters
Coheiresses to wit, ELIZABETH, the Wife of RICHARD TODD and three others; And Whereas the said JOSEPH WINLOCK is Son and Heir of the said JANE by virtue of which
premises the said JOSEPH WINLOCK is intitled and seized in one undivided third part of
the aforesaid Eighty acres of land amounting to near twenty seven acres and the said
RICHARD TODD and ELIZABETH his Wife in right of said ELIZABETH are intitled to &
seized in one fourth part of one third part of the said Eighty acres of land undivided

amounting to near seven acres; NOW THIS INDENTURE WITNESSETH that JOSEPH WIN-
LOCK and MARGARET his Wife and RICHD: TODD and ELIZABETH his Wife in consideration
of Six pounds, fifteen shillings to him the sd. JOS: WINLOCK in hand paid by JAMES
DAVIS, and of the consideration of the sum of one pound, fifteen shillings to RICHARD
TODD and ELIZABETH his Wife in hand paid by JAMES DAVIS, by these presents do bargain and sell unto JAMES DAVIS his heirs one third part and one fourth of one third
part of the aforesaid Eighty acres of land undivided in the whole to about thirty four
acres more or less and the rents issues and profits thereof; To have and to hold the
third part of eighty acres of the undivided part of one fourth part of one third part of
said eight acres undivided with the appurtenances unto JAMES DAVIS his heirs; And
JOSEPH WINLOCK and his heirs shall warrant and defend the one third part of the
eighty acres of undivided land unto JAMES DAVIS his heirs against every person and
RICHARD TODD and ELIZABETH his Wife for themselves & their heirs shall warrant &
defend the one fourth part of the one third part of the eighty acres of land unto JAMES
DAVIS his heirs against all persons; In Testimony whereof the sd. JOSEPH WINLOCK and
MARGRET his Wife and RICHARD TODD and ELIZABETH his Wife have hereunto set their
hands and seals the day and year first above written
Signed Sealed and Delivered in presence of

THOMAS BERRY,	JOSEPH his mark X WINLOCK
JOHN POLLARD, JUNR.	MARGT. her mark × WINLOCK
JAMES RODGERS,	RICHARD TODD
ANTHONY STROTHER.	ELIZABETH her mark X TODD
JOSEPH RODGERS	

Recd. of JAMES DAVIS the within mentioned sum of six pounds, fifteen shillings,
being the consideration to be by him paid to me.
Test THOMAS BERRY & JOHN POLLLARD   JOSEPH his mark X   WINLOCK
    Then recd. of JAMES DAVIS the sum of one pound, fifteen shillings, being the con-
sideration money in the within mentioned to be by him paid to us; Witness our hands &
seals
Test   THOMAS BERRY,   RICHD: TODD
        JOHN POLLARD, JUNR.
    In the name of the Commonwealth of Virginia to THOMAS BERRY, JOHN POLLARD &
GEORGE FITZHUGH, Gent. Justices of County of King George, Greeting. Whereas JOSEPH
WINLOCK and MARGARET his Wife and RICHARD TODD and ELIZABETH his Wife of your
said County by their certain Deed of Bargain and Sale (the Commission for the privy exami-
nations of MARGARET, the Wife of JOSEPH WINLOCK and ELIZABETH, the Wife of RICHARD TODD);
Witness JOSEPH ROBINSON Clerk of our said County Court of King George this 19th day of
Septr: 1777, in the second year of this Commonwealth
                                                JOS: ROBINSON, C. K. G. C.
    By virtue of the within Writ to us directed, we caused the said MARGARET WINLOCK,
Wife of JOSEPH WINLOCK, and ELIZABETH TODD, Wife of RICHARD TODD, to appear before
us and examined them privately and apart from their said Husbands touching the con-
veyance of the within mentioned Land (the return of the execution of the privy examination of
MARGARET WINLOCK and ELIZABETH TODD);   THOMAS BERRY
                                                JOHN POLLARD, JUNR.
    At a Court held for King George County the (blank) day of (blank) 1777
JOSEPH WINLOCK and MARGARET his Wife, RICHARD TODD & ELIZABETH his Wife
This Deed from under the hands and seals of the sd. parties, the said MARGARET &
ELIZABETH being first privately examined by a Commission, was presented into Court by
JAMES DAVIS and proved by the Oaths of THOMAS BERRY, JOHN POLLARD JUNR. & JAMES

RODGERS, and on the motion of the said DAVIS was ordered to be recorded
Test   JOS: ROBINSON, C. K. G. C.

pp. 1210-1211   THIS INDENTURE made the Third day of September in the year of our Lord one thousand seven hundred and seventy eight Between BALDWIN BERRY of LOW-DON & JENNY his Wife of the one part and AARON THORNLEY of County of King George of other part; Whareas the said BALDWIN BERRY & JENNY his Wife are at this time seized and possessed of a certain tract of land in County of King George containing by estimation one hundred and Ninety six acres, and being disposed to sell the same, have contracted with AARON THORNLEY for the purchase thereof for the consideration herein after mentioned. THIS INDENTURE THEREFORE WITNESSETH that the said BALDWIN BERRY and JENNY his Wife for sum of Three hundred pounds in hand paid by AARON THORNLEY by these presents do bargain and sell unto AARON THORNLEY his heirs all that tract of Land whereon BALDWIN BERRY lately lived containing by estimation One hundred and Ninety six acres be the same more or less and bounded; Begining on a Branch of CHINGOTEAGUE near a Crossing Place formerly called ALLENS BRIDGE and running up the said Branch N. 7d. E. 12 poles, thence leaving the Branch and binding on the land of SAMUEL KENDALL, vizt. (series of degrees and poles); to another Branch of CHINGOTEAGUE, thence down the Branch according to the meanders thereof into the line of ANDREW HARRISONs Land, thence binding on the sd. HARRISONs Land S. 14d. W. 28 po. to a Hickory, thence S. 7 1/2 Wt. 107 po: to the Main Branch of CHINGO-TEAGUE, thence down the Branch to the land of SAMUEL KENDALL at the mouth of a small Branch mentioned in FRANCIS WOFFENDALEs Deed of Gift to the said KENDALL, thence up the said Branch vizt. N. 45d. E. 35 po., N. 28 Et. 17 po., N. 35 1/2 Et. 48 po. to a Hickory mentioned in the sd. Deed of Gift, thence S. 80 Et. 18 po., S. 69d. Et. 26 po. S. 43d. Et. 22 po. to a Mulberry Tree standing in a bottom mentioned in the said Deed of Gift, thence by a line mutually agreed on between BALDWIN BERRY and SAMUEL KENDALL vizt. S. 5d. Wt. 15 po., S. 18d. W. 10 po. to a Post on the side of a small Branch, thence S. 24d. W. 182 po. to a doubled bodies live Oak standing in a Branch, thence down the Branch S. 50d. E. 14 po. to another live Oak, S. 17d. E. 6 po. 20 links to another live Oak, S. 62d. Et. into the line of TABITHA STROTHER, thence binding on the said STROTHERs N. 80 Et. to the beginning, together with all water courses rights & appurtenances belonging To have and to hold the tract of land with the appurtenances unto AARON THORNLEY his heirs and BALDWIN BERRY and JENNY his Wife for themselves their heirs the tract of land with appurtenances unto AARON THORNLEY his heirs from the claim of every person shall warrant and forever defend; In Witness whereof the said BALDWIN BERRY and JENNY his Wife have hereunto set their hands and seals the day and year above written
Sealed and Delivered in the presence of
        (no witnesses recorded)   BALDWIN BERRY
                                             JENNY BERRY
   Received the day and year within written of and from the within named AARON THORNLEY the sum of three hundred pounds currt. money the consideration money within mentioned

                                             BALDWIN BERRY
   At a Court held for King George County the (blank) day of (blank) 1778
This Indented Deed of bargain & sale from under the hands and seals of BALDWIN BERRY and JENNY his Wife was presented into Court by AARON THORNLEY & ackd. by BALDWIN & JENNY, she being first privately examined, with the Receipt thereon endorsed & on the motion of the said THORNLEY was ordered to be recorded

pp.   THIS INDENTURE made the 2d. day of April in the year of our Lord one thousand
1211-   seven hundred & seventy seven Between WILLIAM GRIGSBY of Parish of Bruns-
1212   wick and County of King George and his Son, HORATIO GRIGSBY, of the same
         Parish and County aforesaid; Witnesseth that WILLIAM GRIGSBY in considera-
tion of the sum of five shillings current money of Virginia to him in hand paid by
HORATIO GRIGSBY, his Son, has bargained and sold unto HORATIO GRIGSBY, his Son, one
certain parcel of land situate in the Parish & County aforesd. containing by estimation
Fifty acres be the same more or less bounded by the Lands of MICHAEL WALLACE and
ROSE DADE lying all of it of the North side of the Ditch & Branch of (   ) SWAMP with
all its rights members and appurtenances; To have and to hold the fifty acres of land
with appurtenances unto HORATIO GRIGSBY his heirs; And WILLIAM GRIGSBY for himself his heirs will warrant and defend the Land and premises unto HORATIO GRIGSBY
his Son, his heirs against the claim of all manner of persons; In Witness whereof the
sd. WILLIAM GRIGSBY have hereunto set his hand and seal the day and year first above
written
Sealed and Delivered in the presence of us
         ROBERT HARRISON,   (no signature recorded for WILLIAM GRIGSBY)
         ANDREW HARRISON,
         WILLIAM HOOE,   AARON MARDERS
   At a Court held for King George County the (blank) day of Octo: 177 (blank)
This Indented Deed from under the hand and seal of WM. GRIGSBY to HORATIO GRIGSBY
was presented into Court by HORATIO GRIGSBY & proved by the Oaths of ANDREW HAR-
RISON & WM. HOOE, two of the witnesses thereto which on motion of the sd. HORATIO was
ordered to be recorded.

pp.   THIS INDENTURE made the 7th day of March one thousand seven hundred &
1213-   seventy seven Between JOHN WREN of County of King George of one part and
1214   ELIZA: ARNOLD of the same County of other part; Witnesseth that JOHN WREN for
         the sum of Sixteen pounds, ten shillings current money in hand paid by ELIZA-
BETH ARNOLD by these presents doth bargain and sell unto ELIZABETH ARNOLD her
heirs a certain Plantation and tract of land situate in Parish of Hanover & County afsd.
containing by estimation thirteen acres, which land fell by heirship to JOHN WREN as
heir at Law to his Brother, WILLIAM WREN, which land hereby conveyed or meant to
be conveyed begins at a corner Hiccory line to THORNLEY and STROTHER, running
thence along STROTHERs line to a small red Oak near a large white Oak, thence across
GINGOTEAGUE SWAMP to two small sweet Gum Bushes upon the brow of a Hill near the
Swamp, thence a straight course to a large Javin Tree by the head of a Gully near
THONRLIEs line, thence along THORNLEYs line to the beginning, containing by estimation about thirteen acres be the same more or less together with all houses orchards
and appurtenances in any ways belonging; To have and to hold the Plantation and tract
of land and all the premises unto ELIZABETH ARNOLD her heirs and JOHN WREN for
himself his heirs the Plantation and tract of land with appurtenances unto ELIZABETH
ARNOLD her heirs against all persons shall warrant and forever defend by these presents; In Witness whereof the said JOHN WREN hath hereunto set his hand and seal the
day & year first mentioned
Sealed and acknowledged in presence of
         NUMEY her mark + ARNOLD,   JOHN WREN
         LETTIS her mark ⅄ CULLOM
         WILLIAM BOON, THOMAS SMITH,
         WILLIAM GREEN, WILLIAM SHROPSHIRE

Received this 7th day of March 1777 of ELIZA: ARNOLD the sum of sixteen pounds, ten shillings current money the sd. sum being the consideration mentioned in this Deed
(Same six witnesses recorded)   JOHN WREN
At a Court held for King George County the 6 day of February 1777
This Indented Deed of Bargain and Sale from under the hand and seal of JOHN WREN to ELIZA: ARNOLD was presented into Court by the sd. ELIZA: ARNOLD & was ackd. by the said WREN & on the motion of the said ELIZABETH was ordered to be recorded

pp.   THIS INDENTURE made the third day of March in year of our Lord one thousand
1214   seven hundred & seventy seven Between JOSEPH JONES of County of King George
1215   and MARY his Wife of one part and JOHN TALIAFERRO of same County, Gentleman
        of other part; Whareas JOSEPH JONES hath agreed to sell unto JOHN TALIAFERRO
that part of the tract of land called GILBERTS where FICKLIN formerly lived containing Ninety six acres being the back part of sd. tract of land for the price of Forty seven shillings & six pence p acre; THIS INDENTURE WITNESSETH that JOSEPH JONES for sum of Forty seven shillings and six pence p acre for ninety six acres of the Tract called GIL-BERTS, in hand paid by JOHN TALIAFERRO, by these presents doth bargain and sell unto JOHN TALIAFERRO his heirs all that parcel of land where the said FICKLIN formerly lives. being the back part of the Tract called GILBERTS, & containing Ninety six acres according to a Survey made thereof by Colonel JAMES TAYLOR the (blank) day of (blank) 1777; Together with all houses rights members and appurtenances to the same apper-taining; To have and to hold the tract of land and premises with the appurtenances unto JOHN TALIAFERRO his heirs and JOSEPH JONES for himself his heirs the land and premises with appurtenances unto JOHN TALIAFERRO his heirs against the claim of any person shall warrant and forever defend; In Witness whereof the said JOSEPH JONES and MARY his Wife have hereunto set their hands & seals the day and year above written
Sealed and Delivered in the presence of
    JOS: ROBINSON, RICHD: BAYNHAM,   JOS: JONES
    JNO: TALIAFERRO, WILLM. WOODFORD,   MARY JONES
    JAMES DAVIS
At a Court held for King George County the 6th of Feby. 177(blank)
This Indented Deed of Bargain and Sale from under the hands & seals of JOS: JONES & MARY his Wife to JOHN TALIAFERRO, she being first privately examined, was presented into Court by the sd. TALIAFERRO & was acknowledged by the sd. JOS: & MARY, & on the motion of said TALIAFERRO was ordered to be recorded

pp.   THIS INDENTURE made this first day of April one thousand seven hundred and
1215-   seventy seven Between THOMAS JETT and ELIZA: his Wife of County of King
1216   George of one part & ANDREW CRAWFORD of LEEDS TOWN of the other part; Wit-
        nesseth that THOMAS JETT and ELIZABETH his Wife for sum of Seventy five
pounds current money of Virginia to them in hand paid by these presents do bargain and sell unto ANDREW CRAWFORD and to his heirs one certain lott or half acre of land lying in the Town of LEEDS distinguished in the Plan of said Town by the number (34), and on the Lott on which BRAYS WAREHOUSES stand, Together with all houses and im-provements thereon. To have and to hold the lott or half acre of Land hereby con-veyed with appurtenances unto ANDREW CRAWFORD his heirs and THOMAS JETT & ELIZABETH his Wife and their heirs do covenant with ANDREW CRAWFORD that they will warrant and forever defend the lott of land and premises to ANDREW CRAWFORD his heirs against the claim of all persons; In Witness whereof the said THOMAS JETT and

ELIZABETH his Wife have hereunto set their hands & seals the day and year before
written
Sealed & Deliver'd in the presence of
      CHARLES DEANE, JUNR.,   THOMAS JETT
      BENJAMIN STROTHER,   ELIZA: JETT
      WILLIAM JETT
    Received this first day of April 1777 the sum of Seventy five pounds from Mr. ANDRFW
CRAWFORD being the consideration money mention'd in the Deed to be paid by him to
      (no witnesses recorded)   THOS: JETT
    At a Court held for King George County the 6 day of February 1777
This Indented Deed of Bargain and SAle from under the hands and seals of THOMAS JETT
and ELIZABETH his Wife with the Receipt thereon endorsed was presented into Court by
ANDREW CRAWFORD & proved by the witnesses thereto and on the motion of the said
CRAWFORD was ordered to be recorded

pp.   THIS INDENTURE made the fifth day of December one thousand seven hundred
1216- and seventy seven Between DANIEL LOVELL and ELIZA: his Wife of the Parish of
1217   CAMDEN in County of PITTSYLVANIA of one part and AARON WEBB of Parish of
        DRISDALE in County of CAROLINE of other part; Witnesseth that DANIEL LOVELL
and ELIZA: his Wife for sum of Fifty pounds current money of Virginia in hand paid by
these presents doth bargain and sell unto AARON WEBB & to his heirs all that parcel of
land situate in Parish of Hanover and County of King George containing by estimation
One hundred and fifty acres more or less and bounded, Beginning on the line of MOSES
PITMAN, thence along the said PITMANs line to lines of Capt. SAMUEL OLDHAM, thence
along the lines of said OLDHAMs Land to the line of WILLIAM DODGIN, thence along the
lines of said DODGIN to the line of DANIEL RIDING, deced., thence along the said RIDINGs
lines to the beginning, it being the property of SAMUEL MOON deced., and all houses
profits and advantages to the same belonging; To have and to hold the land and premises unto AARON WEBB his heirs and DANIEL LOVELL & ELIZA: his Wife for themselves
their heirs doth agree with AARON WEBB his heirs that they will well and truly defend
the land unto AARON WEBB his heirs against themselves and their heirs; In Witness
whereof the said DANIEL LOVELL and ELIZA: his Wife hath to this Indenture set their
hands & seals the day month and year first before written
Sign'd Seal'd and Deliver'd in the presence of
      WILLIAM CLATOR, WILLIAM RIDING,   DANIEL LOVELL
      MOSES WEBB, WILLIAM BOON,   ELIZA: LOVELL
      ALEXANDR: HANSFORD, JOS: ROBINSON,
      JOSIAH FERGUSON
    Recd. this fifth day of December 1776 of AARON WEBB the sum of fifty pounds currt.
money being the consideration mention'd in this Deed
Witness   WM: BOON, THOMS: GRANT,   DANIEL LOVELL
      JOS: ROBINSON, ALEX: HANSFORD
    At a Court held for King George County the 6th day of February 1777
This Indented Deed of Bargain and Sale from under the hands and seals of DANL:
LOVELL & ELIZABETH LOVELL to AARON WEBB with the Receipt thereon endorsed was
presented into Court by the said WEBB & proved by the Oaths of WM: RIDING, MOSES
WEBB, WM. BOON & ALEX: HANSFORD and on the motion of the said WEBB was ordered to
be recorded   Test JOS: ROBINSON, C. K. G. C.

p.
1217

THIS INDENTURE made the Seventh day of August in year of our Lord one thou-
sand seven hundred and seventy seven Between the Church Wardens of the
Parish of Hanover in County of King George of one part and BENJAMIN MAR-
SHALL of the same Parish of other part; Witnesseth that the Church Wardens doth put
and bind unto BENJAMIN MARSHALL his heirs, four Mulatto Children born of MARY
JENKINSON now a Servant of BENJAMIN MARSHALL whose names is as followeth. vizt.
DAVID JENKINSON born April the 1st day 1770, CLARY JENKINSON born July 4th day
1772, DOLLY JENKINSON born July the 10th 1774, REUBEN JENKINSON born November 2d.
day 1776, for the term of years as the Law directs in such cases and BENJAMIN MAR-
SHALL doth agree to find them sufficient diet and cloathing during their service and as
they shall severally arrive of age to give them what the Law requires in such cases! In
Witness whereof the parties have set their hands and seals the day and year first above
written
Witness J. SKINKER.   THOMAS JETT
       W. BOON,   HORATIO DADE
       GEO: MARSHALL   BENJN: MARSHALL
   At a Court held for King George County the (blank) day of (blank) 1777
This Indenture from under the hands and seals of THOMAS JETT, HORATIO DADE & BEN-
JAMIN MARSHALL was presented into Court by the parties thereof & proved by the
Oaths of JOHN SKINKER and WILLIAM BOON and ordered to be recorded

p.
1218

THIS INDENTURE madethe Second day of October in the year 1777 and in the
Second year of the Commonwalth Between JOHN ELKINS of County of CAROLINE,
Planter, & LUCY his Wife of one part and WILLIAM PRICE of County aforesaid
of other. Witnesseth that JOHN ELKINS in consideration of the sum of Forty pounds current money of Virginia to him in hand paid by WILLIAM PRICE, by these presents doth
bargain and sell unto WILLIAM PRICE a certain tract of land situate in County of King
George and bounded and bordered on the Lands of Colo. WILLIAM CHAMPE and REUBEN
OWENS as by a Survey thereof made by JOHN TRIPLET, Surveyor of the said County, will
appear and containing One hundred and Twenty nine acres more or less which Land
lying and bounded as aforesaid was by Deed duly proved and recorded given and conveyed to (by in text) JOHN ELKINS by his Mother, MARY ELKINS as by said Deed will fully
appear; To have and to hold the land bounded and bordering as aforesaid and the rents
issues and profits thereof unto WILLIAM PRICE his heirs and JOHN ELKINS and LUCY his
Wife for themselves their heirs the one hundred and twenty nine acres of Land unto
WILLIAM PRICE (with the appurtenances) and to his heirs against the claim of every
person shall warrant and by these presents forever defend; In Witness whereof the
said JOHN ELKINS and LUCY his Wife have hereunto set their hands and seals the day &
year first above written
Signd. Sealed & Delivd: in presence of
       CHARLES, SCOGGINS,   JOHN his mark + ELKINS
       THOMAS JORDAN,   LUCY her mark + ELKINS
       THO; G.L. TYLER
   Oct. 2, 1777 Then received of WILLIAM PRICE the sum of Forty pounds current
money being the consideration within mentioned to be by him paid to.
Teste THO: G.L. TYLER,   JOHN his mark + ELKINS
       CHARLES SCOGGINS   LUCY her mark + ELKINS
   At a Court held for King George County the 6th day of November 1777
This Indenture of Bargain & Sale from under the hands and seals of JOHN ELKINS and
LUCY his Wife, she being first privately examined, with the Receipt thereon endorsed,

were presented into Court by WILLIAM PRICE JUNR., and acknowledged by the said
JOHN & LUCY, and on the motion of the said WILLIAM PRICE was ordered to be recorded
Test JOS: ROBINSON, C. K. G. C.

p.   THIS INDENTURE made the Eighth day of May in the year of our Lord one thou-
1219   sand seven hundred and seventy three and in the thirteenth year of our
        Sovereign Lord George the third by the grace of God King of Britain France and
Ireland, Defender of the faith &c., Between DAVID PANNILL of the Parish of Hanover
and County of King George of one part and ALEXANDER THOM of Parish and County
aforesaid of other part; Witnesseth that DAVID PANNILL for sum of Twenty pounds cur-
rent money of Virginia to him in hand paid by ALEXANDER THOM by these presents
doth bargain and sell unto ALEXANDER THOM and assigns all that tract of land lying in
County and Parish aforesaid being the remaining part of a tract of land I purchased of
JOHN TILLER containing Sixty acres more or less and bounded, adjoining the Land of
THOMAS DRAKE on one side, then by the Lands called SYDENHAMs and Mr. THOMAS JETT's
Land he purchased of Majr. THOMAS VIVION, touching upon the Land of JOHN EDRING-
TON and adjoining the Land of said ALEXANDER THOM he purchased of JOHN SHORT and
now lives on; Together with all houses orchards profits and appurtenances belonging;
To have and to hold the ddparcel of land and all the premises with the rights members
and appurtenances unto ALEXANDER THOM his heirs; And DAVID PANNILL for himself
his heirs the land and premises against all persons unto ALEXANDER THOM shall warrant and forever defend by these presents; In Witness whereof the said DAVID PAN-
NILL hath hereunto set his hand and seal the day and year above written
Sealed and Delivered in presence of
        JAMES TRIPLETT,   DAVID PANNILL
        JOHN EDRINGTON,
        GEORGE his mark X   THEEDS
    Received of the within named ALEXANDER THOM the sum of Twenty pounds current
money of Virginia, being the consideration within mentioned as Witness my hand this
(blank) day of (blank) one thousand seven hundred and (blank)
Sealed and delivered in the presence of
        JAMES TRIPLETT,   JOHN EDRINGTON,   DAVID PANNILL
        GEORGE his mark X   THEEDS
    At a Court held for King George County the (blank) day of (blank) 1777
This Deed of Bargain and Sale from under the hand and seal of DAVID PANNILL to
ALEXANDER THOM with the Receipt thereon endorsed was presented into Court by the
said THOM and proved by the Oaths of the witnesses thereto subscribed, which on the
motion of the said ALEXANDER THOM was ordered to be recorded
                    Test JOS: ROBINSON, C. K. G. C.

p.   THIS INDENTURE made the Twenty seventh day of August one thousand seven
1220   hundred and seventy seven Between GRACE STEWARD of the Parish and County
        of FREDERICK of one part and WILLIAM THORNTON of Parish of Hanover and
County of King George of other part; Witnesseth that GRACE STEWARD for sum of Thirty
seven pounds current money of Virginia in hand paid by these presents doth bargain
and sell unto WILLIAM THORNTON and to his heirs during my natural life my right of
Dower in the Land my Husband, JEREMIAH STEWARD, purchased of THOMAS ROBINS
lying in King George and WESTMORELAND joining the land of Mr. GEORGE RIDING containing by survey thereof made Sixty seven acres & one third and bounded, Begining at
a small Cedar at the head of a Gully and runing agreeable to the courses made by the

Surveyor of the County, And all houses profits & advantages belonging unto WILLIAM THORNTON his heirs during my life; To have and to hold the parcel of land unto WILLIAM THORNTON his heirs for the term of my life. In Witness whereof the said GRACE STEWARD hath to this Indenture set her hand and seal the day month & year first above written
Signed sealed & delivered in the presence of
    JOHN LOVELL, FRANCIS THORNTON,   GRACE her mark X STEWARD
    WILLIAM MARSHALL, JAMES RODGER
   Received of Mr. WILLIAM THORNTON Thirty seven pounds current money for the land mentioned in this Deed as Witness my hand the day & year before written
    (same four witnesses)   GRACE her mark X STEWARD
   At a Court held for King George County the (blank) day of (blank) 1777
This Indented Deed of Bargain and Sale from under the hand and seal of GRACE STEWARD to WILLIAM THORNTON with the Rect. thereon indorsed was presented into Court by the said THORNTON and proved by the Oaths of JOHN LOVELL, FRANCIS THORNTON & WILLIAM MARSHALL and on the motion of the said WM. THORNTON was ordered to be recorded   Test JOS: ROBINSON, C. K. G. C.

pp.   THIS INDENTURE made the first day of April one thousand seven hundred and
1220- seventy seven Between THOMAS CASON and SARAH his Wife of the County of
1221   STAFFORD of one part and CELEY SAUNDERS of LEEDS TOWN in County of King
      George of other part; Witnesseth that THOMAS CASON and SARAH his Wife for sum of Twenty pounds current money of Virginia to them in hand paid by these presents doth & each of them doth bargain & sell unto CELEY SAUNDERS and his heirs one certain Lott or half acre of land lying in Town of LEEDS distinguished in the Plan of the Town by the number (14) and is the Lott on which CELEY SAUNDERS now lives and all houses gardens and other improvements thereon; To have and to hold the half acre of land hereby conveyed with the appurtenances unto CELEY SAUNDERS her heirs and THOMAS CASON and SARAH his Wife for themselves and their heirs do covenant to warrant and forever defend the lott or half acre of land to him the said CELEY SAUNDERS his heirs against the claim of all persons
Sealed and delivered in the presence of
    (no witnesses recorded)   THOMAS CASON
   Received this first day of April 1777 the sum of Twenty pounds from Mr. CELEY SAUNDERS being the consideration money mentioned in this Deed to be by him paid to
                    (no signature recorded)
   At a Court held for King George County the 3d day of April 1777
This Indented Deed of Bargain and Sale from under the hand and seal of THOMAS CASON to CELEY SAUNDERS with the Receipt thereon indorsed was presented into Court by the said SAUNDERS and acknowledged by the said CASON and on the motion of the said CELEY SAUNDERS was ordered to be recorded
         Test JOS: ROBINSON, C. K. G. Court

p   THIS INDENTURE made this XXIV day of September in the year of our Lord
1221   MDCCLXXVII Between JOHN TURNER of Saint Pauls Parish and King George
      County (late STAFFORD) in Virginia of one part and SEYMOUR HOOE of the same Parish and County, Attorney at Law, of other part; Witnesseth that JOHN TURNER for the sum of Fifty pounds and eighty shillings lawfull money by this Indenture doth bargain and sell unto SEYMOUR HOOE and his heirs all that tract of land whereon said JOHN TURNER now dwells situate near DODSONS CREEK in said Parish and County and

containing One hundred acres, Together with all Estate right title and demand of JOHN
TURNER in the Plantation and tract of land; To have and to hold the tract of land together with the premises unto SEYMOUR HOOE and his heirs, PROVIDED always and this
Indenture is upon this express condition, that if JOHN TURNER his heirs shall pay or
cause to be paid unto SEYMOUR HOOE his heirs on or before the XXIV day of September
which shall be in the year of our Lord one thousand seven hundred and seventy nine
the sum of Fifty pounds, eight shillings legal money with legal Interest thereon from
the date of these presents, Then this Indenture to cease and be utterly void and of none
effect as though the same had never been made; In Testimony whereof the said JOHN
TURNER hath hereunto set his hand and affixed his seal the day and year first above
written
Sealed and Delivered by the within named JOHN TURNER
in presence of us SARAH HOOE   JOHN TURNER
     WILLIAM SMOD, JOHN MARTIN,
     GARRARD HOOE, RICHD. his mark x KING
  I do acknowledge that I received the sum of Fifty pounds, eight shillings from the
within mentioned SEYMOUR HOOE the day of the date of this Indenture, Witness my
hand
Test   SARAH HOOE,   JOHN TURNER
     WILLIAM SMOD,
     GARRARD HOOE & JOHN MARTIN
  At a Court held for King George County the 6th day of November 1777
This Deed of Mortgage from under the hand and seal of JOHN TURNER to SEYMOUR HOOE
and the Receipt thereon indorsed was presented into Court by the said HOOE and acknowledged by the said JOHN TURNER and on motion of the said HOOE is ordered to be
recorded   Test JOS: ROBINSON, C. K. G. C.

pp.   THIS INDENTURE made this fifth day of November in the year of our Lord 1776
1221a- Between HAY TALIAFERRO of ORANGE and Colony of Virginia, Gent., and
1222   MARTHA his Wife of one part and JOHN TALIAFERRO of County of King George
           and Colony aforesaid of other part. Whereas FRANCIS TALIAFERRO, Gent., deced.,
late of the County of SPOTSYLVANIA being in his life time and at the time of his death
seised in his demense as of fee simple in a certain tract of land lying on RAPPAHAN-
NOCK RIVER near MORTONS WAREHOUSE in the County of King George; and FRANCIS
TALIAFERRO being of the said tract of land so as aforesaid seised did by his Last Will and
Testament in Writing dated the xxv day of February in the year of our Lord MDCCLVII
give and bequeath the tract of land unto said HAY TALIAFERRO in fee simple as by the
said Last Will and Testament of Record in the Court of County of SPOTSYLVANIA may
more fully appear; And Whereas HAY TALIAFERRO did also purchase to himself and his
heirs in fee simple one tract of land containing by estimation one hundred acres
situate in County of King George and commonly called by the name of HACKLEYS FERRY
from a certain JUDITH HACKLEY, Widow and Executrix of the Last Will and Testament of
JOHN HACKLEY, deceased, to which said JUDITH power and authority to sell the land last
above mentioned were given in and by the Last Will and Testament of JOHN HACKLEY
but the Deeds of Lease and Release from said JUDITH unto said HAY bearing date the
Lease the eighth day of June in the year of our Lord MDCCLXIII and the Release the
ninth day of July in the same year being recorded by mistake in the Court of the County of CULPEPER, said HAY TALIAFERRO did procure a confirmation of his title in and to
the last above mentioned tract of land from JAMES HACKLEY, Son and Heir at Law of the
said JOHN HACKLEY by Deed bearing date the xix day of June MDCLXXIV as in and by the

same now of record in the Court of the County of King George may fully appear; NOW
THIS INDENTURE WITNESSETH that HAY TALIAFERRO and MARTHA his Wife for sum of
One thousand and five hundred pounds current money of Virginia by JOHN TALIAFER-
RO to HAY TALIAFERRO in hand paid, by these present Indenture do bargain and sell
unto JOHN TALIAFERRO and his heirs the aforesaid tracts of land, viz. as well the tract of
land devised by FRANCIS TALIAFERRO unto HAY TALIAFERRO as that tract of land purchased by said HAY of and from JUDITH HACKLEY together with all their rights members and appurtenances; To have and to hold the tracts of land unto JOHN TALIAFERRO
and his heirs discharged and acquitted of all manner of Rents charges and incumbrances except the annual Quit Rents reserved and payable to the Lord Proprietor of
the Northern Neck of Virginia; And HAY TALIAFERRO for the consideration herein
before mentioned & his heirs the tracts of land unto JOHN TALIAFERRO his heirs shall
warrant and will by these presents Indenture warrant and for ever defend; In Testimony whereof the said HAY TALIAFERRO and MARTHA his Wife have hereunto set their
hands and affixed their seals the day and year first above written
Sealed and delivered in presence of
    JAMES BOWEN,   HAY TALIAFERRO
    THOMAS BOXLEY,   TERRY RAWLINGS,   MARTHA TALIAFERRO
    JOHN GIBSON,   DORREL TURNER
   Received the day and year within written the within mentioned sum of fifteen
hundred pounds p me
Test (same five witnesses)   HAY TALIAFERRO
   At a Court held for King George County the (blank) day of (blank) 177(blank)
This Indented Deed of Bargain and Sale from under the hands and seals of HAY TALIA-
FERRO and MARTHA his Wife, she being first privately examined, to JOHN TALIAFERRO
with the Receipt thereon indorsed was presented into Court by JOHN TALIAFERRO &
proved by the Oaths of JAMES BOWEN, THOMAS BOXLEY, TERRY RAWLING and DORRELL
TURNER, and on the motion of the said JOHN was ordered to be recorded
         Test JOS: ROBINSON, Cl Cur

pp.   THIS INDENTURE made this 17th day of October in the year of our Lord one
1222- thousand seven hundred & seventy six Between WILLIAM NEWTON SENR. of
1223   Parish of Brunswick and County of King George, Gent., of one part and ABRA-
       HAM NEWTON, Son of the said WILLIAM, of other part; Witnesseth that WIL-
LIAM NEWTON in consideration of the natural live and affection which he hath for his
Son, ABRAHAM NEWTON, and in consideration of the sum of five shillings current
money to him in hand paid by these presents doth bargain and sell unto ABRAHAM
NEWTON and his heirs a certain tract of land situate in said Parish and County containing 250 acres more or less being half of that tract of land whereon WILLIAM NEWTON
JUNR. now lives, which tract of land I bought of ARTHUR MORSON and the Deed recorded in King George Court, and also these following slaves; vizt. Jack, Dick and Patty,
with the future increase of said Patty, together with one mare colt already delivered by
him to ABRAHAM NEWTON & all profits and appurtenances to the tract of land belonging To have and to hold the tract of land and Negroes unto ABRAHAM NEWTON & his
heirs and WILLIAM NEWTON and his heirs the land & premises unto ABRAHAM NEWTON
and his heirs from the claim & demand of every person shall warrant and forever defend by these presents. In Witness whereof the said WILLIAM NEWTON hath hereunto
set his hand and seal the day and year first above written
Signed sealed and delivered in presence of us
    JOHN NEWTON   WILLIAM NEWTON

At a Court held for King George County the (blank) day of November 1776
This Indented Deed from under the hand and seal of WILLIAM NEWTON to ABRAHAM
NEWTON was presented into Court by the said ABRAHAM NEWTON and acknowledged by
the said WILLIAM NEWTON and on the motion of the said ABRAHAM NEWTON was ordered
to be recorded   Test JOS: ROBINSON, Cl Cur

p.   THIS INDENTURE made this fifth day of August one thousand seven hundred
1223   and seventy seven Between JOSEPH BURGES of County of King George of one
          part and WILLIAM MARSHALL of the same County of other part; Witnesseth that
JOSEPH BURGESS in consideration of the Rents hereinafter mentioned to be paid by
WILLIAM MARSHALL by these presents doth lease unto WILLIAM MARSHALL during
the said JOSEPH BURGESS's natural life all that parcel of land sitaute in County of King
George adjoining the Land of THOMAS JETT and bounded by the Road that leads from
MATTOX and contains Twenty five acres; To have and to hold the parcel of land to
WILLIAM MARSHALL during the life of JOSEPH BURGESS paying yearly the annual rent
of two pounds, ten shillings current money and JOSEPH BURGESS doth covenant and
agree that WILLIAM MARSHALL shall and may make use of such Timber on said land as
will build the necessary houses thereon and for what need he has occasion for his
Smiths Shop and WILLIAM MARSHALL promises to deliver up the land and premises in
proper order at the expiration of this Lease. In Witness whereof the parties have here-
unto set their hands and seals the day and eyar before written
Sealed and delivered in the presence of
          WILLIAM BOON,   JOS: his mark ✕ BURGESS
          BENJAMIN STROTHER,   WILLIAM MARSHALL
          SAMUEL his mark ✕ WOOD
At a Court held for King George County the 7th day of Augt. 1777
This Indented Lease from under the hand and seal of JOSEPH BURGESS to WILLIAM
MARSHALL was presented into Court by the said MARSHALL & proved by the Oaths of
WILLIAM BOON & SAMUEL WOOD and on the motion of the said WILLIAM MARSHALL was
ordered to be recorded   Teste JOS: ROBINSON, Cl Court

pp.   TO ALL PEOPLE to whome these presents shall come, Know ye that I MARY
1223-   STONE of County of King George in consideration of the natural affection and
1224   for other divers good cause and considerations me thereunto moving by these
          presents do give & grant unto JOHN FARGUSON of same County, one Yoak of
Steers and Cart now in use, two Cows & yearlings, one Desk and all my stock of Sheep, To
have and to hold the above mentioned goods & chattels and I MARY STONE do & will
warrant & forever defend the goods to JOHN FARGUSON and his heirs, As Witness my
hand & seal this 16th day of January 1776
Signed sealed and delivered in presence of
          JOHN RICHARDSON, & MOURNING RICHARDSON   MARY her mark +STONE
     At a Court held for King George County the 3d. day of October 1776
MARY STONEs Deed of Gift to JOHN FARGUSON was presented into Court by the said FAR-
GUSON and proved by the Oaths of JNO: RICHARDSON and MOURNING RICHARDSON and on
the motion of the said JOHN FARGUSON was ordered to be recorded
                    Test JOS: ROBINSON, Cl Court

p.   THIS INDENTURE made the 7th day of August one thousand seven hundred &
1224   seventy seven Between JAMES DAVIS, Lieutenant in the Third Regiment of this
          Commonwealth of one part & THOMAS CASON of County of STAFFORD of other

part, Witnesseth that JAMES DAVIS for sum of One hundred and twenty pounds to him in hand paid by THOMAS CASON hath bargained and sold unto THOMAS CASON all that tract of land lying in County of King George and Parish of Hanover, it being the land said DAVIS purchased of WILLIAM MONDAY and given by ROBERT MONDAY and CATHARINE his Wife by their certain Deed of Gift recorded in the County Court of King George will more fully appear; containing one hundred acres of land be the same more or less with all its appurtenances and all houses rents & services; To have and to hold the land and premises unto THOMAS CASON his heirs and JAMES DAVIS for himself his heirs the one hundred acres of land shall warrant & by these presents defend; In Witness whereof the said JAMES DAVIS hath hereunto set his hand and seal the day & year first above written

Signed Sealed &c.in presence of us
          (no witnesses recorded)   JAMES DAVIS
     August 7th 1777. Then received of THOMAS CASON the sum of One hundred and twenty pounds being the consideration within mentioned
                                                          JAMES DAVIS
     At a Court held for King George County the 7th day of August 1777
This Indented Deed of Bargain and Sale from under the hand and seal of JAMES DAVIS to THOMAS CASON and the Receipt thereon indorsed was presented into the Court by the said CASON & acknowledged by the said DAVIS and on the motion of the said THOMAS CASON was ordered to be recorded
                    Test JOS: ROBINSON, Cl Court

pp   THIS INDENTURE made this Second day of August one thousand seven hundred
1224-   & seventy seven Between JOHN WASHINGTON and CONSTANT his Wife of County
1225   of King George of one part and DANIEL BRISCOE of same County of other part;
          Witnesseth that JOHN WASHINGTON and CONSTANT his Wife for sum of Ninety
three pounds current money to them in hand paid by DANIEL BRISCOE by these pre-
sents do bargain and sell unto DANIEL BRISCOE his heirs all that parcel of land lying in County of King George containing Thirty one acres & nineteen poles of Land, being part of the tract of land JOHN WASHINGTON now lives on & lies between the MAIN COUNTY ROAD and the land of THOMAS HODGE and further bounded as by a Survey thereof made by BENJA: WEEKS, Gentn., the twenty first day of July last; Together with all commodities appurtenances & profits thereof; To have and to hold the parcel of land unto DANIEL BRISCOE his heirs, and JOHN WASHINGTON and CONSTANT his Wife for themselves & their heirs do covenant with DANIEL BRISCOE his heirs that they will warrant the parcel of land and premises unto DANIEL BRISCOE and his heirs against the claim of all persons; In Witness whereof the said JOHN WASHINGTON and CONSTANT his Wife have hereunto set their hands and seals the day month & year first above written
Sealed & Delivered in presence of
          THOMAS JETT, JOHN LOVELL,   JOHN WASHINGTON
          GEO: MARSHALL, WILLIAM MARSHALL   CONSTANT WASHINGTON
     Received from the within named DANIEL BRISCOE the sum of Ninety three pounds current money, being the consideration within mentioned to be by him paid to
Witness (the same four witnesses)   JOHN WASHINGTON
     At a Court held for King George County the 7th day of August 1777
This Indented Deed of Bargain and Sale from under the hand and seal of JOHN WASHINGTON & CONSTANT his Wife to DANIEL BRISCOE with the Receipt thereon indorsed was presented into Court by DANIEL BRISCOE and proved by the Oaths of JOHN LOVELL, GEORGE MARSHALL & WILLIAM MARSHALL and on the motion of the said

DANIEL was ordered to be recorded
                    Test JOS: ROBINSON, Cl Court

pp.   THIS INDENTURE made this 7th day of August one thousand seven hundred and
1225-   seventy seven Between THOMAS JETT and HORATIO DADE, Gent., Church Wardens
1226   for the Parish of Hanover and County of King George of one part and JAMES
          DODD of the other part; Witnesseth that THOMAS JETT and HORATIO DADE in pur-
suance of the Act of Assembly directing that all bastard males shall be bound to serve
the masters to the age of twenty one years and the females to the age of eighteen, the
said THOMAS JETT and HORATIO DADE by these presents doth put & bind unto JAMES DODD
a bastard male Child named JAMES McFARLING as an Apprentice during such term and
JAMES DODD in consideration of the service of said JAMES McFARLING doth covenant
with THOMAS JETT and HORATIO DADE for the service of JAMES McFARLING, the said
JAMES DODD will find & provide for JAMES McFARLING good & sufficient meat drink
washing cloathing and lodging and also learn him the Trade of a Weaver and further
that he will cause JAMES McFARLING to read & wright and at the expiration of his service pay him lawfull Freedom Dues; In Witness whereof the said THOMAS JETT and
HORATIO DADE and the said JAMES DODD hath hereunto set their hands & seals the day &
year first before written
Sealed & Delivered in the presence of
      WILLIAM BOON   THOMAS JETT
                                                      HORATIO DADE
                                                      JAMES DODD

      At a Court held for King George County the 7th day of August 1777
This Indenture from under the hand and seal of THOMAS JETT & HORATIO DADE & JAMES
DODD was presented into Court by the said DODD and acknowledged by the parties &
ordered to be recorded   Test JOS: ROBINSON, Cl Court

p.   THIS INDENTURE made this Seventh day of August one thousand seven hundred
1226   & seventy seven Between THOMAS JETT and HORATIO DADE Gent., Church War-
          dens of Parish of Hanover in County of King George of one part & JAMES ED-
WARDS of same Parish and County of other part; Witnesseth that THOMAS JETT and
HORATIO DADE in pursuance of the Act of Assembly directing that all bastard Children
shall be bound to service, the males to the age of twenty one years and the females to
the age of eighteen, by these presents doth put & bind unto JAMES EDWARDS a bastard
Child named BENJAMIN McFARLING an Apprentice during such term as said BENJAMIN
shall arrive to the age of twenty one years to learn the Trade of a Carpenter and JAMES
EDWARDS in consideration of the service of BENJAMIN McFARLING doth covenant with
THOMAS JETT and HORATIO DADE that said JAMES EDWARDS will learn said BENJAMIN the
Trade of a Carpenter as aforesaid & further that he will cause BENJAMIN McFARLING to
be learned to read and write and that he will during his service find & provide for for
him good and sufficient cloaths meat drink washing and lodging and at the expiration
of his service to pay him lawfull Freedom Dues; In Witness whereof THOMAS JETT &
HORATIO DADE & the said JAMES EDWARDS hath hereunto set their hands and seals the
day & year first above written
Sealed and delivered in the presence of
      (no witnesses recorded)   THOMAS JETT
                                                       HORATIO DADE
                                                       JAMES EDWARDS

At a Court held for King George County the 7th day of August 1777
This Indented Deed from under the hands & seals of THOMAS JETT & HORATIO DADE and
JAMES EDWARDS was presented into Court by JAMES EDWARDS and acknowledged by the
parties and ordered to be recorded

Test JOS: ROBINSON, Cl Court

pp.   THIS INDENTURE made the fifth dy of January in the year of our Lord one
1226- thousand seven hundred and seventy seven Between ALEXANDER HANSFORD of
1227   County of King George and ANN his Wife of one part and THOMAS OLIVER of
       County of STAFFORD and ELIZABETH his Wife of other part; Witnesseth that
ALEXANDER HANSFORD and ANN his Wife for sum of One hundred and fifty one pounds,
seventeen shillings and six pence current money of Virginia to ALEXANDER HANSFORD
in hand paid by THOMAS OLIVER and ELIZABETH his Wife, by these presents do bargain
and sell unto THOMAS OLIVER and his Wife all that certain tract of land lying in County
of King George and bounded as by a Survey thereof made by TRAVERSE DANIEL, Gent.,
of County of STAFFORD; Begining at a white Oak near a small Branch corner of THOMAS
FICKLINs Tenement in the line of FITZHUGH, thence So. 41d. Et. 46 1/4 poles to a red Oak
corner to this Land, thence So. 71 Et. 24 ps. to a Stake, thence So. 74 Et. 126 ps. to another
State suposed to be in the line of tract whereof this is part, thence with or near that
line No. 4 Wt. 211 ps. to another Stake by the Road that leads to FALMOUTH, thence with
or along that Road No. 70 Wt. 54 ps. five links to a marked red Oak in the line of the said
FITZHUGH, thence with FITZHUGHs line Et. 44 poles to the begining, containing by the
Survey one hundred & thirty five acres and being part of a larger tract which ALEXAN-
DER HANSFORD puchased of JAMES HUBARD of the City of WILLIAMSBURG, Attorney at
Law, and his Wife as by their Deed now of Record among the Recors of the Honble. the
General Court may appear; and the houses orchards profits & appurtenances to the pre-
mises belonging; To have and to hold the land and appurtenances unto THOMAS OLIVER
and ELIZABETH his Wife and the longest liver of them and to the use of the survivor; In
Witness whereof the said ALEXANDER HANSFORD & ANN his Wife have hereunto set
their hands and seals the day and year first before written
Sealed and Delivered in presence of
      WILLIAM CHADWELL,   ALEXR: HANSFORD
      TERRY RAWLINS,   WILLIAM HARRISON   ANN HANSFORD
At a Court held for King George County the 7th day of Augt. 1777
This Indented Deed of bargain and sale from under the hands and seals of ALEXANDER
HANSFORD & ANN his Wife to THOMAS OLIVER, she being first privately examined, was
presented in Court by the said OLIVER and acknowledged by the said HANSFORD & his
Wife, ANN, and on the motion of THOMAS OLIVER was ordered to be recorded
                   Test JOS: ROBINSON, Cl Court

p.   THIS INDENTURE made this fifteenth day of August in the year of our Lord one
1228   thousand seven hundred and seventy eight Between JOHN TALOE, Esqr., and
       REBECCA his Wife of County of RICHMOND of one part and LAURANCE ASHTON of
County of King George of other part; Witnesseth that JOHN TAYLOE for sum of four
hundred and twenty pounds current money of Virginia hath bargained and sold unto
LAURANCE ASHTON his heirs a certain parcel of land situate in County of King George
containing Forty two acres or thereabouts and bounded Easterly by a tract of land belonging to LAURANCE ASHTON and Northerly and Westerly by the Land formerly belonging to WILLIAM CHAMPE but now to LEWIS WILLIS Esqr., Together with all houses
profits and advantages thereunto belonging; To have and to hold the parcel of land

with its appurtenances unto LAURANCE ASHTON his heirs and JOHN TAYLOE for himself
his heirs doth covenant with LAURANCE ASHTON that he will warrant and defend the
parcel of land against all persons; In Witness whereof the said JOHN TAYLOE and
REBECCA his Wife have hereunto set their hands and seals the day & year above written
Signed Sealed and Delivered in prsence of

WILLIAM HENDREN,	JOHN WHELDON,	JOHN TAYLOE
FRANCIS LIGHTFOOT LEE,		REBECCA TAYLOE
GRIFFIN GARLAND, GEORGE DYE,		
CHARLES ASHTON JUNR., and LANGHORNE DADE		

Received of the within LAURANCE ASHTON Four hundred and twenty pounds, the
consideration within mentioned. Witness my hand the day and year within written

Witness WM: HENDREN, JOHN WELDON   JOHN TAYLOE
         FRANCIS LIGHTFOOT LEE,
         GRIFFIN GARLAND, GEO: DYE

At a Court held for King George County the 4th day of March 1779
This Indented Deed of Bargain & Sale from under the hands & seals of JOHN TAYLOE &
REBECCA his Wife to LAURANCE ASHTON was presented into Court by the said LAURANCE
& proved by the Oaths of LANGHORNE DADE, CHARLES ASHTON JUNR. and GEORGE DYE &
on motion of the said LAURANCE ASHTON was ordered to be recorded

                    Test   JOS: ROBINSON, Cl: Court

pp.   THIS INDENTURE made the Twenty third day of December in the year of our
1228-   Lord one thousand seven hundred and seventy eight Between JOB POPHAM of
1229   BRUMFIELD in County of CULPEPER of one part and GEORGE JOHNSON of King
         George County in Parish of Washington of other part; Witnesseth that JOB POP-
HAM for sum of Two hundred & fifty pounds current money to him in hand paid by
GEORGE JOHNSON, by these presents doth bargain and sell unto GEORGE JOHNSON his
heirs a certain part of land lying in County of King George containing the tract of land
willed to me by JOHN POPHAM, which was purchased of TOWNSHEND HOOE by an Indenture of bargain & sale Recorded in the County Court of WESTMORELAND and therein said
to contain One hundred acres more or less, the bounds of which are also therein particularly mentioned and set forth; Together with all houses profits and advantages to
the same belonging; To have and to hold the land and premises with the appurtenances unto GEORGE JOHNSON his heirs and JOB POPHAM for himself his heirs shall
warrant and defend the premises against the claim & title of every person; In Witness
whereof the said JOB POPHAM have hereunto set his hand and seal the day & year above
mentioned
Sealed and Delivered in presence of

        ROBERT MASSEY, EVIN P. JOHNSON   JOB POPHAM
        FRANCIS his mark ⅂ ROSE,
        SARAH JOHNSON and
        ANTHONY his mark + ROLLINGS

Received December 23d. 1778 of the within named GEORGE JOHNSON the consideration
within mentioned. Witness my hand
        (same five witnesses, no marks.)   JOB POPHAM

At a Court held for King George County the 4th day of March 1779
This Indented Deed of Bargain and Sale from under the hand and seal of JOB POPHAM to
GEORGE JOHNSON with the Receipt thereon indorsed was presented into Court by the said
JOHNSON & proved by the Oaths of ROBERT MASSEY, FRANCIS ROSE and ANTHONY ROL-
LINGS and on the motion of said GEORGE JOHNSON was ordered to be recorded

                    Test JOS: ROBINSON, Cl. Court

pp.   THIS INDENTURE made this twenty fifth day of November one thousand seven
1229-   hundred and seventy seven Between THOMAS DOUGLAS of LEEDS TOWN in Coun-
1230   ty of King George of one part and Captain WILLIAM SAUNDERS of said Town and
          County of other part; Witnesseth that THOMAS DOUGLAS for sum of Two hun-
dred and fifty pounds current money of Virginia to him in hand paid by Capt. WILLIAM
SAUNDERS by these presents doth bargain and sell unto WILLIAM SAUNDERS his heirs
all that lot and land situate in Town of LEEDS and County aforesaid containing (blank)
acres and bounded by the Lands of Col. THOMAS JETT Northerly and on all the other
points according to the boundary shewn to WILLIAM SAUNDERS, the premises including all the landed property of THOMAS DOUGLAS in the Town of LEEDS and all houses
gardens profits commodities and appurtenances belonging; To have and to hold the lots
and houses lands and appurtenances unto WILLIAM SAUNDERS his heirs and THOMAS
DOUGLAS doth covenant that he will defend the aforesaid lotts and houses lands and
appurtenances unto WILLIAM SAUNDERS his heirs against every person; In Witness
whereof the said THOMAS DOUGLASS hath hereunto set his hand and seal the day and
year first before written
Sealed & Delivered in presence of
        AL: ROSE,   ANDREW CRAWFORD,   THOMAS DOUGLAS
        REUBIN BULLARD,   BENJA: STROTHER
    Received from C. WILLIAM SAUDNERS the sum of Two hundred and fifty pounds being
the consideration in the annexed Deed to be paid by him to
Witness (same four witnesses)   THOMAS DOUGLAS
    At a Court held for King George County the 3d. day of February 1778
This Indented Deed of Bargain and Sale from under the hand and seal of THOMAS DOUG-
LAS to WM: SAUNDERS with the Receipt thereon indorsed was presented into Court by
said SAUNDERS & proved by the Oaths of ALEXANDER ROSE, ANDREW CRAWFORD and
RUEBIN BULLARD and on the motion of the said SAUNDERS was ordered to be recorded
                        Test JOS: ROBINSON, Cl. Court

pp.   THIS INDENTURE made and bearing date this fourth day of March in the year
1230-   of our Lord Christ one thousand seven hundred and seventy nine Between JOHN
1231   GRIGSBY & ELIZABETH his Wife of County of King George and Parish of Bruns-
          wick of one part and FRANKY WILTON ROBINSON of the aforesd. County & Parish
of other part; Witnesseth that JOHN GRIGSBY & ELIZABETH GRIGSBY for the natural love
good will and parently affection which we do bear towards FRANKY WILTON ROBINSON
by these presents do give grant and release unto FRANKY WILTON ROBINSON when she
arrives to the age of twenty one years to her and her heirs two certain tracts of Land
lying in County of King George and Parishes of Brunswick and Overwharton on which
JOHN GRIGSBY and ELIZABETH now live, the first tract is bounded, Beginning at a Hickory
standing in a Bottom and runing South one hundred and fifty four poles to an Oak standing in the head of a small glade and near unto a red Oak and Hickory sapling, thence
East one hundred & four poles to a red Oak standing on a Ridge, thence North one hundred and fifty four poles to a small Oak standing near an old Spanish Oak Stump, the reputed corner tree of a tract of land formerly belonging to PETER GALLON, thence one
hundred and four poles to the begining; and is part of Four hundred acres formerly
given by JOHN and GEORGE MOTTs unto JOHN VICARS; The second is a tract of land purchased of BARNETT FOWLEY contiguous the other tract and bounded; Begining near the
Road and a Branch and runs from thence South seventy five East two hundred and fifty
four poles near where it was reported the corner stood, thence South thirty seven & a
half West eighty six where it mett with MOTTs line, thence North twenty nine West

twenty one and a half pole, thence North seventy one West thirty nine poles to a
marked Hickory said to be one of MOTTs corners, thence South eighty nine West one
hundred & twenty eight poles near a marked white Oak, thence North fourteen West to
the begining; containing in the aforesaid bounds and courses of both tracts of land two
hundred and one acres sixteen poles; Together with all houses orchards profits and
appurtenances belonging; To have and to hold the parcels of land and premises unto
FRANKY WILTON ROBINSON to her and her heirs; In Witness whereof the said JOHN
GRIGSBY and ELIZABETH have hereunto set their hands and seals the day and year first
above written
Signed Sealed and Delivered in the presence of

JAMES MONTEITH, MOTT DARMITT,   JOHN GRIGSBY
MARY DARMITT,   ELIZABETH GRIGSBY
THOMAS his mark + JONES

At a Court held for King George County the 4th day of March 1779
This Indented Deed of Gift from under the hands and seals of JOHN GRIGSBY & ELIZA-
BETH GRIGSBY to FRANKY WILTON ROBINSON, the said ELIZABETH being first privately
examined, was acknowledged in Court by the said parties and ordered to be recorded
Test JOS: ROBINSON, Cl: Court

pp.   THIS INDENTURE TRIPARTITE made the Sixteenth day of February in the year
1231-   one thousand seven hundred and seventy nine Between GEORGE RIDING Gent.,
1232   of the first part and JOHN LOVELL of the second part and JOHN COURTS, Grandson
        of GEORGE RIDING of the third part, all parties residing in County of King George
Witnesseth that GEORGE RIDING as well for the love and affection he hath to the said
JOHN COURTS as in consideration of a certain promise made in favour of the said JOHN
COURTS by a certain Letter written and sent by GEORGE RIDING to Mr. WILLIAM THORN-
TON previous to the Marriage of JOHN COURTS with SUSANNAH, Daughter of said WIL-
LIAM THORNTON, which said letter is recorded in the Office of this County, for settling
and securing the lands and slaves herein after mentioned upon the Trusts and uses
after mentioned and for the consideration of Ten shillings to GEORGE RIDING in hand
paid by JOHN LOVELL said GEORGE RIDING doth by these presents bargain sell and release unto JOHN LOVELL his heirs all that tract of land whereon GEORGE RIDING now
lives containing Four hundred and one acres more or less situate in Parish of Hanover
and County of King George and all houses priviledges and emoluments to said land in
any way belonging; Also five slaves, to wit, a Negro or dark Mulattoe named Phil, a
Carpenter by Trade, a Negro woman named Lucy, two Negro boys named Tom and Simon,
and a Negro girl named Rose; the said Tom, Simon and Rose being the offspring of said
Lucy; To have and to hold the plantation and tract of land with appurtenances and also
the five slaves unto JOHN LOVELL his heirs IN TRUST nevertheless and for the use of
GEORGE RIDING in Trust and for the sole use of JOHN COURTS his heirs and for no other
or further use and GEORGE RIDING the Plantation land and slaves unto JOHN LOVELL his
heirs in trust for the uses aforesaid against all persons shall warrant and forever defend by these presents; In Witness whereof the parties have hereunto put their hands
and seals the say and year before written
Signed Sealed & Delivered in presence of

PETER HANSBROUGH,   GEORGE RIDING
WILLIAM RIDING,   JOHN LOVELL
SAMUEL OWENS,   JOHN COURTS
FRANCIS THORNTON

1779 February. Received from JOHN LOVELL Ten shillings the consideration in the Deed specified
    (same four witnesses)   GEORGE RIDING
  At a Court held for King George County the 4th day of March 1779
This Indented Deed of Trust from under the hand & seal of GEORGE RIDING to JOHN LOVELL & JOHN COURTS presented into Court by the said LOVELL & proved by the Oathes of P. HANSBROUGH, WILLIAM RIDING & SAMUEL OWENS & on the motion of the said JOHN was ordered to be recorded
            Test   JOS: ROBINSON, Cl: Court

pp. 1233-1234 THIS INDENTURE made this Second dy of January in the year of our Lord one thousand seven hundred and Eighty one Between DAVID GALLOWAY and MARGARET his Wife of one part and THACKER WASHINGTON of County of King George of other part. Whereas JAMES BLAIR of County of WESTMORELAND died seised and possessed among other things, intestate, of a certain parcel of land whereon he resided in County of King George containing four hundred and eighty acres or there abouts in fee simple, leaving issue the said MARGARET, party hereto, SARAH intermarried with BURDIT ASHTON, ELIZABETH and ANNE BLAIR, to whom the said Tract of Land descended in coparceny; And Whereas DAVID GALLOWAY in right of his Wife and for the benefit of said ELIZABETH and ANNE BLAIR, who are Infants, to whome the said GALLOWAY is Guardian, has covenanted and agreed with THACKER WASHINGTON to sell and convey to him three undivided fourth parts of said tract of land to which the said MARGARET, ELIZABETH and ANNE are intitled as coheiresses or Copartners as aforesaid; with warranty against the claims of MARGARET, ELIZABETH and ANNE and of all persons claiming from them; THIS INDENTURE Therefore Witnesseth that DAVID GALLOWAY and MARGARET his Wife for quantity of sixty seven thousand five hundred pounds of crop tobacco to DAVID GALLOWAY in hand paid, by these presents do and each of them doth bargain and sell unto THACKER WASHINGTON his heirs three undivided of the Manor Plantation and tract of land herein before described; Together with all houses orchards profits and advantages belonging; To have and to hold the three undivided fourth parts of said tract of land and premises unto THACKER WASHINGTON his heirs and DAVID GALLOWAY for himself his heirs doth covenant the three fourth parts of said tract of land and premises with appurtenances unto THACKER WASHINGTON his heirs against all persons shall warrant and forever defend by these presents; In Witness whereof the said DAVID GALLOWAY and MARGARET his Wife have hereunto set their hands and seals the day and year above written
Signed sealed & acknowledged in presence of
    WILLIAM BARNARD,   DAVID GALLOWAY
    RICHARD BARNARD, JOHN THORNTON,   MARGARET GALLOWAY
    FRANCIS WILSON, CHARLES ASHTON
  Received of the within named THACKER WASHINGTON the consideration within mentioned; Witness my hand the day & year within written
Witness WILLIAM BARNARD,   DAVID GALLOWAY
    FRANCIS WILSON, RICHARD BARNARD
  At a Court held for King George County the 5th day of July 1781
This Indented Deed of Bargain and Sale from under the hands and seals of DAVID GALLOWAY JUNR., and MARGARET his Wife, she being first privately examined by virtue of a Commission. with the Receipt thereon indorsed to THACKER WASHINGTON was presented into Court by said WASHINGTON and proved by the Oaths of WILLIAM BARNARD, CHARLES ASHTON and RICHARD BARNARD, and on motion of said THACKER WASHINGTON was ordered to be recorded   Test JOS: ROBINSON, Cl: Court

pp.   THIS INDENTURE made this Sixth day of February in the year of our Lord one
1234- thousand seven hundred and Eighty two Between GEORGE RIDING and WINNI-
1235   FRED his Wife of County of King George of one part and BENJAMIN JOHNSON of
       same County of other part: Witnesseth that in consideration of fifteen thousand
weight of Crop Tobacco to GEORGE RIDING in hand paid by BENJAMIN JOHNSON, by these
presents do bargain and sell unto BENJAMIN JOHNSON his heirs all that Plantation tract
of land situate in County aforesaid, of part of which Land said BENJAMIN hath before
purchased the reversion in fee; the tract of land begins at a Chesnut tree on a Hill near
the corner of GEORGE RIDINGs Peach Orchard, the Chesnut being a corner to the land
formerly ROBINS now DUNLAPs and to the Mannor Plantation of GEORGE RIDING,
runing thence Northerly along the line of said ROBINS or DUNLAPs Land to a white Oak
on the edge of the RIDGE ROAD corner to the Land now herein mentioned to be conveyed and to the Land formerly PITMANs now WILLIAM RIDINGs, thence along PIT-
MANs or RIDINGs Line returning to the Chesnut or begining aforesaid, runing thence
along the line of FRANCIS THORNTONs Land (the remaining bounds of the Land not
being yet ascertained) and the reversion of the part of the land together with the profits thereof with the appurtenances; To have and to hold the land and premises (sup-
posed to be Five hundred acres more or less) unto BENJAMIN JOHNSON and his heirs;
And the said GEORGE and his heirs to BENJAMIN JOHNSON his heirs the land and premises according to the nature of said GEORGEs present Estate and Interest the land and
premises will warrant and defend against any claim: In Witness whereof the said
GEORGE RIDING and WINNIFRED his Wife have hereunto put their hands and seals the
day and year aforesaid
Signed Sealed & Delivered in presence of
    YOUNGER JOHNSON,   GEORGE RIDING
    WEEDON ARNOLD, JAMES CARTER   WINNEY RIDING
  Received of BENJAMIN JOHNSON fifteen thousand weight of Crop Tobacco being the
consideration expressed in the said Deed February 1782
Witness YOUNGER JOHNSON,   GEORGE RIDING
    WEEDON ARNOLD, JAMES CARTER
  At a Court held for King George County the 7th day of February 1782
This Indented Deed of Bargain and Sale from under the hands and seals of GEORGE
RIDING and WINNIFRED his Wife with the Receipt thereon indorsed, to BENJAMIN JOHN-
SON was presented into Court by the said JOHNSON and proved by the Oaths of YOUNGER
JOHNSON, WEEDON ARNOLD and JAMES CARTER, And on the motion of the said BENJAMIN
JOHNSON was ordered to be recorded
            Test JOS: ROBINSON, Cl: Court

pp.   THIS INDENTURE made this twenty first day of January in the year of our Lord
1235- one thousand seven hundred and Eighty two Between JOHN COURTS and SUSAN-
1237   NA his Wife of County of FAIRFAX of one part and BENJAMIN JOHNSON of County
      of King George of other part; Whereas JOHN COURTS is intitled after the decease
of said JOHN COURTS's Grandfather, GEORGE RIDING, by virtue of a Marriage Contract
and since by virtue of a Deed of Trust recorded in King George Court to the tract of land
whereon said GEORGE RIDING now lives and heretofore has lived with the appurtenances containing Four hundred and one acres more or less. NOW THIS INDENTURE
WITNESSETH that JOHN COURTS and SUSANNA his Wife for sum of forty two thousand
pounds of tobacco to them paid or secured to be paid by BENJAMIN JOHNSON by these
presents do bargain and sell unto BENJAMIN JOHNSON his heirs all that his the said
JOHN COURTS right title claim and demand in and to the tract of land with the appurte-

nances, also his the said JOHN COURTS right title claim and demand in and to all houses orchards profits & emoluments to said land belonging; To have and to hold the tract of land containing Four hundred and one acres more or less and all the premises with the appurtenances unto BENJAMIN JOHNSON his heirs; And JOHN COURTS for himself and his heirs doth grant that he and his heirs the tract of land unto BENJAMIN JOHNSON his heirs against every person claiming or to claim the same by or under them shall warrant and forever defend by these presents; In Testimony whereof we the said JOHN COURTS and SUSANNA his Wife have hereunto put their hands and seals the day and year first before written

Signed Sealed and Delivered in presence of

FRANCIS THORNTON,	JOHN COURTS
JAMES CARTER, YOUNGER JOHNSON	SUSANNA COURTS

January 21st 1782. Received of BENJAMIN JOHNSON the sum of forty two thousand pounds of tobacco, the consideration in this Deed mentioned

Test FRANCIS THORNTON	JOHN COURTS
JAMES CARTER, YOUNGER JOHNSON	SUSANNA COURTS

In the Name of the Commonwealth of Virginia to SAMUEL OLDHAM and THOMAS BERRY, Gentlemen, Greeting. Whereas JOHN COURTS and SUSANNA his Wife late of County of King George, now of the County of FAIRFAX by their certain Deed of Bargain and Sale (the Commission for the privy examination of SUSANNA, the Wife of JOHN COURTS); Witness JOSEPH ROBINSON, Clerk of our said Court of King George this 17th day of January 1782, in the Seventh year of this Commonwealth   JOS: ROBINSON, C. Court

By virtue of the within Writ to us directed, we caused the said SUSANNA COURTS, Wife of JOHN COURTS, Gent., to appear before us and examined her privately and apart from her Husband touching the conveyance of the within mentioned land (the return of the execution of the privy examination of SUSANNA COURTS); Given under our hands and seals this 23d day of February 1782   SAMUEL OLDHAM
                                                                THOMAS BERRY

At a Court held for King George County the 7th day of February 1782
This Indented Deed of Bargain and Sale from under the hands and seals of JOHN COURTS & SUSANNA his Wife with the Receipt thereon indorsed to BENJAMIN JOHNSON, she being first privately examined by virtue of a Commission, was presented into Court by the said JOHNSON, was proved by the Oaths of FRANCIS THORNTON, JAMES CARTER and YOUNGER JOHNSON, the witnesses thereto, and on the motion of the said BENJAMIN JOHNSON was ordered to be recorded

                                Test JOS: ROBINSON, C: Court

pp.   THIS INDENTURE made this Sixth day of February one thousand seven hundred
1237-   and Eighty two Between GEORGE MARSHALL and ANN his Wife of County of King
1237a   George of one part and BENJAMIN JOHNSON of said County of other part; Witnes-
1238   seth that GEORGE MARSHALL and ANN his Wife in consideration of the sum of
               Twenty five pounds Specie to him in hand paid by these presents do bargain and
sell unto BENJAMIN JOHNSON his heirs our right title & interest of a certain Plantation and tract of land situate in Parish of Hanover in County of King George containing One hundred acres, which Land WILLIAM MARSHALL SENR. deceased, purchased of JOHN INGLAND and divised the same to his Son, BENJAMIN MARSHALL during his life and after his decease to descend to his four Sons, GEORGE, RUSH, HUDSON & MERRYMAN MARSHALL or the survivors of them to be equally divided amongst them as they shall think proper and which was recorded in County Court of King George which land hereby conveyed or meant to be conveyed be the same more or less lieth between the Lands

of THOMAS TURNER, SAMUEL KENDALL JUNR. and ANDREW HARRISON containing One
hundred acres by estimation, Together with all houses orchards profits & emoluments
to said Land with appurtenances; To have and to hold the Plantation and tract of Land
unto BENJAMIN JOHNSON his heirs; And GEORGE MARSHALL and ANN his Wife their
heirs the Plantation and tract of land with the appurtenances unto BENJAMIN JOHNSON
and his heirs against said GEORGE MARSHALL and ANN his Wife and their heirs will
warrant and defend against the claim of every person; In Witness whereof the said
GEORGE MARSHALL and ANN his Wife have hereunto put their hands and seals the day
and year aforesaid
Signed Sealed and Delivered in presence of
          JAMES CARTER,   GEORGE MARSHALL
          FRANCIS THORNTON,   YOUNGER JOHNSON   ANN MARSHALL
     Received of BENJAMIN JOHNSON Twenty five pounds Specie being the consideration
expressed in the aforesaid Deed February 6th day 1782
Test   JAMES CARTER,   GEORGE MARSHALL
          FRANCIS THORNTON,   YOUNGER JOHNSON
     In the Name of the Commonwealth of Virginia to THOMAS BERRY, WILLIAM HOOE and
BURDIT ASHTON Gentlemen, Greeting. Whereas GEORGE MARSHALL & ANN MARSHALL
of County of King George by their certain Deed of Bargain & Sale (the Commission for the
privy examination of ANN, the Wife of GEORGE MARSHALL); Witness JOSEPH ROBINSON, Clerk
of our said County Court of King George the 17th day of January 1782, in the Seventh
year of this Commonwealth   JOS: ROBINSON, C: Court
     By virtue of the within Writ to us directed, we the Subscribers went to the House of
Mr. GEORGE MARSHALL and then and there examined the within mentioned ANN MAR-
SHALL, Wife to said GEORGE MARSHALL, seperately and apart from her said Husband (the
return of the execution of the privy examination of ANN MARSHALL); Given under our hands
and seals at King George County the 1st day of May 1782
                                        THOMAS BERRY
                                        WILLIAM HOOE
     At a Court held for King George County the 7th day of February 1782
This Indented Deed of Bargain and Sale from under the hands and seals of GEORGE MAR-
SHALL and ANN his Wife to BENJAMIN JOHNSON with the Rect. thereon Indorsed, she
being first privately examined by virtue of a Commission, was presented into Court by
the said BENJAMIN JOHNSON and proved by the Oathes of JAMES CARTER, FRANCIS
THORNTON and YOUNGER JOHNSON, witnesses thereto, and on the motion of the said BEN-
JAMIN was ordered to be recorded
                    Test JOS: ROBINSON, C: Court

pp.   THIS INDENTURE made the 24th day of May one thousand seven hundred &
1238-   Eighty one Between MERRYMAN MARSHALL and PEGGY his Wife of County of
1240   ORANGE of one part and BENJAMIN JOHNSON of King George County of other
            part; Witnesseth that MERRYMAN MARSHALL and PEGGY his Wife for sum of
two thousand five hundred pounds of tobacco to them in hand paid by these presents do
bargain and sell unto BENJAMIN JOHNSON and his heirs our right title and Interest of a
certain Plantation & tract of land situait in the Parish of Hanover in King George County, containing One hundred acres, which land WM: MARSHALL SENR. purchased of JOHN
INGLAND and devised the same to his Son, BENJAMIN MARSHALL, during his natural
life and after his decease to descend to his four Sons, GEORGE, RUSH, HUDSON and
MERRYMAN or the Survivors of them to be equally divided amongst them as they shall
think proper; and which was recorded in the County Court of King George; which land

hereby conveyed or intended to be conveyed be the same more or less lyeth between the lands of THOMAS TURNER, SAMUEL KENDALL JUNR. and WILLIAM GREEN, containing by estimation one hundred acres, Together with all houses orchards profits & emoluments belonging; To have and to hold the Plantation and tract of land unto BENJAMIN JOHNSON his heirs and MERRYMAN MARSHALL and PEGGY his Wife doth hereby grant for themselves and their heirs that they and their heirs the Plantation and tract of land unto BENJAMIN JOHNSON his heirs against them and their heris shall warrant and forever defend; In Witness whereof the said MERRYMAN MARSHALL and PEGGY his Wife have hereunto put their hands and seals the day and year first mentioned

Signed Sealed and Acknowledged in presence of

   LAURANCE BAULTHROPE   MERRYMAN MARSHALL
   JOHN RANKINS,   PEGGY MARSHALL
   WILLIAM WILLIS

  Received this 24th day of May 1781, the sum of Two thousand five hundred pounds of tobacco of BENJAMIN JOHNSON this sum being the consideration mentioned in this Deed
Witness   LAURANCE BAULTHROPE   MERRYMAN MARSHALL
   JOHN RANKINS

  In the name of the Commonwealth of Virginia to HORATIO DADE and GEORGE FITZ-HUGH, Gent., Greeting. Whereas MERRYMAN MARSHALL and PEGGY his Wife of the County of King George by their certain Deed of Bargain and Sale (the Commission for the privy examination of PEGGY, the Wife of MERRYMAN MARSHALL); Witness JOSEPH ROBINSON, Clerk of our said County Court of King George this 23d day of May 1781, in the Sixth year of this Commonwealth   Test   JOS: ROBINSON, Cl: Court

  Personally appeared before us HORATIO DADE and GEORGE FITZHUGH, two of the Justices of the Peace for the County aforesaid, the within named PEGGY MARSHALL and being by us privately examined and apart from her Husband (the return of the execution of the privy examination of PEGGY MARSHALL); Given under our hands this 25th day of May 1781   HORATIO DADE
             GEORGE FITZHUGH

  At a Court held for King George County the 5th day of July 1782
This Indented Deed from under the hands and seals of MERRYMAN MARSHALL and PEGGY his Wife to BENJAMIN JOHNSON with the Rect. thereon indorsed, she being first privately examined by virtue of a Commission, was presented into Court by the said BENJAMIN JOHNSON and proved by the Oaths of LAURANCE BAULTHROPE, JOHN RANKINS and WILLIAM WILLIS and on the motion of the said BENJAMIN was ordered to be recorded   Test JOS: ROBINSON, Cl: Court

pp. THIS INDENTURE made this 26th day of September in the year of our Lord one
1240- thousand seven hundred & Eighty one Between ASTEN COMBS of County of King
1241 George of one part & THOMAS SMITH of aforesaid County of other part; Witnes-
   seth that ASTEN COMBS for sum of sixteen pounds Specie current money of Virginia to him in hand paid, by these presents doth bargain and sell unto THOMAS SMITH his heirs all that tract of land lying in County aforesaid containing by estimation Thirty acres more or less and bounded on said THOMAS SMITHs line, GARRARD WILLIAMSON & DANIEL WHITE's lines; To have and to hold the tract of land with all the appurtenames thereunto appertaining and said ASTEN COMBS his heirs doth by these presents warrant & forever defend the tract of land to THOMAS SMITH his heirs from the claim of any person, In Witness whereof the said ASTEN COMBS has hereunto set his hand & seal the day & year first above written

Signed Sealed and Delivered in presence of
  GEORGE STROTHER,   ASTEN his mark X COMBS
  NATHAN SMITH, FRANKY CARTER
  Received of THOMAS SMITH sixteen pounds current money it being the consideration
money within mentioned. As Witness my hand this twenty six day of September 1781
Test GEORGE STROTHER,   ASTEN his mark X COMBS
  NATHAN SMITH, FRANKY CARTER
  At a Court held for King George County the 1st day of November 1781
This Indented Deed of Bargain and Sale from under the hand and seal of ASTEN COMBS to
THOMAS SMITH with the Receipt thereon indorsed was presented into Court by the said
SMITH and acknowledged by the said ASTEN COMBS and on the motion of the said THO-
MAS SMITH was ordered to be recorded
      Test JOS: ROBINSON, Cl. Court

pp. THIS INDENTURE made the Seventh day of March one thousand seven hundred
1241- & eighty two Between JOHN KENDALL and SARAH his Wife of County of King
1242 George of one part and THOMAS SMITH of said County of other part; Witnesseth
    that JOHN KENDALL and SARAH his Wife for sum of Fifteen pounds specie to
them in hand paid by THOMAS SMITH by these presents do bargain and sell unto THO-
MAS SMITH his heirs a certain Plantaion and tract of land situaite in Parish of Hanover
and County aforesaid containing by estimation twenty five acres which land was sold
by DANIEL WHITE to JOHN KENDALL and Deed recorded in County Court of King George;
it is also part of a tract of Land sold by RICHARD & JOHN STROTHER to DANIEL WHITE,
deceased, and recorded in the County Court of King George; be the same more or less,
begins in said THOMAS SMITHs line at a Branch, thence runing up said Branch to a
Bottom between where JOSEPH DODD JUNR. formerly lived & JOHN ROSE SENR, deced., to
GREENs line, thence along the line to THOMAS SMITHs Land purchased of JOHN SKATH,
thence along said SMITHs line to the begining, containing by estimation twenty five
acres be the same more or less, Together with all houses orchards profits & emoluments
belonging; To have and to hold the Plantation and tract of land and all other the premises with appurtenances unto THOMAS SMITH his heirs; And JOHN KENDALL & SARAH
his Wife their heirs the plantation & tract of land with appurtenances to THOMAS
SMITH his heirs against all persons shall warrant and forever defend by these presents; In Witness whereof the said JOHN KENDALL & SARAH his Wife have hereunto put
their hands and seals the day and year first above written
Sealed and Delivered in presence of
  (no witnesses recorded)   JOHN KENDALL
              SARAH KENDALL
  Received this 7th day of March 1782 the sum of fifteen pounds specie of the within
named THOMAS SMITH, the said sum being the consideration mentioned in this Deed
          JOHN KENDALL
  At a Court held for King George County the 7th day of March 1782
This Indented Deed of Bargain and Sale from under the hands and seals of JOHN KEN-
DALL and SARAH his Wife, she being first privately examined, with the Receipt thereon
Indorsed to THOMAS SMITH was presented into Court by the said THOMAS and acknow-
ledged by the said JOHN KENDALL and SARAH his Wife to be their act and deed and on
the motion of said THOMAS SMITH was ordered to be recorded
      Test JOS: ROBINSON, C: Court

pp.   THIS INDENTURE made this thirteenth day of July in the year of our Lord 1777
1242-   Between ROBERT WASHINGTON of Saint Pauls Parish and King George County,
1244   Gent., and ALICE his Wife, and LAURANCE WASHINGTON the Younger of sd.
County and CATHARINE his Wife of one part and LUND WASHINGTON of FAIRFAX
County in the Commonwealth, Gent., of other part; Witnesseth that ROBERT WASHING-
TON and ALICE his Wife and LAURANCE WASHINGTON and CATHARINE his Wife for sum
of one thousand and two hundred pounds of lawful money of Virginia to them the said
LAURANCE WASHINGTON and ROBERT WASHINGTON in hand paid by LUND WASHINGTON
doth bargain and sell utno LUND WASHINGTON his heirs all the Plantation and tract of
land whereon MRS. ELIZABETH WASHINGTON, Mother of said ROBERT, LUND & LAURANCE
lately lived and died, situate in Saint Pauls Parish and County of King George and containing by estimation Six hundred acres; To have and to hold the plantation and tract of
land with all the premises unto LUND WASHINGTON his heirs and ROBERT WASHINGTON
and LAURANCE WASHINGTON their respective heirs or any person claiming under them
the plantation and tract of land unto LUND WASHINGTON his heirs against every person
shall warrant and forever defend; In Testimony whereof the said ROBERT WASHINGTON
and ALICE his said Wife, the said LAURANCE WASHINGTON and CATHARINE his Wife have
hereunto set their hands and affixed their seals the day & year first above written
Sealed and Delivered in presence of

JOHN WASHINGTON,	ROBERT WASHINGTON
ROBERT STITH,	LAURANCE WASHINGTON, JUNR.,
GEORGE JOHNSON,	ALICE WASHINGTON
TOWNSHEND DADE	CATHARINE WASHINGTON

Received of LUND WASHINGTON the within consideration of One thousand two hundred pounds current money of Virginia and acknowledge ourselves to be therewith
fully satisfied; Witness our hand this 30th day of July 1777

Test JOHN WASHINGTON,	ROBERT WASHINGTON
ROBERT STITH	LAURANCE WASHINGTON, JUNR.

The Commonwealth of Virginia to JOHN WASHINGTON and ROBERT STITH, Gentlemen,
Justices of King George County, Greeting. Whereas ROBERT WASHINGTON and ALICE his
Wife and LAURANCE WASHINGTON and CATHARINE his Wife of your said County by their
certain Deed of Bargain and Sale (the Commission for the privy examination of ALICE, the Wife
of ROBERT WASHINGTON and of CATHARINE, the Wife of LAURANCE WASHINGTON); Witness
JOSEPH ROBINSON, Clerk of our said Court this 30th day of July 1777, in the first year of
this Commonwealth   JOS: ROBINSON, C. K. G. Court
In Obedience to the within Commission, we did go to the within named ALICE and
CATHARINE severally and them and each of them did examine seperately privately and
apart from their said Husbands according to the requisition of the said Commission; (the
return of the execution of the privy examination of ALICE WASHINGTON and CATHARINE WASHING-
TON); Given under our hands this 30th day of July 1777
                                        JOHN WASHINGTON
                                        ROBERT STITH
At a Court held for King George County the (blank) day of (blank) 177(blank)
This Indented Deed of Bargain & Sale from under the hands and seals of ROBERT
WASHINGTON & ALICE his Wife and LAURANCE WASHINGTON and CATHARINE his Wife,
the said ALICE & CATHARINE being first privately examined by Commission, with the
Rect. thereon Indorsed to LUND WASHINGTON was presented into Court and proved by
the Oaths of the witnesses thereof and ordered to be recorded
                    Test JOS: ROBINSON, C. K. G. Court

pp.   THIS INDENTURE made this 24th day of January in the year of our Lord one
1245-   thousand seven hudnred and seventy eight Between WILLIAM PECK and JANE
1246   his Wife of the first part, JOHN PECK of the second part and GEORGE FITZHUGH,
         all of the County of King George of the third part; Whereas ROBERT PECK, Father
of said WILLIAM and JOHN, whose Eldest Son & heir at Law the said WILLIAM is, was in
his life time seized of a Mill & two acres of land, one acre on each side of the DOGUE
SWAMP, also of the Land covered by the Pond of said Mill, and the Lands adjoining on
all sides of said Pond, and being so seized by a certain Deed or Indenture dated the 14th
day of December in the year 1765 did convey & make over unto JOHN PECK among other
things half the said Mill during his the said JOHNs life, and also the said ROBERT being
so seized by his Last Will and Testament dated the 13th day of August 1771 did give and
bequeath to his Son, JOSEPH PECK, the said Mill with the acre of land on each side and
died so seized; which Deed & Will are recorded in the Office of the County of King
George; And whereas it is morally certain that said JOSEPH PECK is since dead intestate
and without issue, at whose death the said WILLIAM PECK as heir to his said Father and
Brother, JOSEPH, became seized of the said Land with the premises; NOW THIS INDEN-
TURE WITNESSETH that WILLIAM PECK and JOHN for sum of forty five pounds current
money to them in hand paid by GEORGE FITZHUGH, by these presents do bargain and sell
to GEORGE FITZHUGH his heirs all the said Mill, Mill Dam, two acres of Land and the Land
whereon the said Mill Pond may flow and the profits & emoluments to the premises
appertaining; To have and to hold the Mill, Mill Dam, Land and premises with the appurtenances unto GEORGE FITZHUGH his heirs and WILLIAM PECK and JANE his Wife
and JOHN PECK and their heirs the Mill, Mill Dam, Land & Premises unto GEORGE FITZ-
HUGH his heirs against all persons shall warrant and forever defend by these presents;
In Testimony whereof the said WILLIAM PECK & JANE his Wife and JOHN PECK hereunto
set their hands and seals the day and year first above written
Signed Sealed & Delivered in presence of
          THOMAS TYLER   WILLIAM PECK
                                                 JANE her mark X   PECK
                                                 JOHN PECK
     Be it remembered that on the 24th day of January 1778, peaceable and quiet posses-
sion and seisen of the Mill Dam and other the premises in the within Deed contained
was delivered by the within named WILLIAM, JANE & JOHN PECK to the within named
GEORGE FITZHUGH according to the form & effect thereof in presence of
                                                 THOMAS TYLER &
                                                 GEORGE PECK
     24th January 1778. Then received of the within named GEORGE FITZHUGH the sum of
Forty five pounds current money being the consideration within mentioned to be paid
by him to
Test   THOS: TYLER   WILLIAM PECK
                                                 JOHN PECK
     KNOW ALL MEN by these presents that we WILLIAM PECK and JOHN PECK of
County of King George are held and firmly bound unto GEORGE FITZHUGH of said County,
Gent., in the sum of Ninety pounds current money to the which payment well and truly
to be made we bind ourselves our heirs firmly by these presents; Sealed with our seals
and dated this 24th day of January 1778
     THE CONDITION of the above obligation is such tht whereas WILLIAM & JOHN PECK
have this day by Deed of Feoffment conveyed to GEORGE FITZHUGH & his heirs a certain
Mill, two acres of land and the Dam & the land whereon the Water of Mill Pond may flow
with the appurtenances; And whereas by Accident the said Mill was destroyed & by the

default of the said WILLIAM & JOHN in not rebuilding the same within the time limitted by Law, said GEORGE; will be obliged to Petition the County Court for leave to build the said Mill in manner prescribed by Act of Assembly. Now if WILLIAM &JOHN shall refund the said GEORGE his heirs all expences relating to such Petition summoning Jury and any sum of money to which he may be found liable by such Jury, Then this obligation to be void, otherwise to remain in full force
Sealed and Delivered in presence of
    THOMAS TYLER   WILLIAM PECK
                                     JOHN PECK
   At a Court held for King George County the 7th day of March 1778
This Indented Deed with the Livery & Seisin thereon from under the hand and seal of WILLIAM PECK & JANE his Wife and JOHN PECK with the Receipt thereon Indorsed to GEORGE FITZHUGH was presented into Court by the said GEORGE, the said JANE being first privately examined, was acknowledged by the said parties to be their act & deed & on motion of said GEORGE FITZHUGH was ordered to be recorded; And the Endemnification from WILLIAM & JOHN PECK was acknowledged & ordered to be recorded
               Test JOS: ROBINSON, C: Court

p.   THIS INDENTURE made this 19th day of November 1778 and in the Third year of
1247   the Commonwealth of Virginia Between WILLIAM GREEN JUNR. and ELIZABETH
       his Wife of County of CULPEPER of one part and JAMES MARDERS of King George
County of other part; Witnesseth that WILLIAM GREEN & ELIZABETH his Wife for sum of Three hundred pounds current money of Virginia, by these presents doth bargain and sell unto JAMES MARDERS his heirs one certain tract of land lying in Parish of Hanover & Washington containing by estimation one hundred acres be the same more or less; and bounded, Begining at the lower corner of his land, extending thence South seventy four degrees and binding on the land of DANIEL WHITE, fifty nine poles to a white Oak in the line of said WHITE, thence North twenty one & half West two hundred & thirty two poles to two Dogwoods, thence North fifty nine degrees East seventy five poles into the lower line of said GREENs Land, thence in the said line to the begining, Together with all appurtenances rents issues and profits thereof; To have and to hold the hereby granted one hundred acres to JAMES MARDERS hisheirs free from the claim and demand of WILLIAM GREEN his heirs and against the claim and demand of any person and will warrant and forever defend the same; In Witness whereof the said WILLIAM GREEN & ELIZABETH his Wife hath hereunto set their hands and seals the day & year above written
Signed sealed & delivered in presence of
    BENJAMIN JOHNSON,   WILLIAM GREEN
    WOFFENDAL KENDAL,
    AARON THORNLEY & LAURANCE BAULTHROPE
 Received of Mr. JAMES MARDERS three hundred pounds current money of Virginia being the consideration money within mentioned
Test (same four witnesses)   WILLIAM GREEN
   At a Court held for King George County the (blank) day of (blank) 177(blank)
This Indented Deed from under the hand and seal of WILLIAM GREEN was presented into Court & proved by the witnesses thereto & ordered to be recorded
         Test   JOS: ROBINSON C. Court

pp.   THIS INDENTURE TRIPARTITE made this Tenth day of January in the year of
1248- our Lord one thousand seven hundred and seventy eight Between WILLIAM
1249   THORNTON of County of King George of first part; ELISABETH THORNTON, Wife of

the said WILLIAM THORNTON and FRANCIS, ELIZABETH and ANN THORNTON, Children of
the second part; and ANTHONY THORNTON of County of CAROLINE and FRANCIS THORN-
TON, Brother of said WILLIAM THORNTON, Gent., of the third part; Witnesseth that WIL-
LIAM THORNTON for the settling and securing a compleat sufficient and seperate maintenance for ELIZABETH THORNTON, his Wife, and also to make a suitable provision for
the support, maintenance and education of the said three Children, FRANCIS, ELIZA-
BETH & ANN THORNTON, and in consideration of the natural love and affection which he
has for them and for the sum of Five shillings to him in hand paid by ANTHONY &
FRANCIS THORNTON, by these presents doth bargain sell and release unto ANTHONY
THORNTON AND FRANCIS THORNTON and their heirs all said WILLIAM THORNTONs Estate
in the County of King George consisting of the tract of land on which he now resides
with all advantages & privileges thereunto belonging, with all houses orchards and all
other improvements and also the following slaves, to wit, David, Will, Jo, Harry, Stephen, David, Ceasar, Willis, Joan, Lucy, Winney, Avarilla, Reubin, Alice, Willough-
by, Tina, Chloe, Lucy, Avarilla, Sam, Tom, Joshua, Aaron, Simon, Mary, Judy,
Daniel & Thorn with their future increase, all the stocks of horses, cattle, sheep & hogs,
houshold & kitchen furniture, riding chair and harness, Together with two thirds of
the Crop of every kind whatsoever at this time upon the Estate and all the stock of provisions laid in for the use of WILLIAM THORNTONs family and the increase of the stocks
of every kind; To have and to hold the land premises with their appurtenances unto
ANTHONY THORNTON and FRANCIS THORNTON and their heirs for the several uses herein after mentioned limited and declared and for no other use; that is to say, to the use of
ANTHONY THORNTON and FRANCIS THORNTON for the paymt. of two thirds of all sums of
money as other things which may be due and owing from WILLIAM THORNTON on any
Account and from and after the paymt. thereof said ANTHONY THORNTON and FRANCIS
THORNTON shall suffer and permit ELIZABETH THORNTON to receive one half of the profits arising from the Estate and premises during the term of her life if said WILLIAM
THORNTON should survive her, to her sole and seperate use and shall also suffer her to
hold & occupy all or any of the houses and buildings upon the said Estate without inter-
ruption or molestation and ANTHONY THORNTON and FRANCIS THORNTON shall apply the
residue of the profits arising from the Estate to the maintainance & education of the
Children, FRANCIS, ELIZABETH and ANN untill they shall arrive respectively to the age
of twenty one years or are married and from and after the death of said ELIZABETH, the
Wife, then the said FRANCIS, ELIZABETH, ANN & SUSANNA COURTS (another Daughter of
the said WILLIAM THORNTON) or their legal representatives for such Estates as WIL-
LIAM THORNTON by his Last Will and Testament or Instrument of Writing hereby exe-
cuted in his life shall direct and appoint; In Witness whereof the said WILLIAM THORN-
TON, ANTHONY and FRANCIS THORNTON have hereunto set their hands & seals the day
and year first above written
Sealed and Acknowledged in presence of
     HENRY FITZHUGH, WILLIAM BARNARD,   WILLIAM THORNTON
     HENRY WASHINGTON,
     WILLIAM FITZHUGH JUNR., BAILEY WASHINTON JUNR.
  Received the within consideration mentioned; Witness my hand the day & hear within
written
     WILLIAM BARNARD, HENRY FITZHUGH,   WILLIAM THORNTON
     HENRY WASHINGTON & WILLIAM FITZHUGH JUNR.
  At a Court held for King George County the 3d day of April 1778
This Indented Deed from under the hand & seal of WILLIAM THORNTON to ANTHONY
THORNTON &c. with the Receipt thereon was presented into Court & proved by the Oaths

of HENRY WASHINGTON, WILLIAM FITZHUGH JUNR. and BAILEY WASHINGTON JUNR.,
witnesses thereto, and was ordered to be recorded
                    Test JOS: ROBINSON, C: Court

pp.   THIS INDENTURE made the fifth day of October in year of our Lord one thousand
1250-   seven hundred & seventy seven Between MICHAEL WALLACE and LETTICE his
1252   Wife of one part and MOSES ROWLEY of County of King George of other part;
         Whereas the said MOSES ROWLEY being seizen in fee Tail of certain lands in
County of King George has agreed to dispose thereof unto MICHAEL WALLACE and
convey a fee simple Estate therein unto him & his heirs for the performance of which
said agreement MOSES ROWLEY entered into a Bond in the penalty of one thousand
pounds payable to MICHAEL WALLACE which Bond is dated the fifth day of April 1776;
and is now in full force; And whereas the Wife of MOSES ROWLEY hath not yet conveyed unto MICHAEL WALLACE her right of Dower in the lands which remains to be
done to compleat the title, but MICHAEL WALLACE in the mean time is willing to fulfill
his part of the Agreement; THIS INDENTURE WITNESSETH that MICHAEL WALLACE and
LETTICE his Wife in consideration of MOSES ROWLEY's conveying the fee simple Estate to
MICHAEL WALLACE and his heirs of and in three hundred acres of land more or less
according to the recited Agreement, by these presents do bargain and sell and make
over unto MOSES ROWLEY and his heirs all that parcel of land in County of King George
containing Two hundred acres more or less & bounded, Begining at two persimon trees
on South side a Path leading from a New House built for MOSES ROWLEY to the CHURCH
ROAD and runing Et. along to a marked Hiccory, thence to a Maple standing on South
side the head of Gully, thence down the Gully to a Spring Branch, thence down the
Spring Branch to the POPLAR SWAMP, thence down the Swamp to REUBIN OWEN's Line,
thence along the line of OWENS to the corner of ROSSERs Patent, thence a straight
course up JOHN ROWLEYs Spring Branch to the begining; Together with all rights members and appurtenances belonging; To have and to hold the parcel of land to MOSES
ROWLEY his heirs, Provided and upon condition that ANN ROWLEY, the Wife of MOSES
ROWLEY shall convey & release her right of Dower in the said land unto MICHAEL
WALLACE his heirs and be content with the courses of the land as herein before stated
and to which both consented for the conveniences of woodlands although the same does
but contain two hundred acres; And MICHAEL WALLACE and LETTICE his Wife for them-
selves their heirs the tract of land and premises with the appurtenances unto MOSES
ROWLEY his heirs against the claim of every person shall warrant and forever defend;
In Witness whereof the said MICHAEL WALLACE and LETTICE his Wife have hereunto set
their hands & seals the day & year first above written
Sealed & Delivered in presence of
            (no witnesses recorded)   MICHAEL WALLACE
                                                             LETTICE WALLACE
     In the name of the Commonwealth of Virginia to HORATIO DADE & JOHN POLLARD,
Justices of the County of King George, Greeting. Whereas MICHAEL WALLACE and
LETTICE his Wife of your said County by their certain Deed (the Commission for the privy
examination of LETTICE, the Wife of MICHAEL WALLACE); Witness JOSEPH ROBINSON, Clerk of
our said Court of King George this 16th day of October in the Second year of the Commonwealth   Test JOS: ROBINSON, Cl: Court
     By virtue of the within to us directed, we the Subscribers met at the House of
MICHAEL WALLACE and examined LETTICE WALLACE seperate & apart from her Husband
whether she was willing to acknowledge her right in & to the land sold by MICHAEL
WALLACE to MOSES ROWLEY (the return of the execution of the privy examination of LETTICE

WALLACE); In Witness whereof I have hereunto set my hand and seale
Taken before us   LETTICE WALLACE
     HORATIO DADE   )
     JOHN POLLARD JUNR.) 26th Novr. 1777
   At a Court held for King George County the 7th day of May 1778
This Indented Deed from under the hands and seals of MICHAEL WALLACE and LETTICE
his Wife to MOSES ROWLEY, she being first privately examined, was presented into Court
and acknowledged by the said parties to be their act & deed, was ordered to be recorded
                    Test JOS: ROBINSON, Cl: Court

p.   KNOW ALL MEN by these presents that I ZACHARIAH ROSE of CHARLES County
1252   MARYLAND have bargained and sold all my right and title of Negro Nan, Phill
          & Sall now in the possession of TOWNSHEND DADE in Saint Pauls Parish STAFFORD
County and all their increase and by these presents do bargain and sell unto FRANCIS
ROSE in Saint Pauls Parish STAFFORD County all my right and title of Nan, Phill & Bett in
the possession of Mr. TOWNSHEND DADE; In consideration of Ten pounds current money
of Virginia and a Horse or a Mare. In case FRANCIS ROSE do not recover the above
mentioned Negros by Law suit of Mr. TOWNSHEND DADE, the said ZACHARIAH ROSE is not
to have one farthing by Agreement before these evidences; And I do hereby warrant
and forever defend the above mentioned Negros, Nan, Phill & Sall from the claim of
every person claiming by from or under me; In Witness whereof I have hereunto set
my hand seal this 20th day of June 1772
Test   WILLIAM McGILVERY   ZACHARIAH his mark X ROSE
         WILLIAM THOMPSON, JOHN BOWEN
    (No recording shown for this Indenture Bargain and Sale.)

pp.   THIS INDENTURE made the Tenth day of November one thousand seven hundred
1253-   and seventy eight Between JAMES DUNLOP of County of ESSEX, Merchant, of one
1254   part and HUGH GORDON of County of King George of other part; Witnesseth that
           for sum of Three hundred pounds current money of Virginia to JAMES DUNLOP
in hand paid by HUGH GORDON by these presents doth bargain and sell unto HUGH GOR-
DON and his heirs all that tract of land lying in Parish of Hanover & County of King
George containing by estimation one hundred acres more or less and which JAMES
DUNLOP purchased of JOHN BODINGTON and is bounded by the Lands of THOMAS TURNER
Esqr., FRANCIS THORNTON, Gent., and AIMY SETTLE and all houses orchards profits and
appurtenances belonging; To have and to hold the land hereby conveyed with appur-
tenances unto HUGH GORDON his heirs free and clear from all Incumbrances (the Quit-
rents and fees hereafter to become due only excepted); In Witness whereof the said
JAMES DUNLOP hath hereunto set his hand and seal the day and year first above written
Sealed and Delivered in the presence of
        FRANCIS THORNTON,   JAMES DUNLOP
        THOMAS PARKER, JAMES CONDUIT
   Received the day of the date of this Indenture of Mr. HUGH GORDON the sum of Three
hundred pounds current money, being the consideration therein mentioned, reced. by
me;
Test   FRANCIS THORNTON,   JAMES DUNLOP
         THOMAS PARKER, JAMES CONDUIT
   At a Court held for King George County the 1st day of July 1779
This Indented Deed of Bargain and Sale from under the hand and seal of JAMES DUNLOP
with the Receipt thereon Indorsed to HUGH GORDON was presented into Court and

proved by the Oaths of the witnesses thereto & on the motion of the said GORDON was
ordered to be recorded   Test JOS: ROBINSON, Cl: Court

p   THIS INDENTURE made the 6th day of January in the year of our Lord one thou-
1255   sand seven hundred and seventy nine Between ANTHONY PRICE of County of
        King George of one part and JOHN PRICE of same County of other part; Witnes-
seth that ANTHONY PRICE for sum of five shillings current money of Virginia to him in
hand paid by JOHN PRICE, by these presents doth bargain and sell unto JOHN PRICE all
that tract of land situate in Parish of Washington and County of King George containing One hundred acres more or less which tract of land was purchased by my Father,
THOMAS PRICE, of WILLIAM BRUTON and THOMAS MONDAY and conveyed to him by Deed
of Sale which Deed was duly proved among the Records of the General Court; And all
houses orchards profits and appurtenances belonging; To have and to hold the tract of
land & premises unto JOHN PRICE his heirs from the date of these presents during the
term of one full year paying therefore the rent of one year of Indian Corn at the expiration of the said term if lawfully demanded to the intent that by virtue of these presents and of the Statute for transferring uses into possession JOHN PRICE may be in
actual possession of the tract of land and premises and thereby be the better enabled to
accept a release of the reversion and inheritance thereof; In Witness whereof the said
ANTHONY PRICE hath to this Indenture set his hand and seal the day & year first above
written
        COLVERT JONES,   WILLIAM BUNBURY,   ANTHONY PRICE
        JOHN SMITH, JOHN BUNBURY
    At a Court held for King George County the 4th day of August 1779
This Indented Deed of Bargain and Sale from under the hand & seal of ANTHONY PRICE
to JOHN PRICE was presented into Court by JOHN PRICE and proved by the witnesses
thereto & on the motion of the said JOHN PRICE was ordered to be recorded
                        Test JOS: ROBINSON, C: Court

p   THIS INDENTURE made the 5th day of August one thousand seven hundred and
1256   seventy nine Between ROBERT STROTHER of County of King George of one part &
        WILLIAM SHROPSHIRE of aforesaid County of other part; Witnesseth that
ROBERT STROTHER for sum of seven hundred and fifty pounds current money of Virginia to him in hand paid by WILLIAM SHROPSHIRE by these presents do bargain and
sell unto WILLIAM SHROPSHIRE his heirs a certain Plantation and tract of land whereon ROBERT STROTHER now lives, lying in Parish of Hanover & County of King George,
containing Ninety and a half acres, which land hereby conveyed or intended to be conveyed be the same more or less lieth between the Land of Col. JOHN SKINKER, MARGT.
STROTHER and LANDON CARTER and was surveyed by BENJAMIN BERRY the 17th June
1761; Together with all houses orchards profits & emoluments belonging; To have and
to hold the Plantation & tract of land with the appurtenances unto WILLIAM SHROP-
SHRIE his heirs and ROBERT STROTHER and his heirs the Plantation and tract of land
unto WILLIAM SHROPSHIRE his heirs against all persons shall warrant & forever
defend; In Witness whereof the said ROBERT STROTHER have hereunto put his hand &
seal the day & year first above written
Sealed and acknowledged in presence of
        (no witnesses recorded)   ROBERT STROTHER
    Received the 5th day of August 1779 of the above named WILLIAM SHROPSHIRE seven
hundred and fifty pounds current money of Virginia being the consideration in this
Deed mentioned   ROBERT STROTHER

At a Court held for King George County the 5th day of August 1779
ROBERT STROTHER came into Court & acknowledged this Deed with the Receipt thereon
to WILLIAM SHROPSHIRE which on the motion of the said WILLIAM was ordered to be
recorded   Test JOS: ROBINSON, Cl: Cur:

p.   WHEREAS JOHN THORNLEY late of King George County did in his life time put
1257   into the possession of each of his Children, one Negro, namely to his Daughter,
          ELIZABETH, one Negro girl named Alice; to his Daughter, MARY, one Negro girl
named Winny, to his Son, AARON THORNLEY one Negro boy named Daniel; to his Son,
JOHN, one Negro boy named Isaac, and to his Son, EPAPHRODITUS one Negro boy named
Cyrus, and did on his death bed desire that his said Children should keep and possess the
said Negros for ever; And Whereas no such Gift is lawfull and the Widow of the said
JOHN THORNLEY, deceased, have a Right of Dower in the said slaves, We therefore the
Widow and the Children of JOHN THORNLEY, deceased, and their Representatives have
mutually agreed to make over & confirm to each other lawfull right & possession of the
slaves and their increase they are or were in possession of; And do agree by these presents for our selves our heirs to give and grant to each other our Right Title and Claim
to each of the slaves and their increase for ever; And further that this Agreement be
recorded in the County aforesaid. In Witness whereof we have hereunto set our hands
and seals this 2d. day of September 1779.
Sealed and Delivered in the presence of
          GEORGE MARSHALL,   ANNE her mark X THORNLEY
          JOHN WREN   BENJAMIN BERRY
          JOHN PEACH   THOMAS POLLARD
                                           AARON THORNLEY
                                           JOHN THORNLEY
                                           EPAS. THORNLEY
       At a Court held for King George County the 2d day of Sept. 1779
This Agreement between ANNE THORNLEY and others was presented into Court and
proved by the Oaths of the witnesses thereto and on the motion of the said parties then
present, was ordered to be recorded
                        Test JOS: ROBINSON, Cl: Court

p.   THIS INDENTURE made this 16th day of April 1779 Between ANN WHITE of the
1258   Parish of Hanover and County of King George of one part and JOHN LOVELL of
          the same County and Parish of other part; Whereas ANN WHITE hath two fea-
ther beds and furniture, three pewter dishes, four pewter basons, eight pewter plates,
one weaveing loom, three slays and harnesses, one spining wheel, two cows & their
increase, one yearling, five hogs, one Cupboard, one Chest, one large Bible, two iron
potts, on box Iron & heaters, one frying pan, one brass spice mortar. NOW THIS INDEN-
TURE Witnesseth that ANN WHITE as well for the Special Trust and confidence she has
in JOHN LOVELL as also for sum of five shillings current money of Virginia to her in
hand paid by JOHN LOVELL by these presents do bargain & sell unto JOHN LOVELL his
heirs all the above mentioned houshold furniture and stocks of cattle and hogs against
the claim or demand of said ANN WHITE; To have & to hold the above mentioned houshold furniture & stocks of Cattle & hogs unto JOHN LOVELL his heirs &c., In Trust,
nevertheless & to & for the only proper use of ANN WHITE to dispose of as she thinks
proper and for no other purpose; In Witness whereof I have hereunto set my hand and
seal the day and year first above written

Signed sealed and delivered in presence of
          GEORGE RIDINGS   ANN WHITE
          THOMAS SMITH, LOVEL HARRISON
     At a Court held for King George County the 2d day of September 1779
This Deed of Trust from under the hand and seal of ANN WHITE was presented into Court
by JOHN LOVELL & proved by the Oath of THOMAS SMITH and on the motion of the said
LOVELL was ordered to be recorded
                         Test JOS: ROBINSON, C: Court

pp   THIS INDENTURE made the eighth day of March in the year of our Lord
1259-   1779 and in the Third year of the Commonwealth of Virginia Between JOHN
1260   ASHTON SENR. & HANNAH his Wife of County of King George and Parish of Han-
          over of one part and JOHN PRICE of County & Parish aforesaid of other part; Wit-
nesseth that JOHN ASHTON SENR. and HANNAH his Wife for sum of Two hundred pounds
current money of Virginia in hand paid by JOHN PRICE by these presents doth bargain
and sell unto JOHN PRICE his heirs all that tract of land situate in County & Parish
aforesaid containing by estimation One hundred & seventy five acres more or less
which formerly belonged to RICHARD ARROWSMITH being bounded, vizt., on SMITHs
Land Eastward to ANTOPIAN RUN, on the side of ANTOPIAN RUN Southwards to the land
of WILLIAM BUTTON or JOHN PRICE, on the said BUTTONs line Westward to the land of
JAMES DISHMAN and from said DISHMANs Land Northward to the said SMITHs Land, and
the rents & profits thereof; To have and to hold the land and premises with the appurtenances unto JOHN PRICE his heirs clear of all titles and demands and JOHN ASHTON and
HANNAH his Wife for themselves & their heirs unto JOHN PRICE his heirs do warrant &
forever defend the land against the claims and demands of all persons; In Testimony
whereof the said JOHN ASHTON & HANNAH his Wife have hereunto set their hands &
seals the day & year above written
          WILLIAM LOVELL,   COLVERT JONES   JOHN ASHTON
          JAMES DISHMAN,   CHARLES ASHTON JUNR.   HANNAH ASHTON
     March 8th day of 1779. Then received from JOHN PRICE the sum of Two hundred
pounds current money of Virginia, being the consideration above mentioned; Witness
my hand & Seal   JOHN ASHTON
     At a Court held for King George County the 2d. day of September 1779
This Indented Deed of Bargain and Sale from under the hands and seals of JOHN ASHTON
and HANNAH his Wife to JOHN PRICE was presented into Court & fully proved by the
Oaths of the witnesses thereto, and on the motion of the said JOHN PRICE was ordered to
be recorded   Test JOS: ROBINSON, C: Court

pp.   THIS INDENTURE made the twenty ninth day of September in the year 1779 Be-
1260-   tween SAMUEL PECK, Planter, and MARY his Wife of one part and GEORGE FITZ-
1261   HUGH, Gent., both of the Parish of Brunswick in County of King George of the
          other part; Witnesseth that SAMUEL and MARY PECK for sum of Eight hundred
pounds twenty & eight current money of Virginia to them in hand paid by GEORGE
FITZHUGH by these presents do bargain and sell unto GEORGE FITZHUGH and his heirs a
certain tract of land situate in Parish and County aforesaid and is bounded, Beginning
at a marked white Oak standing on East side the DOGUE SWAMP near the mouth of a
Branch, corner to this Land and the land of WILLIAM SHROPSHIRE, extending Westerly
up the meanders of the Branch 140 poles to the land of JAMES KAY, thence leaving the
Branch and binding on KAYs line S. 23 W. 160 poles to a marked white Oak in the said
KAYs line, thence S. 31 West 14 pole to another marked white Oak standing in a Branch

of the COW TAIL SWAMP, thence So. 20 W. 35 poles to the line of Colo: SKINKERs Land and
to this Land and the Land of WILLIAM PECK, thence binding on said PECKs land N. 74 E.
to the lower Corner of the aforesaid SHROPSHIREs Land at the mouth of a small Branch;
thence up the meanders of the Branch to the land thereof, thence N. 61 E. 114 pole to
the begining; To have and to hold the tract of land according to the above bounds together with all houses orchards rights members & appurtenances thereof to GEORGE FITZ-
HUGH his heirs and SAMUEL PECK for himself and for his heirs doth covenant with
GEORGE FITZHUGH his heirs against the claim & demand of every person shall warrant
and by these presents forever defend; In Testimony whereof the said SAMUEL PECK
and MARY his Wife set their hands and fixed their seals the day month & year first
above written
Signed Sealed & Delivered in presence of us
            (no witnesses recorded)   SAMUEL PECK
                                                        MARY PECK
    September xxix 1779. Then received of GEORGE FITZHUGH the sum of eight hundred &
twenty eight pounds current money, the consideration within mentioned to be paid to
us; Witness our hands & seals   SAMUEL PECK
                                                        MARY PECK
    At a Court held for King George County the 7th day of October 1779
This Indented Deed of Bargain and Sale from under the hands and seals of SAMUEL PECK
and MARY his Wife with the Receipt thereon Indorsed to GEORGE FITZHUGH, the said
MARY being first privately examined, was presented into Court by the said GEORGE and
was acknowledged by the said SAMUEL PECK and MARY his Wife to be their proper act &
deed, And on the motion of the said GEORGE FITZHUGH was ordered to be recorded
                    Test JOS: ROBINSON, C: Court

p.   KNOW ALL MEN by these presents that I THOMAS FIGLIN of King George County
1262   in consideration of the affection and regard which I have and bear unto my Son
          in Law, WILLIAM JENKINS of DUMFRIES in PRINCE WILLIAM County in Virginia
and for divers other good causes and considerations me thereunto moving by these presents do give unto WILLIAM JENKINS one Negro boy Child named George and at this
time in the possession of said WILLIAM JENKINS. To have and to hold the Negro boy
George to WILLIAM JENKINS and assigns, and I the said THOMAS FIGLIN the Negro boy
George to WILLIAM JENKINS and assigns against all persons shall warrant and forever
defend by these presents; In Witness whereof I the said THOMAS FIGLIN have hereunto
set my hand & affixed my seal this 9th day of June 1778
Sealed and Delivered in the presence of
        JOHN FICKLIN,   THOMAS FICKLIN
        JOHN SWETNAM
    At a Court held for King George County the 3d day of Decr: 1778
This Deed of Gift from under the hand and seal of THOMAS FICKLIN to WILLIAM JENKINS
was presented into Court by the said JENKINS and proved by the Oaths of JOHN FICKLIN
& JOHN SWETNAM and on the motion of said WILLIAM JENKINS was ordered to be
recorded   Test JOS: ROBINSON C: Court

pp.   THIS INDENTURE made the xix day of May in the year of our Lord one thousand
1263- seven hundred and seventy six Between JAMES HACKLEY of one part and HAY
1265   TALIAFERRO of the other part. Whereas JOHN HACKLEY in and by his Last Will
          and Testament bearing date the eight day of August in the year of our Lord one
thousand seven hundred and sixty among other things devised his whole lands unto his

Wife, JUDITH HACKLEY, during her natural life, And in case his Wife, whom he appointed his sole Executrix of his Last Will and Testament, could not discharge his debts without selling his personal Estate and Negros, that then she should have full power to sell and dispose of his lands in the County of King George wehreon he then lived and the money arising from such sale after discharging his just debts to be placed out at Interest or land or slaves as she should think fit for the purpose mentioned in the said Will and so it was found necessary to make sale of the land to enable JUDITH HACK-LEY to discharge the debts of JOHN HACKLEY and to fulfill the conditions of his said Will; said JUDITH HACKLEY pursuant to the Last Will and Testament of JOHN HACKLEY did for the sum of Four hundred pounds current money to her in hand paid by HAY TALIA-FERRO bargain and sell unto HAY TALIAFERRO all that tract of land whereon JOHN HACKLEY formerly lived and the said JUDITH HACKLEY lately dwelt., situate in County of King George at the place commonly called and known by the name of HACKLEYS FERRY containing in the whole one hundred acres be the same more or less together with all houses fences orchards profits and appurtenances to the same belonging; To have and to hold the tract of land and premises with appurtenances unto HAY TALIAFERRO his heirs which tract of land was conveyed to HAY TALIAFERRO by a Deed of Lease bearing date the eighth day of June in the year one thousand seven hundred & sixty three and by a Deed of Release bearing date the ninth dy of July in the year one thousand seven hundred and sixty three, to which Deeds JUDITH HACKLEY was a party, and which Deeds were duly executed but by mistake were proved & recorded in the Court of CULPEPER contrary to an Act of Assembly made in the nineteenth year of our late Sovereign Lord King George the second, which requires that all Deeds for conveying lands shall be acknowledged or proved & recorded in the General Court or in that County Court where Land to be conveyed lies; NOW THIS INDENTURE WITNESSETH that in performance of a Covenant for further assurance in the said Deed of Release contained as also for the sum of Four hundred pounds current money to JUDITH HACKLEY truly paid by HAY TALIAFERRO and in consideration of the sum of Ten shillings to him JAMES HACKLEY well and truly paid by HAY TALIAFERRO by these presents doth release and forever quit claim unto HAY TALIAFERRO his now being in his actual & peaceable possession by virtue of the before mentioned Deeds of Lease and Release and to his heirs all the afore-said tract of land mentioned in the aforesaid Deeds of Lease and Release; To have and to hold unto HAY TALIAFERRO and JAMES HACKLEY doth hereby promise for himself and his heirs that the premises aforesaid unto HAY TALIAFERRO and his heirs against JAMES HACKLEY and his heirs shall warrant & forever defend by these presents; In Witness whereof the said JAMES HACKLEY hath hereunto set his hand and seal the day and year first above written
Signed Sealed & Delivered in presence of
    A: BUCHANAN,   JAMES HACKLEY
    BENJAMIN DAY,   JOHN ROSE
   At a Court held for King George County the 7th day of October 1779
This Indented Deed from under the hand and seal of JAMES HACKLEY to HAY TALIAFER-RO was presented into Court and proved by the Oaths of the witnesses thereto subscribed and on the motion of the said HAY TALIAFERRO was ordered to be recorded
       Test JOS: ROBINSON, C. Court

p.   TO ALL PEOPLE to whom these presents shall come, I GEORGE RIDING send
1266 Greeting. Know ye that I GEORGE RIDING of the Parish of Hanover in the County
     of King George, Planter, for divers good causes and in consideration of the love
and affection which I have & do bear towards my loving Daughter, ELIZABETH COURTS,

of the same County & Parish, Widow, have given & granted & by these presents do give
and grant unto ELIZABETH COURTS her heirs seven Negros, to wit, Ben, Sarah & her
Child, Cilla, Patt & her three Children, to wit, Bett, James and a boy not Christened & all
their increase all in my possession in the Parish aforesaid for which before the
signing of these presents I have delivered her the sd. ELIZABETH COURTS an Inventory
signed with my own hand & bearing even date; To have and to hold the Negros to
ELIZABETH COURTS her heirs from henceforth as her and their proper Negros absolute-
ly without any manner of condition; In Witness whereof I have hereunto set my hand
and seal this seventeenth day of November 1778
Signed sealed & delivered in presence of us
        JOHN LOVELL,   GEORGE RIDING
        MOSES KENDAL,   FRANCIS THORNTON
    At a Court held for King George County the 2th day of December 1778
This Deed of Gift from under the hand and seal of GEORGE RIDING to ELIZABETH COURTS
was presented into Court & proved by the Oaths of the witnesses thereto subscribed &
ordered to be recorded   Test JOS: ROBINSON, C. Court

pp.   THIS INDENTURE made the first day of April in the year one thousand seven
1267-   hundred & seventy nine Between JOHN MARTIN, JOHN WASHINGTON, THOMAS
1268   TURNER and BECKWITH BUTLER, Gent., of one part and DOCTOR WILLIAM BANK-
         HEAD of the other part; Whereas by an Act intitled "An Act for disposing several
Vestrys" made at an Assembly begun in October last, it was enacted among other things
that the GLEBE of the Parish of Washington with the appurtenances be vested in the
said JOHN MARTIN, JOHN WASHINGTON, THOMAS TURNER & BECKWITH BUTTLER, Gentn.
Commissioners in Trust that they or any three of them shall by Deeds of Bargain & Sale
sell & convey the GLEBE for the best price that can be got for the same to any person or
persons who shall be willing to purchase the said lands to hold to such purchaser or
purchasers his her or their heirs; And whereas the said GLEBE LANDS were exposed to
Publck Sail to the highest bidder, the sale having before that been duly advertised &
the land being struck off to WILLIAM BANKHEAD, the highest bidder at the price of
Eighteen hundred pounds & fifty one pounds currency which sum he then & there bid,
NOW THIS INDENTURE Witnesseth that in consideration of the said sum of current
money L. 1851 to them the aforesaid Commissioners or to the three Subscribing Trustees
in hand paid by WILLIAM BANKHEAD by these presents do bargain and sell unto WIL-
LIAM BANKHEAD his heirs all the GLEBE LAND containing three hundred acres formerly purchased by Washington Parish of JOHN MARSHALL now situate in King George
County & all houses gardens profits & hereditaments belonging; To have and to hold
the three hundred acres of land unto WILLIAM BANKHEAD his heirs and the Trustees or
three of them for themselves their & each of their heirs unto WILLIAM BANKHEAD his
heirs do warrant & defend the land & premises against all persons, In Witness whereof
the Trustees or three of them have hereunto put their hands and seals the day & year
before written, April 1st 1779
Signed Sealed & acknowledged in presence of
        THOMAS JETT, J. SKINKER,   JOHN MARTIN
        ARTHUR MAXWELL,   JOHN WASHINGTON
        REUBIN BULLARD   BECKWITH BUTTLER
    1779 April 1st. Received of Doctor WILLIAM BANKHEAD eighteen hundred & fifty one
pounds, being the consideration within mentioned
Witness THOMAS JETT,   JOHN MARTIN
        J. SKINKER, ARTHUR MAXWELL,   JOHN WASHINGTON
        WILLIAM ROBINSON, REUBIN BULLARD BECKWITH BUTTLER

At a Court held for King George County the 2d. day of September 1779
This Indented Deed of Bargain and Sale from under the hands & seals of JOHN MARTIN,
JOHN WASHINGTON & BECKWITH BUTTLER Gent., to Doctor WILLIAM BANKHEAD was
presented into Court & proved by the Oaths of JOHN SKINKER, ARTHUR MAXWELL,
WILLIAM ROBINSON & REUBIN BULLARD and on the motion of the said WILLIAM BANK-
HEAD was ordered to be recorded

Test JOS: ROBINSON, C: Court

pp.　　THIS INDENTURE made the 26th day of November in the year of our Lord one
1269-　thousand seven hundred & seventy eight Between ROBERT WASHINGTON & ALICE
1271　　his Wife and LUND WASHINGTON of County of FAIRFAX, Gent., of one part and
　　　　HENRY FITZHUGH Esqr., of County of King George of other part; Witnesseth that
in consideration of the sum of Six thousand five hundred pounds current money of
Virginia by HENRY FITZHUGH to ROBT: WASHINGTON and LUND WASHINGTON in hand
paid, by these presents do bargain and sell unto HENRY FITZHUGH his heirs a certain
tract of land containing Six hundred acres more or less lying in Parish of Saint Pauls
and County of King George and bounded Northerly on the Land of said HENRY FITZHUGH
called BLACK CASTLE, Easterly on the Land where said FITZHUGH now lives, Southerly &
Westerly on the Land of Col. JOHN WASHINGTON and Mr. ALVIN MOXLEY, formerly Majr.
RICHARD HOOE, it being the land whereon MRS. ELIZABETH WASHINGTON, deceased,
Mother of said ROBERT & LUND WASHINGTON formerly lived; Together with all houses
orchards profits and appurtenances belonging; To have and to hold the three hundred
acres of land more or less & premises with the appurtenances unto HENRY FITZHUGH
his heirs and ROBERT WASHINGTON and LUND WASHINGTON for themselves and their
heirs doth further covenant and agree with HENRY FITZHUGH his heirs that they shall
warrant and forever defend by these presents against every person lawfully claiming
the same under the Last Wills of CHRISTOPHER & THOMAS LUND, deceased, or of either of
them; In Witness whereof the said ROBERT WASHINGTON & ALICE his Wife & LUND
WASHINGTON have hereunto set their hands and seals the day and year first above
written
Sealed and delivered in presence of

　　　　ROBERT STITH, GEORGE FITZHUGH,　　　　ROBERT WASHINGTON
　　　　JOHN B. FITZHUGH, AL: ROSE　　　　　　　LUND WASHINGTON
　　　　WILLIAM FITZHUGH
　　　　P. HANSBROUGH

　Received of the within named HENRY FITZHUGH six thousand five hundred pounds
current money of Virginia, being the consideration for the within mentioned lands,
Witness my hand this Twenty sixth day of November one thousand seven hundred and
seventy eight

Witness P. HANSBROUGH, ALEXR: ROSE,　　　　LUND WASHINGTON
　　　ROBERT STITH, WILLIAM FITZHUGH　　　　ROBERT WASHINGTON

　At a Court held for King George County the 3d. day of December 1778
This Indented Deed from under the hands and seals of ROBERT WASHINGTON and LUND
WASHINGTON with the Receipt thereon Indorsed to HENRY FITZHUGH was presented into
Court by the said FITZHUGH and proved by the Oaths of ROBERT STITH, ALEXANDER ROSE,
WM: FITZHUGH and PETER HANSBROUGH and on the motion of the said HENRY FITZHUGH
was ordered to be recorded　　Test JOS: ROBINSON, C: Court

pp.   THIS INDENTURE made this 5th day of January in the year of our Lord one
1271-   seven hundred & seventy eight Between FRANCES STORKE of County of WEST-
1272   MORELAND and Commonwealth of Virginia, Widow, of one part & ROBERT YATES
        of King George County, Son & heir at Law of ROBERT YATES, Gent., deceased, of
other part; Whereas the said ROBERT YATES the Elder did in his life time (to wit) upon
the seventh day of July in the year of our Lord one thousand seven hundred & sixty
nine by Indenture then bearing date and now of Record in the Court of the County of
STAFFORD as may fully appear had conveyed to FRANCES STORKE for the uses in the
Indenture expressed & for the consideration therein mentioned a certain Plantation &
tract of Land whereon said YATES then lived & sundry slaves to wit, Great Jack, Luke,
Will, Hannah, Cate, Little Jack, Harry, Sarah, Bess & Sarah & their future increase
upon condition that if the said ROBERT YATES the Elder his heirs should pay or cause to
be paid unto said FRANCES STORKE for the use & benefit of WILLIAM & JOHN STORKE, her
Sons then under the age of twenty one years, the sum of Two hundred pounds current
money with Interest from the date of the aforesaid Indenture that then the said Indenture should cease determine & be utterly void. NOW THIS INDENTURE WITNESSETH that
for sum of Three hundred & twenty seven pounds & fifteen shillings currency being
the principal sum & Interest due upon the aforesaid Indenture paid by the aforesaid
ROBERT YATES, Eldest Son & heir at Law of the aforesaid ROBERT YATES deceased, unto
FRANCES STORKE to & for the use of WILLIAM & JOHN STORKE, the said FRANCES STORKE
by these presents doth bargain & sell unto ROBERT YATES, Eldest Son & heir at Law of
ROBERT YATES, deceased, the aforesaid Plantation and tract of land and all the aforesaid
slaves and their increase; To have & to hold the Plantation & tract of land & sd. slaves
and their increase unto ROBERT YATES & his heirs discharged of the aforesaid Mortgage
In Witness whereof the said FRANCES STORKE hath hereunto set her hand & seal the day
and year first above written
Sealed and Delivered in presence of us
    SEYMOUR HOOE,   FRANCES STORKE
    JACOB SMITH, FRANCIS THORNTON JUNR.
  Received on the day of the date of this Indenture from ROBERT YATES, Eldest Son &
heir at Law of ROBERT YATES, deceased, & for the use & benefit of my Sons, JOHN &
WILLIAM STORKE, the sum of three hundred & twenty seven pounds, fifteen shillings
current money being the principal & Interest due this day upon a Mortgage executed to
me by the said ROBERT YATES, deceased, bearing date the 7th day of July 1769, &
recorded in the Court of the County of STAFFORD
Test   SEYMOUR HOOE,   FRANCES STORKE
    JACOB SMITH,   FRANCIS THORNTON JUNR.
  At a Court held for King George County the 3d. day of September 1778
This Indented Deed from under the hand and seal of FRANCES STORKE with the Rect.
thereon to ROBERT YATES, was presented into Court & proved by the Oaths of the witnesses thereto & on the motion of the said ROBERT YATES ordered to be recorded
              Test JOS: ROBINSON, C. Court

p   THIS INDENTURE made this third day of September 1779 Between WILLIAM
1273   MARSHALL and MARY his Wife and ANN PIPER of County of King George of one
        part and BENJAMIN ETHERINGTON of the same County of other part; Witnesseth
that WILLIAM MARSHALL & MARY his Wife and ANN PIPER for sum of one hundred
pounds current money of Virginia to them in hand paid, by these presents doth bargain and sell unto BENJAMIN ETHERINGTON his heirs all that parcel of land situate in
County of King George containing One hundred acres more or less which parcel of land

was given by JONATHAN PIPER to his Daughter, Wife of the said WILLIAM MARSHALL,
party to these presents, and is the land whereof the said WILLIAM lately lived, And all
houses orchards thereon belonging; To have & to hold the parcel of land with appurtenances unto BENJAMIN ETHERINGTON his heirs; And WILLIAM MARSHALL and MARY
his Wife and ANNE PIPER for themselves their heirs will warrant & defend the parcel of
land & premises to BENJAMIN ETHERINGTON his heirs against the claim of all persons;
In Witness whereof the said WILLIAM MARSHALL & MARY his Wife & ANN PIPER hath
hereunto set their hands & seals the day & year first above written
Sealed and Delivered in presence of
     (no witnesses recorded)   WILLIAM MARSHALL
                                MARY MARSHALL
                                ANNE PIPER
    Received this 3d. day of September 1778 from BENJAMIN ETHERINGTON the within
mentioned sum of One hundred pounds current money of Virginia, being the consideration mentioned in the within Deed to be by him paid to
                                WILLIAM MARSHALL
                                ANNE PIPER
    At a Court held for King George County the 3d. day of September 1778
This Indented Deed fromunder the hands and seals of WILLIAM MARSHALL & MARY
MARSHALL & ANN PIPER was presented in Court & acknowledged by the parties &
ordered to be recorded   Test JOS: ROBINSON, Cl: Court

p.   THIS INDENTURE made the 1st day of October 1777 Between GEORGE MARSHALL
1274   and JUDITH his Wife of County of CAROLINE of one part and WILLIAM MAR-
       SHALL of County of King George of other part; Witnesseth that GEORGE MAR-
SHALL and JUDITH his Wife for sum of Sixty pounds current money of Virginia to them
in hand paid by GEORGE MARSHALL by these presents doth bargain and sell unto
GEORGE MARSHALL his heirs a certain tract of land, except the Grave Land, situate in
the Parish of Hanover and County of King George, containing by estimation one
hundred & fifty acres which land hereby conveyed or meant to be conveyed be the
same more or less lies between the land of Col. THOMAS TURNER, TABITHA STROTHER,
THOMAS SMITH, AMY SETTLEs, BODINGTONs & the Land of WILLIAM MARSHALL,
deceased, purchased of WILLIAM THORNTON containing by estimation One hundred &
fifty acres of land be the same more or less, Together with all houses orchards profits
and appurtenances belonging; To have and to hold the Plantation & tract of land unto
GEORGE MARSHALL his heirs and WILLIAM MARSHALL for himself his heirs that the
said WILLIAM MARSHALL & his heirs the Plantation & tract of land unto GEORGE MAR-
SHALL his heirs against every person shall warrant and forever defend by these
presents. In Witness whereof the said WILLIAM MARSHALL and MARY his Wife have
hereunto set their hands and seals the day & year first written
Signed sealed & acknowledged in presence of
    GEORGE JOHNSON,   GEORGE MARSHALL
    DAVID MONROE, ELIJAH DICKERSON
   At a Court held for King George County the 1st day of October 1778
This Indented Deed from under the hand and seal of GEORGE MARSHALL JUNR. to WIL-
LIAM MARSHALL was presented into Court & acknowledged by the said GEORGE MAR-
SHALL & on the motion of the said WILLIAM MARSHALL was ordered to be recorded
                  Test JOS: ROBINSON, Cl: Court

pp.   THIS INDENTURE made this Twenty first day of October 1778 Between JOHN
1275-   BLACKISTON of Parish of Saint Paul and County of King George and MARY his
1276   Wife of the one part and FRANCIS DADE the Younger, the only Son and Heir at
        Law of CADWALLADER DADE, late of the same place, Gent., deceased, of the other
part; Witnesseth that JOHN BLACKISTON and MARY his Wife for the sum of eight pounds
current money of Virginia to JOHN BLACKISTON in hand paid by FRANCIS DADE the
Younger, by this Indenture doth bargain & sell unto FRANCIS DADE his heirs all that
one third part of a tract of two hundred acres of land situate on POTOWMACK RIVER in
County & Parish aforesaid, which hath been allotted unto JOHN BLACKISTON and MARY
his said Wife for the Dower of said MARY in the tract of two hundred acres of land of
which tract of two hundred acres of land said CADWALLADER DADE, former Husband of
said MARY died seised of an Estate of Inheritance of which the said MARY was endow-
able, Together with all the Estate title & interest which said MARY ever had & JOHN
BLACKISTON now have; To have and to hold the one third part of the tract of two hundred acres of land together with all the premises unto FRANCIS DADE his heirs; In
Testimony whereof the said JOHN BLACKISTON & the said MARY his Wife have hereunto
set their hands & affixed their seals the day and year first above written
Signed sealed & delivered in presence of
        ROBERT YATES,   JOHN BLAKISTONE
        W. GIBBONS STUART,   MARY BLAKISTONE
        LAURANCE WASHINGTON
    I do acknowledge that I did receive of the within mentioned FRANCIS DADE by the
hands of TOWNSHEND DADE, Guardian of the said FRANCIS, the sum of Eighty pounds
current money of Virginia, the consideration expressed in this Indenture on the day of
the date thereof
Test   ROBERT YATES   JOHN BLAKISTONE
    The Commonwealth of Virginia to ROBERT WASHINGTON, WILLIAM HOOE, ROBERT
STITH Gent., Greeting. Whereas JOHN BLAKISTONE and MARY his Wife by their certain
Deed Indented have conveyed unto TOWNSHEND DADE, Gent., Guardian of FRANCIS DADE
the Younger, in Trust, for the said FRANCIS all right of Dower of her the said MARY
BLAKISTONE of & in 200 acres of land late the Property of CADWALLADER DADE, deced.,
Husband of said MARY & Father of the said FRANCIS (the Commission for the privy examination of MARY, the Wife of JOHN BLAKISTONE); Witness JOSEPH ROBINSON Clerk of our Court
of King George this 21st day of October 1778
                                        JOS: ROBINSON, C: K: G: Court
    By virtue of the within Commission we the subscribers personally went to the within
named MARY DADE BLAKISTON, the Wife of the within named JOHN BLAKISTON & received her acknowledgment of the Indenture of Bargain & Sale hereunto annexed (the
return of the execution of the privy examination of MARY BLAKISTONE). Certified under our
Seals this 21st day of October 1778   ROBT. WASHINGTON
                                                   ROBERT STITH
    At a Court held for King George County the 5th day of November 1778
This Indented Deed from under the hands and seals of JOHN BLAKISTONE and MARY his
Wife, she being first privately examined, with the Receipt thereon to FRANCIS DADE
was presented in Court & proved by the Oaths of the witnesses thereto subscribed & on
the motion of the said DADE was ordered to be recorded
                        Test JOS: ROBINSON, Cl: Court

p.   KNOW ALL MEN by these presents that I JAMES MARTIN of King George County
1277   in consideration of the sum of Three thousand one hundred and eighty pounds
       of Crop tobacco and eight pounds, fourteen shillings & six pence three farthings
paid by JOHN GREEN, Exr. of Col. WILLIAM GREEN, deceased, of CULPEPER County, the
Rect. of which I do acknowledge do by these presents bargain & sell unto JOHN GREEN
&c., the following goods & chattels, two cows & calves marked with two crops, a hole and
two underkeels, eight head of hogs in the same marks, one feather bed & furniture, six
pewter plates & one pewter dish & one bason, one Loom & table, two chairs & two Chests;
To have & to hold the goods & chattels unto JOHN GREEN &c., their heirs and I the said
JAMES MARTIN my heirs against the claim of all persons shall warrant and forever
defend the said JOHN GREEN in full possession of the premises by delivering to
WILLIAM BOON, Attorney for the said GREEN &c., the pewter Bason before mentioned in
the name of the whole; In Witness whereof I have hereunto set my hand and seal this
23d day of March 1778
Sealed & acknowledged in presence of
        THOMAS SMITH   JAMES his mark X MARTIN
        JOHN BUTTEREDGE, WILLIAM GREEN
    At a Court held for King George County the 5th day of November 1778
This Indented Mortgage from under the hand and seal of JAMES MARTIN to JOHN GREEN
was presented into Court by WILLIAM BOON & proved by the Oaths of THOMAS SMITH and
JOHN BUTTERAGE & on the motion of the said BOON was ordered to be recorded
            Test JOS: ROBINSON, C.K.G. Court

p.   THIS INDENTURE made the 19th day of October 1778 Between WILLIAM STORKE
1278   of County of King George and Parish of Saint Paul of one part and TAYLOR
       WILKERSON of Washington Parish in said County & MARY WILKERSON his Wife
of other part; Witnesseth that WILLIAM STORKE for the Annual Rent of One thousand
pounds of crop tobacco & cask by TAYLOR WILLIAMS and MARY his Wife to be rendered
& paid to WILLIAM STORKE and his heirs by these Indenture doth give & demise unto
TAYLOR WILKERSON and to the said MARY his Wife a certain Plantation & tract of land
whereon said TAYLOR WILKERSON and MARY his said Wife now reside situate in Parish
of Washington containing Two hundred acres; To have and to hold the plantation and
tract of land unto TAYLOR WILKERSON and MARY his Wife during the term of the
natural lives of said TAYLOR WILKERSON and said MARY his Wife & no longer; In Testimony whereof the said parties have hereunto set their hands and seals interchangeably the day & year above written
Signed sealed & acknowledged in presence of
        WOFFENDAL KENDALL,   WILLIAM STORKE
        STEPHEN BAILEY, JOHN WILKERSON
    At a Court held for King George County the 5th day of November 1778
This Lease from under the hand & seal of WILLIAM STORKE to TAYLOR WILKERSON &
MARY his Wife was presented into Court & proved by the Oaths of the witnesses thereto
and ordered to be recorded   Test JOS: ROBINSON, Cl: Court

p.   THIS INDENTURE made this Twenty third day of July one thousand seven hun-
1279   dred and seventy one Between GEORGE RIDING and URSULA his Wife of Parish
       of Hanover and County of King George of one part and JOHN LOVELL of same
Parish and County of other part; Witnesseth that GEORGE RIDING & URSULA his Wife for
sum of Thirteen pounds ten shillings curt. money of Virginia to them in hand paid by
JOHN LOVELL, by these presents do bargain and sell unto JOHN LOVELL his heirs all that

parcel of land lying in the Parish and County aforesaid, Begining at two red Oaks being
a corner of the said RIDINGs, WM. THORNTONs and JOHN PIPERs Lands, runing from
thence N. 4d. W. 34 poles to a Hickory standing by the Main Road being a line tree of
said PIPERs Land, thence up the Road N. 76 1/2 W. 40 poles, thence along said Road S. 75
1/2 W. 6 poles, thence along said Road S. 70 W. 14 poles, thence along said Road S. 55 W. 8
poles, thence continuing along said Road S. 35 W. 15 poles, thence along said Road S. 12
1/2 W. 23 1/2 poles to a red Oak, thence along said THORNTONs line to the beginning, containing eighteen acres one rod & twenty one perches of land, and all houses fences,
rents issues and profits thereof; To have and to hold the tract of land and premises unto
JOHN LOVEL his heirs and GEORGE RIDING and URSULA his Wife for themselves and
their heirs doth covenant with JOHN LOVEL his heirs that they will warrant and forever defend by these presents the tract of land and premises against all persons; In
Witness whereof the said GEORGE RIDING and URSULA his Wife have hereunto set their
hands and seals the day and eyar above written
Sealed & Delivered in presence of
    ROBT. LOVELL JUNR. GEORGE JONES,   GEORGE RIDING
    THOMAS APPLEBE, WM: PITTMAN   URSULA RIDING
    WILL: ROBINSON, WILL: NELSON
    Received of the within named JOHN LOVELL the sum of Thirteen pounds current
money being the consideration within mentioned; Witness my hand this twenty third
day of July 1771
Witness   WILL: ROBINSON, WILL: NELSON,   GEORGE RIDING
    GEO: JONES, WM: PITTMAN,
    ROBT. LOVELL, THOS: APPLEBE
    At a Court held for King George County the 1st day of August 1771
This Indentured Deed of Bargain and Sale as aforegoing with the rect. thereon from
under the hands & seals of GEORGE RIDING & URSULA his Wife to JOHN LOVELL was then
presented into Court, proved by the Oaths of three witnesses, & ordered to be recorded
          Test JOS: ROBINSON, Clk.

p.   The Commonwealth of Virginia to WILLIAM McWILLIAMS & JOHN JULIAN,
1280   Gentlemen, Greeting. Whereas DAVID GALLOWAY JUNIOR, Gent., and MARGARET
      his Wife, late of County of King George by their certain Deed of Bargain and Sale
bearing date the first day of January 17 hundred and eighty one did convey unto
THACKER WASHINGTON,.Gent., of County of King George the fee simple Estate of and in a
certain tract of land situate in Parish of Hanover and County of King George containing
by estimation seven hundred and twenty one acres, and Whereas the said MARGARET
cannot conveniently travel to our County Court of King George to make her personal
acknowledgement of the said Conveyance (the Commission for the privy examination of
MARGARET, the Wife of DAVID GALLOWAY JUNR.); Witness JOSEPH ROBINSON, Clerk of our
said Court of King George this 24th day of July 1783 in the 8th year of the Commonwealth   JOS: ROBINSON, C. K. G. C.
    We WILLIAM McWILLIAMS and JOHN JULIAN do hereby certify that agreeable to the
within Order of King George Court have this day examined MARGARETT GALLOWAY,
Wife of DAVID GALLOWAY seperately and apart from her Husband (the return of the execution of the privy examination of MARGRET GALLOWAY); Given under our hands in the
Corporation of FREDERICKSBURG this 26th day of July one thousand seven hundred and
eighty three   WM: McWILLIAMS
                        JOHN JULIAN

          END

CHINN. Charles (Gent. Justice of Fauquier Co. -55).

CLATOR. William 71.

CLAYTON. John 57.

CLELAND. James 1, 28.

CLIFTON. -60.

COCKRANE. Andrew, William Cunninghame & Co. of Glasgow) 7, 8, 11, 12.

COCKSHUTT. John 8, 17-20, 23, 24, 48-52.

COLHAM. John 56.

COLQUHOUN. Walter 45.

COMBS. Asten 88, 89; John 39.

CONDUIT. James 95.

CONNELLES. Daniel 59.

CONWAY. -62, 63.

COOK(E). John 38, 39; Mr. 58.

COUNTIES: Albemarle 5; Caroline 14, 26, 43, 71, 72, 104; Culpeper 6, 9, 29, 30, 54, 56, 57, 75, 81, 92, 100; Essex 95; Fairfax 85, 86, 103; Fauquier 55; Frederick 73; Gloucester 36; Goochland 61, 62; Hanover 33, 48; Loudoun 68; Orange 37, 75; Pittsylvania 71; Prince William 57, 59, 60, 99; Richmond 4, 9, 58, 80; Spotsylvania 29, 75; Stafford 3, 11, 18, 27, 29, 30, 53, 59-61, 65, 66, 74, 78; Westmoreland 32, 33, 47, 49, 61, 73, 81, 84, 103.

COURTS. Elizabeth 100, 101; John 83, (of Fairfax Co. -85), 86; Susannah (Thornton) 83; (of Fairfax Co. -85), 86, 93.

COX. John 41; Vincen(t). 2, 50.

CRAPP. James 16, 17.

CRAWFORD. Andrew 33, 36, 41 (of Leeds Town -70), 71, 82.

CREEKS. Dodsons 74; Muddy 41; Paspatanzy 64; Thatchers 38.

CULLEN. Lettis 69.

CUNNINGHAME. William (of Glasgow) 7, 8, 44, 45.

DADE. Cadwallader (Gent., deced.-105; Francis (the Younger) 105; Horatio 72, 80; Horatio (Gent. Just.) 17, 40, 79, 88, 94, 95; Langhorne 81; Rose 69; Townshend 90, 95, 105.

DALE. Samuel 54.

DANIEL. Traverse 80.

DAVENPORT. Burkett 4; Burkett (Gent. Just.) 26, 34.

DAVIS. James 41, 45, 65-68, 70, (Lieut. in 3rd. Virginia Regiment -77), 78; Samuel 66.

DAY. Benjamin 10, 11, 19, 21, 100; Francis 11, 12; John 15.

DEACONS. William 32.

DEANE. Charles 26, 47, 48, 53; Charles Junr. 36, 46, 47, 52, 71; Charles Senr. 37, 38; Mary 46, 47.

DEARING. John 48.

DERMITT/DARMITT. Mary 83; Mott 58, 83.

DICK. Charles 28.

DICKERSON. Elijah 104.

DICKIE. John 20, 21, 41.

DISHMAN. James 98.

DIXON. John (Reverend, of College of William & Mary) 1, 15, 25, 54; John (the Elder, deced. -25)

DOAKE. Thomas 34.

DODD. James 79; Joseph Junr. 89.

DODGIN. William 71.

DONIPHAN. Magdelain 65; Mott 64.

DONNE. Mary (deced.-29), 30.

DOUGLASS. Thomas 25, 26 (of Leeds Town -82).

DRAKE. James 16, 17; Thomas 36, 38, 46-48, 73.

DUNLAP -85; James (of Essex Co., Mercht. -95).

DYE. George 81.

EDRINGTON. John 73.

EDWARDS. James 79, 80; Richard Sevan 7.

ELKINS. John (of Caroline Co.-72), 73; Lucy (of Caroline Co. -72), 73; Mary 72.

ETHERINGON. Benjamin 103, 104.

EUSTACE. John 6, 9, 24.

FALMOUTH. Ann Street 6, 9; Cambridge Street 9, 15; Caroline Street 6, 9, 42, 43; Carter Street 25; King Street 25; Town of 1, 6, 7, 9, 11, 12, 14, 15, 25, 40, 42, 43, 80.

FAUNTLEROY. Moore (Capt. of Richmond Co. -58), 59.

FERGUSON/FARGUSON. John 77; Josiah 71.

FICKLIN/FIGLIN. -70; John 99; Thomas 80, 99.

FITZHUGH. -5, 59, 80; Ann (of Stafford Co. -60), 61; Daniel 61; George (Gent. Just.) 67, 88; George 91, (Gent.-98), 99, 102; Henry 93, (Esqr.-102); John B. 102; William 31, 35, 102; William (of Stafford Co. -60), 61; William Junr. 93, 94.

FLOWERS. William 5.

FOLIE. Bryant 65.

FOLLIS. Jacob 46.

FOWKE. Chandler 59; Richard Senr. 59, 60.

FOWLEY. Barnett 82; Richard 66.

O'BANNON. Bryon 7.

OLDHAM. Samuel 71, (Gent. -86).

OLIVER. Elizabeth (of Stafford Co. -80); Thomas (of Stafford Co. -80).

O'NEAL. -27.

ORR. John 4, 33.

OSWALD. Thomas 13, 33.

OWENS. Aaron 57; Ann 55; Jeremiah (deced. -57); Joshua (of Prince William Co. -57); Lettice 57; Reuben 16, 72, 94; Richard 57; Richard Junr. (deced. -57); Samuel 83, 84; William 55, 57.

PALMER. Joseph 44.

PANNILL. Ann (of Orange Co. -37), 38, 39; David 38, 73; William (of Orange Co. -37), 38, 39.

PARKER. Thomas 95.

PAYNE. -31; Daniel 54; George 17, 18; Reuben 8; Richard 13, 27, 41.

PEACH. John 97.

PECK. George 91; Jane 91; John 8, 9, 91, 92; Joseph (deced.-91); Mary 98, 99; Robert (deced. -91); Samuel 9, 98, 99; William 16, 91, 92, 99.

PEED/PEAD. Philip 58, 59, 63, 64; Thomas (Son of Philip -59); Thomas (of Richmond Co. -9), 10, 58, 59.

PENDLETON. Nathaniel (Gent. Just. of Culpeper Co.-57).

PERKINS. John 32; William 21, 22.

PEYTON/PAYTON. Evan 5, 6; Henry (Gent. Just. of Fauquier Co.) 55; James 5, 6, 9; Jn: 10, 21, 46.

PIPER. Ann 103, 104; John 107; Jonathan 104.

PITMAN. -85; John 62; Moses 71; William 107.

PLACES: Allens Bridge 68; Black Castle 102; Brays Warehouse in Leeds Town 70; College of William & Mary 1, 25; Falls Run Bride in Falmouth 1; Fredericksburg 25, 29, 107; Hackleys Ferry 75, 100; Hangallies 62; Mortons Warehouse 75; Williamsburg 54, 80.

PLAYL. John 2.

POLLARD -5; John 28; John (Gent. Just.) 66, 67; John Junr. 16; John Junr. (Gent. Just.) 94, 95; John Senr. 2; Thomas 97.

POPHAM. Job (of Culpeper Co. -81); John (deced. -81).

PORTER. William 32.

POWELL. Cordall 21, 22; William 21, 22.

PRATT -60, 61.

PRICE. Anthony 96; John 96, 98; Thomas 96; William 16; William Junr. (of Caroline Co. -72), 73.

PULLIN. Jedediah 56.

QUISENBERRY. Ann (of Westmoreland Co.-47, 48; James (of Westmoreland Co. -47), 48.

RAMEY. Jacob 10, 11.

RANDOLPH. Ann (of Goochland Co. -61), 62; Thomas Mann (of Goochland Co. -61), 62; William 2, 3.

RANKINS. John 28, 88.

RAWLINGS/RAWLINS. Terry 76, 80.

REDDOCK/RIDDOCK. Collin 4, 13, (Doctor of Hanover Co.-33), 48; Jane (of Hanover Co. -33), 48.

REVELEY. William 18.

RICHARDS. John 54.

RICHARDSON. Daniel 4, 26, 33 (of Leeds Town -36), 41, 46; John 77; Mourning 77; Nancy 36.

RIDING. Daniel (deced.-71); George 39, (Gent., Marriage Contract-53), 73, 83-85, 98, 100, 101, 106, 107; Ursula 106, 107; William 71, 83-85; Winnefred 85.

RIVERS: Falls of Rappahannock 55; Potomack 59, 60, 105; Rappahannock 26, 29, 30, 46, 47, 75.

ROADS: Church 94; Main County 37, 38, 78; Old 32; Ridge 85.

ROBERTS. Benjamin 9.

ROBERTSON. Benjamin Junr. 6; John 2, 3, 6, 9, 13, 14, 20, 23, 24, 28.

ROBINS -85; Thomas 73.

ROBINSON. Franky Wilton 82; James (of Falmouth -7), 8, 25, 44, 45; Joseph 65, 70, 71; Maximilian 4, 38; William 4, 26, 27, 36, 37, 41, 47, 107; William (Gent. Just.) 33, 34, 47.

ROBISON. Thomas 54.

RODGERS. James 67, 74; Joseph 67.

ROLLINGS. Anthony 81.

ROSE. Alexander 82, 102; Francis 81; John 54, 100; John Senr. (deced. -89); William 20; Zachariah (of Charles Co. in Maryland -95).

ROWE. Alexander 46; William 50, 51.

ROWLEY. Ann 94; John 94; Moses 94, 95; William (Marriage Contract-30, 31); William (deced. -65).

ROY. Mungo 26.
RUNS. Antopian 98; Falls 2, 15; Rappahannock 25; Reed Swamp 32; Richland 13.

SAMPSON. Stephen (Gent. Just. of Goochland Co.
   -62).
SAUNDERS. Celey (of Leeds Town -74);
   William (Capt., of Leeds Town -82).
SCOGGINS. Charles 72.
SEAL. John 41.
SEAY. John Thomas 2.
SETTLE. Aimy 95, 104; Sarah (deced.-56).
SHARPE. Hannah 7, 8; John Junr. 42, 43, 51;
   John Senr. 51; Lincefield (deced. -7);
   Thomas 7, 8; Thomas June. 51, 52.
SHARPLES. John 26.
SHELTON. Meriwether (Gent. Just. of Hanover
   Co. -48).
SHEPARD. Andrew 38; Andrew (Gent. Just. of
   Orange Co.) 38, 39.
SHORT. John 38, 73; Winifred 38.
SHROPSHIRE. William 69, 96-98.
SIMPSON. Diana (deced.-5); Margaret 5;
   Sampson (of Albemarle Co. -5), 6;
   William (deced. -5).
SKATH. John 89.
SKINKER. Colo. 99; John 35, 37, 39, 72,
   (Colo: -96), 101, 102; John (Gent. Just.) 17;
SLAUGHTER. George (of Culpeper Co. -6), 7, 9;
   James (Gent. Just. Culpeper Co.) 54; John
   (Gent. Just. Culpeper Co.) 54; Mary (of Cul-
   peper Co. -6), 9.
SMALLWOOD. William 64.
SMITH. Jacob 103; John 16, 17, 96;
   Nathan 89; Thomas 53, 56, 57, 63, 64, 69,
   88, 89, 98, 104, 106; William 57;
   Winny (Marriage Contract -53).
SMOD. William 75.
SNELSON. John (Gent. Just. Hanover Co.) 48.
SPARK, Alexander (of Westmoreland Co. -32).
SPENCER. Joseph 38.
STEVENS. Edward (Gent. Just. Culpeper Co.) 57.
STIGLER. Benjamin 56; James (deced. -56);
   Martha 56.
STEWARD. Grace (of Frederick Co. -73), 74;
   Jeremiah (deced.-73); William 59, 60.
STITH. Robert (Gent. Just.) 90, 102, 105.
STONE. Mary 77.
STORKE. Frances (of Westmoreland Co.-103;
   John 103; William 103, 106.

STRINGFELLOW. George 15.
STROTHER. -69; Anthony 20, 41, 67; Anthony
   (Gent. Just.) 40, 42; Benjamin 71, 77, 82;
   George 89; John 89; Margaret 96;
   Richard 89; Robert 96, 97; Tabitha 68, 104;
   W. D. 38, 39.
STUART. W. Gibbons 105.
SUITER. Andrew 16, 17.
SULLIVAN. William 49, 50.
SUMNER. Joseph 64.
SWETNAM. John 99; John (of Stafford Co. -18);
   William 8.
SYDENHAM -73.

TALIAFERRO. Francis 39, 40; Francis (Gent., of
   Spotsylvania Co., deced.-75), 76; Hay (of Orange
   Co. -75), 76, 99, 100; John 16, (Marriage Con-
   tract -29, 30), 39-41, 65, 66, 70, 75; John (Gent.
   Just.) 40, 42; John June. 65; John Junr. (Gent.
   Just.) 66); John Senr. 64; Lawrence 30;
   Martha (of Orange Co. -75), 76; Walker (of
   Caroline Co. -43), 44.
TAYLOE/TALOE. John Esqr. (of Richmond Co.
   -80), 81; Rebecca (of Richmond Co. -80), 81.
TAYLOR. Catharine (of Caroline Co.-65), 66;
   James 41, (Colo: -70); John 43; Richard 31;
   Richard (of Caroline Co. -65), 66.
TEMPLEMAN. William 48.
THEEDS. George 73.
THOM. Alexander 73.
THOMAS -38.
THOMPSON. William 95.
THORNLEY. -62, 69; Aaron 37, 68, 92, 97;
   Aaron (Son of Aaron -97); Anne 97;
   Elizabeth 97; Epaphroditus 97; John 36, 37,
   97; John (deced. -97); Mary 97.
THORNTON. Ann 93; Anthony (of Caroline Co.
   -93); Elizabeth 92, 93; Elizabeth (Dau: of
   William) 93; Francis (Gent.-39), 62, 74, 83,
   85-87, 93, 95, 101; Francis (Son of William
   -93); George 30; John 28, 84; Sarah 34, 35;
   Sukey 39; Susannah 83, 93; William 34, 35,
   39, 47, 73, 74, 83, 92, 93, 104, 107;
   William (Gent. Just.) 17, 33, 34.
TILLER. John 73.
TIMBERLAKE. Joseph Junr. 15.
TODD. -25; Elizabeth 66, 67; Richard 66, 67;
   Samuel 4, 9.
TRIPLETT. James 73; John 2, (Co. Surveyor-16),
   32, 33, 72; John (of Culpeper Co.-54). (contd.)

Heritage Books by Ruth and Sam Sparacio:

Abstracts of Account Books of Edward Dixon, Merchant of Port Royal, Virginia, Volume I: 1743–1747

Abstracts of Account Books of Edward Dixon, Merchant of Port Royal, Virginia, Volume II

Albemarle County, Virginia Deed and Will Book Abstracts, 1748–1752

Albemarle County, Virginia Deed Book Abstracts, 1758–1761

Albemarle County, Virginia Deed Book Abstracts, 1761–1764

Albemarle County, Virginia Deed Book Abstracts, 1764–1768

Albemarle County, Virginia Deed Book Abstracts, 1768–1770

Albemarle County, Virginia Deed Book Abstracts, 1776–1778

Albemarle County, Virginia Deed Book Abstracts, 1778–1780

Albemarle County, Virginia Deed Book Abstracts, 1780–1783

Albemarle County, Virginia Deed Book Abstracts, 1787–1790

Albemarle County, Virginia Deed Book Abstracts, 1790–1791

Albemarle County, Virginia Deed Book Abstracts, 1791–1793

Augusta County, Virginia Land Tax Books, 1782–1788

Augusta County, Virginia Land Tax Books, 1788–1790

Amherst County, Virginia Land Tax Books, 1789–1791

Caroline County, Virginia Order Book Abstracts, 1765

Caroline County, Virginia Order Book Abstracts, 1767–1768

Caroline County, Virginia Order Book Abstracts, 1768–1770

Caroline County, Virginia Order Book Abstracts, 1770–1771

Caroline County, Virginia Order Book, 1765–1767

Caroline County, Virginia Order Book, 1771–1772

Caroline County, Virginia Order Book, 1772–1773

Caroline County, Virginia Order Book, 1773

Caroline County, Virginia Order Book, 1773–1774

Caroline County, Virginia Order Book, 1774–1778

Caroline County, Virginia Order Book, 1778–1781

Caroline County, Virginia Order Book, 1781–1783

Caroline County, Virginia Order Book, 1786–1787

Caroline County, Virginia Order Book, 1787, Part 1

Caroline County, Virginia Order Book, 1788

Culpeper County, Virginia Deed Book Abstracts, 1795–1796

Culpeper County, Virginia Land Tax Book, 1782–1786

Culpeper County, Virginia Land Tax Book, 1787–1789

Culpeper County, Virginia Minute Book, 1763–1764

Digest of Family Relationships, 1650–1692, from Virginia County Court Records

Digest of Family Relationships, 1720–1750, from Virginia County Court Records

Digest of Family Relationships, 1750–1763, from Virginia County Court Records

Digest of Family Relationships, 1764–1775, from Virginia County Court Records

Essex County, Virginia Deed and Will Abstracts, 1695–1697

Essex County, Virginia Deed and Will Abstracts, 1697–1699

Essex County, Virginia Deed and Will Abstracts, 1699–1701

Essex County, Virginia Deed and Will Abstracts, 1701–1703

Essex County, Virginia Deed and Will Abstracts, 1745–1749

Essex County, Virginia Deed and Will Book, 1692–1693

Essex County, Virginia Deed and Will Book, 1693–1694

Essex County, Virginia Deed and Will Book, 1694–1695

Essex County, Virginia Deed and Will Book, 1753–1754 and 1750

Essex County, Virginia Deed Book, 1724–1728

Essex County, Virginia Deed Book, 1728–1733

Essex County, Virginia Deed Book, 1733–1738

Essex County, Virginia Deed Book, 1738–1742

Essex County, Virginia Deed Book, 1742–1745

Lancaster County, Virginia Order Book, 1701–1703

Lancaster County, Virginia Order Book, 1703–1706

Lancaster County, Virginia Order Book, 1732–1736

Lancaster County, Virginia Will Book, 1675–1689

Loudoun County, Virginia Order Book, 1763–1764

Loudoun County, Virginia Order Book, 1764

Louisa County, Virginia Deed Book, 1744–1746

Louisa County, Virginia Order Book, 1742–1744

Madison County, Virginia Deed Book Abstracts, 1793–1804

Madison County, Virginia Deed Book, 1793–1813, and Marriage Bonds, 1793–1800

Middlesex County, Virginia Deed Book, 1679–1688

Middlesex County, Virginia Deed Book, 1688–1694

Middlesex County, Virginia Deed Book, 1694–1703

Middlesex County, Virginia Deed Book, 1703–1709

Middlesex County, Virginia Deed Book, 1709–1720

Middlesex County, Virginia Order Book, 1686–1690

Middlesex County, Virginia Record Book, 1721–1813

Northumberland County, Virginia Deed and Will Book, 1650–1655

Northumberland County, Virginia Deed and Will Book, 1655–1658

Northumberland County, Virginia Deed and Will Book, 1662–1666

Northumberland County, Virginia Deed and Will Book, 1666–1670

Northumberland County, Virginia Deed and Will Book, 1670–1672 and 1706–1711

Northumberland County, Virginia Deed and Will Book, 1711–1712

Northumberland County, Virginia Order Book, 1652–1657

Northumberland County, Virginia Order Book, 1657–1661

Northumberland County, Virginia Order Book, 1665–1669

Northumberland County, Virginia Order Book, 1669–1673

Northumberland County, Virginia Order Book, 1680–1683

Northumberland County, Virginia Order Book, 1683–1686

Northumberland County, Virginia Order Book, 1699–1700

Northumberland County, Virginia Order Book, 1700–1702

Northumberland County, Virginia Order Book, 1702–1704

Orange County, Virginia Deeds, 1743–1759

Orange County, Virginia Order Book Abstracts 1747–1748

Orange County, Virginia Order Book Abstracts 1752–1753

Prince William County, Virginia Deed Book, 1749–1752

Prince William County, Virginia Order Book Abstracts, 1752–1753

Prince William County, Virginia Order Book Abstracts, 1753–1757

(Old) Rappahannock County, Virginia Deed and Will Book Abstracts, 1656–1662

(Old) Rappahannock County, Virginia Deed and Will Book Abstracts, 1662–1665

(Old) Rappahannock County, Virginia Deed and Will Book Abstracts, 1663–1668

(Old) Rappahannock County, Virginia Deed and Will Book Abstracts, 1665–1677

(Old) Rappahannock County, Virginia Deed and Will Book Abstracts, 1668–1670

(Old) Rappahannock County, Virginia Deed and Will Book Abstracts, 1670–1672

(Old) Rappahannock County, Virginia Deed and Will Book Abstracts, 1672–1673/4

(Old) Rappahannock County, Virginia Deed and Will Book Abstracts, 1673/4–1676

(Old) Rappahannock County, Virginia Deed and Will Book Abstracts, 1677–1678/9

(Old) Rappahannock County, Virginia Deed and Will Book Abstracts, 1678/9–1682

(Old) Rappahannock County, Virginia Deed and Will Book Abstracts, 1682–1686

(Old) Rappahannock County, Virginia Deed and Will Book Abstracts, 1686–1688

(Old) Rappahannock County, Virginia Deed and Will Book Abstracts, 1688–1692

(Old) Rappahannock County, Virginia Order Book Abstracts, 1683–1685

(Old) Rappahannock County, Virginia Order Book, 1689–1692

(Old) Rappahannock County, Virginia Will Book, 1682–1687

Richmond County, Virginia Deed Book Abstracts, 1692–1695

Richmond County, Virginia Deed Book Abstracts, 1695–1701

Richmond County, Virginia Deed Book Abstracts, 1701–1704

Richmond County, Virginia Deed Book Abstracts, 1705–1708

Richmond County, Virginia Deed Book Abstracts, 1708–1711

Richmond County, Virginia Deed Book Abstracts, 1711–1714

Richmond County, Virginia Deed Book Abstracts, 1715–1718

Richmond County, Virginia Deed Book Abstracts, 1718–1719

Richmond County, Virginia Deed Book Abstracts, 1719–1721

Richmond County, Virginia Deed Book Abstracts, 1721–1725

Richmond County, Virginia Order Book Abstracts, 1694–1697

Richmond County, Virginia Order Book Abstracts, 1697–1699

Richmond County, Virginia Order Book abstracts, 1699–1701

Richmond County, Virginia Order Book Abstracts, 1714–1715

Richmond County, Virginia Order Book Abstracts, 1719–1721

Richmond County, Virginia Order Book, 1692–1694

Richmond County, Virginia Order Book, 1702–1704

Richmond County, Virginia Order Book, 1717–1718

Richmond County, Virginia Order Book, 1718–1719

Spotsylvania County, Virginia Deed Book, 1722–1725

Spotsylvania County, Virginia Deed Book, 1725–1728

Spotsylvania County, Virginia Deed Book: 1730–1731

Spotsylvania County, Virginia Order Book Abstracts, 1742–1744

Spotsylvania County, Virginia Order Book Abstracts, 1744–1746

Stafford County, Virginia Deed and Will Book, 1686–1689

Stafford County, Virginia Deed and Will Book, 1689–1693

Stafford County, Virginia Deed and Will Book, 1699–1709

Stafford County, Virginia Deed and Will Book, 1780–1786, and Scheme Book Orders, 1790–1793

Stafford County, Virginia Deed Book, 1722–1728 and 1755–1765

Stafford County, Virginia Order Book, 1664–1668 and 1689–1690

Stafford County, Virginia Order Book, 1691–1692

Stafford County, Virginia Order Book, 1692–1693

Stafford County, Virginia Will Book, 1729–1748

Stafford County, Virginia Will Book, 1748–1767

Westmoreland County, Virginia Deed and Will Abstracts, 1723–1726

Westmoreland County, Virginia Deed and Will Abstracts, 1726–1729

Westmoreland County, Virginia Deed and Will Abstracts, 1729–1732

Westmoreland County, Virginia Deed and Will Abstracts, 1732–1734

Westmoreland County, Virginia Deed and Will Abstracts, 1734–1736

Westmoreland County, Virginia Deed and Will Abstracts, 1736–1740

Westmoreland County, Virginia Deed and Will Abstracts, 1740–1742

Westmoreland County, Virginia Deed and Will Abstracts, 1742–1745

Westmoreland County, Virginia Deed and Will Abstracts, 1745–1747

Westmoreland County, Virginia Deed and Will Abstracts, 1747–1748

Westmoreland County, Virginia Deed and Will Abstracts, 1749–1751

Westmoreland County, Virginia Deed and Will Abstracts, 1751–1754

Westmoreland County, Virginia Deed and Will Abstracts, 1754–1756

Westmoreland County, Virginia Order Book, 1705–1707

Westmoreland County, Virginia Order Book, 1707–1709

Westmoreland County, Virginia Order Book, 1709–1712

www.ingramcontent.com/pod-product-compliance
Lightning Source LLC
Chambersburg PA
CBHW082359270326
41935CB00013B/1690